"Sweeping in scope and teeming with insights, this creative and compelling book shows us the horror of a world without Christianity. An eye-opening work that should be read with pen in hand to mark points to remember. Truly powerful and persuasive."

Lee Strobel, bestselling author of *The Case for Christ* and *The Case for Faith*

"This brilliant book is a wake-up call to a world that refuses to see the impact of the life, death, and resurrection of Jesus Christ and to a church that has too often forgotten who we are and what we believe."

Sheila Walsh, co-host, *Life Today*

"In today's politically correct environment, Christianity is the militant secularists' default scapegoat, blamed for every societal problem. A sober review of history into the modern era exposes this calculated effort to demonize Christianity. *Unimaginable* documents Christianity's overwhelmingly positive influence on the world and, contrastingly, describes the horror anti-Christian forces have inflicted on mankind. Refreshingly, Johnston corrects the record."

David Limbaugh, bestselling author, attorney, and commentator

"A sophisticated, thoughtful book based on a profound assumption—and it entertains as well as instructs."

Dr. Rodney Stark, Distinguished Professor of the Social Sciences and Co-Director, Institute for Studies of Religion, Baylor University

"Brilliantly conceived and beautifully written, *Unimaginable* is a splendid book for both Christians and non-Christians. . . . I heartily commend Johnston for this outstanding work."

David S. Dockery, President, Trinity International University/ Trinity Evangelical Divinity School

"For half a century, America has been moving away from its Christian heritage. Many apparently are oblivious to the value of this heritage and how it laid the very foundation on which this great nation was built. I am pleased to recommend this compelling and fascinating book."

Mike Huckabee, former governor of Arkansas

"This book joins *What If Jesus Had Never Been Born?* and *Who Is This Man?* as historical affirmations of the positive effects of the Christian faith. Easy to read and thoroughly documented, *Unimaginable* shows how the fundamental values humans hold dear are traceable to Christianity. Where we find a rejection of those values we find death, destruction, and despair. Far from being a detriment to the world or the source of all ills, Christianity is foundational to our concepts of freedom, equality, and human dignity."

Thom S. Rainer, President and CEO, LifeWay Christian Resources

"Much of the way we interpret reality is determined by how we view the world, and the Christian worldview has shaped millions of lives across the globe. If you want to make the case for what you believe as a Christian, or simply want to investigate the truth for yourself, this book will help you in a new and meaningful way."

J. Warner Wallace, cold-case detective, Senior Fellow at the Colson Center for Christian Worldview, and author *of Cold-Case Christianity, God's Crime Scene,* and *Forensic Faith*

"*Unimaginable* is brimming with hope as the author proves not only the relevance of Christ to culture but also the heart-healing, spirit-restoring power available through the Savior. Bravo!"

Janet Parshall, nationally syndicated talk show host

"A timely, well-researched, and fascinating book . . . the definitive response to the claim that Christianity is 'poisonous' for the world."

Sean McDowell, PhD, Biola University Professor, speaker, and author of fifteen books, including *A New Kind of Apologist*

"Wow! This book is a FastPass to the epic ride known as the Christian faith . . . a must-read for anyone who wants to 'give an answer for the hope that lies within us' (1 Peter 3:15). The author's scholarly detail encourages parents, students, teachers, and pastors to dig deep."

Dr. Jay Strack, President and Founder of Student Leadership University

"Western culture is under assault, and it may not survive. That's why *Unimaginable* is so critical to this moment in history. I encourage you to share it with someone who thinks the Christian faith is outdated and irrelevant, because what comes after Christianity may be the end of us all."

Phil Cooke, PhD, filmmaker and author of *Unique: Telling Your Story in the Age of Brands and Social Media*

"What a difference the gospel makes! The book presents not only a powerful apologetic for a culture that takes for granted the legacy of the Christian faith but also a clear vision of the transforming power the gospel can bring to any society."

Paul Copan, Pledger Family Chair of Philosophy and Ethics, Palm Beach Atlantic University; coeditor of *The Dictionary of Christianity and Science*

"*Unimaginable* contains insights into human history and culture that to my knowledge have not been perceived before. Some of it is simply terrifying. Today's atheists and nihilists do not know they are playing with fire, a fire that could destroy our civilization. What ended slavery? What ended systemic abuse of children and women? What ended gross ignorance and superstition? Read this book and you will find the answers."

Craig A. Evans, PhD, DHabil, John Bisagno Distinguished Professor of Christian Origins, Houston Baptist University

"With scholarly research and imaginative flair, Jeremiah Johnston asks us to consider the unimaginable: What if Christianity had not won the war of competing ideologies? What if it were not to continue as a world-changing influence? This insightful book will help you to understand why Christianity makes sense for us and the world we live in."

Justin Brierley, presenter of the *Unbelievable* radio show and podcast and Senior Editor of *Premier Christianity* magazine

"As we live in a world desirous of scourging religion from life, Dr. Johnston shows that without difference-making believers in Jesus, many of the greatest elements of our world would be missing. Atheist, agnostic, or lifelong churchgoer—read this book and realize the importance and power of Christianity."

Gregg Matte, Pastor, Houston's First Baptist Church

"A remarkably clear account of the often underestimated impact of Christianity on a culture and on individuals. As an educator, I welcome this engaging text as a primer for anyone interested in the historical, social, and personal effect of the powerful message of Christianity."

Dr. Carlos Campo, President, Ashland University; Chair of the Hispanic Education Alliance for the National Hispanic Christian Leadership Conference

"*Unimaginable* is one of those rare books that successfully combines cutting-edge scholarship on the origins of Christianity with meaningful and thought-provoking reflections on the place of religion in the contemporary world. In a bold way, Johnston presents the strong and unflinching case that in terms of ethics, social values, and human equality the world is a better place because of the contributions of Christianity."

Paul Foster, Professor of New Testament and Early Christianity, School of Divinity, University of Edinburgh

"Someone once asked: What if you woke up tomorrow with only the things you thanked God for today? We tend to take advantage of the stabilizing factors in our lives and communities. If Christianity never existed, what would people miss out on, long for, or worry about? *Unimaginable* will not only compel you to thank God for his influence but also inspire you to reflect Christ's heart to a world very much in need of a Savior."

Susie Larson, talk radio host and author of *Your Powerful Prayers*

"It is essential that we understand the influence of Christ and the Christian faith upon civilization and culture. Our witness in the world is at stake, and one of the most significant reasons we believe and share our message is the massive impact of Christianity upon the lives of millions. . . . I highly recommend this book."

Jack Graham, Pastor, Prestonwood Baptist Church

"Jeremiah Johnston takes you on a sweeping ride through history to reveal how Jesus Christ has infused our lives with goodness in ways you may never have imagined. I can't recommend this book highly enough!"

Frank Turek, Crossexamined.org and co-author of *I Don't Have Enough Faith to Be an Atheist*

"Always the scholar who keeps his finger on the pulse of real-world society and culture, Jeremiah Johnston has produced a volume that addresses the myriad of blessings Christianity provides. It immediately reminded me of the 'New Atheist' complaints in recent years that religion never produces good results. Read this book and you'll have more answers than you'll ever need!"

Gary R. Habermas, Distinguished Research Professor and Chair, Department of Philosophy, Liberty University

"Jeremiah Johnston brilliantly shows us what a world without Christianity has been and would be. I was struck in new ways by just how miserable the lives of most of Christianity's most famous opponents have been. Don't be a miserable opponent of Christianity. Read this book."

Dr. Peter J. Williams, Principal, Tyndale House, Cambridge, UK

"Counterfactual studies are always fascinating, but *Unimaginable* is especially so. Contemplating a world without Christianity reminds us anew of all the gospel of the Lord Jesus Christ has accomplished and all that his church has done for the world's good."

Dr. Jason K. Allen, President, Midwestern Baptist Theological Seminary

"Johnston's readers have reason to be pleased with his new work that highlights the cultural impact of the Christian faith. Of particular relevance are the sections on eugenics, slavery, and racism, and the historic Christian rejection of these evils. May we take his words to heart in our day."

Dr. Holly Ordway, faculty, Houston Baptist University;
author of *Apologetics and the Christian Imagination*

"Jeremiah Johnston is one of the brightest young Christian apologists today. *Unimaginable* will prove to be an invaluable resource for believers who desire to be more effective defenders of the faith. I highly recommend this book."

Dr. Harold Rawlings, Assistant Director of The Rawlings Foundation

"For the past few decades, Western society has been on a path to purge itself of Christian influence. If the trend continues, will progressives want what they get? Engaging and informative, this timely volume considers what our world and even modern Western society might look like without the tremendously positive impact of Christianity. I love the concept! Christian and non-Christian readers alike will walk away with a conviction similar to that of militant atheist Richard Dawkins: Christianity may very well be the barrier preventing the world from becoming a place where freedom and justice are things of the past."

Michael R. Licona, PhD, Associate Professor of
Theology, Houston Baptist University

"More than one hundred of the foremost atheists, agnostics, secularists, and philosophers have filmed interviews with me. Collectively, their accusation is that Christians do not know how to think critically. Jeremiah Johnston not only refutes the error, but presents the positive, seismic, irrefutable changes Christianity has brought to our world. Every Christian needs to know the crucial truths in this book."

Dr. Jerry Johnston, jerryjohnston.com

"Many say Christianity is outdated and bigoted, based on a book of ancient myths. Jeremiah Johnston beautifully and biblically outlines that from politics to education to the hope of eternal life through Jesus Christ, Christianity is actually the world's greatest force for good."

Janet Mefferd, radio host, *Janet Mefferd Today* and *Janet Mefferd Live*

"*Unimaginable* is essential reading. My trusted friend Jeremiah gives us a clear and compelling defense for the positive impact of Christianity on history and society. It is a book that will empower believers and answer skeptics. Read it and share it immediately."

Philip Nation, author of *Habits for Our Holinesss*

UNIMAGINABLE

WHAT OUR WORLD WOULD BE LIKE
WITHOUT CHRISTIANITY

JEREMIAH J. JOHNSTON

BETHANYHOUSE
a division of Baker Publishing Group
Minneapolis, Minnesota

Published by Bethany House Publishers
11400 Hampshire Avenue South
Bloomington, Minnesota 554378
www.bethanyhouse.com

Bethany House Publishers is a division of
Baker Publishing Group, Grand Rapids, Michigan

Paperback edition published 2019

Printed in the United States of America

ISBN 978-0-7642-3081-3 (cloth)
ISBN 978-0-7642-3137-7 (ITPE)
ISBN 978-0-7642-3216-9 (trade paper)

The Library of Congress has cataloged the hardcover edition as follows:
Names: Johnston, Jeremiah, author.
Title: Unimaginable : what our world would be like without Christianity / Jeremiah J.
   Johnston.
Description: Minneapolis, Minnesota : Bethany House, 2017. | Includes bibliographical
   references.
Identifiers: LCCN 2017036882 | ISBN 9780764230813 (cloth : alk. paper)
Subjects: LCSH: Church and the world. | Christianity—Influence. | Christianity—Controversial
   literature.
Classification: LCC BR115.W6 J63 2017 | DDC 270—dc23
LC record available at https://lccn.loc.gov/2017036882

Cover design by LOOK Design Studio

Author is represented by the Law Office of Curtis W. Wallace, P.C.

19 20 21 22 23 24 25   7 6 5 4 3 2 1

For my friend Cary Summers,
President of the Museum of the Bible,
whose life exemplifies the impact and difference
faith makes in the world.

CONTENTS

Foreword   11

Introduction   15

Part I: The World Before Christianity

1. Our Sense of the Divine   25

2. A World of Suffering   32

3. A World of Fear   40

4. A World of Inequality   51

5. A World of Bondage: Racism   62

Part II: The World Without Christianity

6. A Slippery Slope   73

7. Dehumanizing Humanity   86

8. Atheism and the Broken Soul   96

9. "Superman" Arrives   108

10. Hitler's Hell on Earth   119

11. When Truth Is What You Want It to Be   129

Contents

Part III: The World With Christianity

12. Jesus' Tour de Force: Good News for All People   149
13. New Hope: Jesus and His Proclamation   159
14. New Life: What Made Christianity Irresistible?   169
15. Christianity Ends Racism and Slavery   180
16. Without Jesus, Women Would Not Be Free   187
17. Healing the Unimaginable in Your Life   195

Acknowledgments   203
Notes   205
About the Author   237

FOREWORD

Just before the turn of this century, the editors of *Life* magazine published a ranking of what they called the "100 Most Important Events and People of the Past 1,000 Years." Their top ten included things like Galileo's telescope, the Declaration of Independence, Columbus's voyage, and, at number nine, "Hitler comes to power." Calling that event *important* doesn't feel right; *impactful* seems better. Still, the number one event of the last millennium according to *Life* magazine was "Gutenberg prints the Bible." Good choice.

Of all the books printed on a Gutenberg press, the Bible was by far the most important and most influential. And it continues to benefit the world immensely.

Some will argue we would be better off without the Bible or Christianity. I couldn't disagree more. The fact is, there will always be conflict between differing worldviews, just as there will always be political differences and conflicts. The question is, on which worldview should we build our society? Every society is built on one. Imagine for a moment if the founders of America had a Hindu worldview; our nation would look very different. What about a Muslim worldview or an atheistic worldview? All you have to do is look at societies that are primarily influenced by those worldviews to get an idea of what our country might look like.

Our founders, for the most part, had a biblical worldview. That's not to say that all of them were Christians (most were), but the Bible had an undeniable effect on them. It also isn't to say that they got it all right. This nation has never been perfect and it never will be. But what they built became one of the freest, most powerful and wealthy nations on earth.

The intent of the Museum of the Bible in Washington, D.C., is to show how the Bible has had an impact on every area of life. Our education efforts only scratch the surface, as no building, not even a state-of-the-art eight-floor, 430,000-square-foot museum, can contain the whole of its story. On the Impact floor, we show the Bible's influence on everything from the most powerful nation on earth down to an individual life. With billions of people touched by the Bible, the whole museum could be filled with just those stories.

In this fascinating book, Dr. Jeremiah J. Johnston takes us on a tour around the world and throughout history as he considers the impact the Bible and the Christian faith have had on humanity. What would our world be like without Christianity? Quite simply, *unimaginable*.

Of course, many people in today's increasingly secular society think the Bible is obsolete and that Christianity is out-of-date. These beliefs are not new. Today's so-called "New Atheism" is rooted in the nineteenth century when a number of bad ideas were advanced, but it goes even farther back than that. People of all ages need to know this information. And this is why I am thrilled by the appearance of Dr. Johnston's stimulating and well-written book.

Dr. Johnston first shows what the world was like before Jesus and the Christian movement arrived on the scene. It was not a pretty place. Poverty, slavery, prostitution, and the abuse of women and children were commonplace. It was a world of suffering and a world of fear. Racism and gross inequities were widespread and human life was cheap.

What changed that world? The evidence, says Dr. Johnston, is clear: Jesus and his movement set the world in a new direction that led to an enormous improvement in the quality of life. But before he highlights the many benefits of Christianity, he presents six important chapters that in graphic and disturbing terms show us what has happened in modern times when Christianity is shoved to the side to make room for a new worldview, one that is based on atheism and its many social and scientific corollaries. Again and again, Dr. Johnston digs down into the original sources of the "new" ideas of the nineteenth century and shows how almost always they were based on the pre-Christian ideas and practices of late antiquity. Far from representing advances in science and enlightenment, these bad ideas reflect the warped and evil thinking of a bygone era.

The depravity of men like Friedrich Nietzsche laid the foundation for the Nazi and Communist regimes of the twentieth century. These regimes, inspired by anti-Christian ethics and policies, were responsible for the deaths of almost 150 million people. For all their talk of science and education, if the New Atheists have their way they will take us back to a dark time. A return to the philosophies, ideologies, and bogus science of the nineteenth century will not be progress but a tragic regression.

The third part of this important book outlines the benefits that Jesus and the Christian movement have brought to humanity. Dr. Johnston shows how revolutionary the preaching and ministry of Jesus was from the norms of his day. The Roman world simply couldn't resist the life-changing message of Jesus, and within three centuries, this nonviolent movement had swept the Roman Empire. Doctrines of racism were laid aside, crucifixions and the cruel gladiator games of the arenas were ended, the dignity of life was taken to new levels, the seeds of the emancipation of slaves were planted, and the groundwork of modern science was laid. It was the beginning of countless blessings bestowed on the world by the Christian church. Why would anyone want to see that end?

I am impressed by the depth and breadth of the scholarship throughout this book. Dr. Johnston is tackling complex, important topics. Behind the claims and conclusions lie careful research, as evidenced by the first editions, original-language editions, and other technical sources cited in the notes section. Reading this great book took me back to school for further education. What a treat!

Dr. Johnston writes like a leader—a leader for the church and the academy. He communicates as a statesman, speaking directly and effectively to the challenges of our time. Under his leadership, the Christian Thinkers Society has formed strategic partnerships and opened doors for fruitful and effective ministry. *Unimaginable* is a book for our time; it is a book that is urgently needed.

Steve Green
President, Hobby Lobby
Chairman, Museum of the Bible

INTRODUCTION

I t was our second day in Turkey, and we were driving on a highway that had seen better days, when it hit me: *I don't see any crosses.*

Two thousand years ago, present-day Turkey was the cradle of Christianity. It was at Antioch (known now as Antakya) where the followers of Jesus were first called Christians. The Nicene Creed, the foundational statement of the Christian faith, was adopted in northwestern Turkey in AD 325. This is the country where all seven churches addressed in Revelation were founded along the Aegean coast, not to mention some of the earliest places of worship dating to the book of Acts. But during my visit, I was hard-pressed to spot any vestiges of Turkey's once thriving Christian community. It has been pushed out by conflicts, warfare, genocide, and Islamic jihad.

On another trip, this time to Cuba, I witnessed a place where the distribution of Bibles was banned for more than forty years. Only recently has the government lifted the restriction as part of an "experimental program." I had flown to Cuba with other scholars and leaders to celebrate the opening of a traveling exhibit of the Museum of the Bible. For five weeks, Cubans had unprecedented freedom to see biblical artifacts and rare manuscripts, including the first complete Bible in Spanish. The exhibit's inauguration included a public performance by Cuban singers, dancers, and actors paying tribute to the narrative of the Bible. We sat among the Cuban people as they cheered, some overwhelmed with emotion. It was a stunning reminder of the impact Christianity has on society, especially on individuals.

Mark Zuckerberg, the billionaire founder of Facebook and one-time self-described atheist, shocked many of his followers on a recent Christmas Day when he changed his Facebook status to "celebrating Christmas" and wrote that he now believes "religion is very important." Five months later, as Harvard's commencement speaker, Zuckerberg (a Harvard dropout) talked about the importance of prayer and even quoted a Jewish prayer, "Mi Shebeirach," which he says whenever he faces major challenges and also when he puts his daughter to bed.[1]

In North America, we still have freedom of religion, worshiping in our preferred manner and where we desire. Bibles are still found in some hotel rooms in nightstands. At this point, churches still seem to be the bedrock of many communities. But frighteningly, there is growing, undeniable hostility toward Christianity and its followers. Analogous to the 9/11 attackers who were determined to crack the foundation of America's security, we see the undermining of the Judeo-Christian ethic in our nation. There are innumerable expressions of this, from Richard Dawkins' *The God Delusion*, a three-million-copy bestselling book, and Bill Maher's *Real Time* on HBO, to countless lawsuits to remove Nativity scenes or Christian symbols from government buildings, trying to erase our nation's heritage. In public schools, "Christmas" has been replaced by "winter holiday." It is all reminiscent of Malcolm Muggeridge's parable of a frog in a kettle that is gradually heated to boiling—most seem unaware of what is happening.

The seeds of this book were planted as my wife, Audrey, and I enjoyed one of our favorite pastimes: binge-watching television shows.

Amazon Prime's *The Man in the High Castle* is a disturbing dystopian series set in 1960s America. It envisions what the country and everyday life would be like if the Axis powers, primarily Japan and Germany, had won World War II and ruled over the United States. Certain plot twists in the series brought to my mind the various ways Jesus and the Christian movement have radically changed the world and civilization. Audrey made a striking statement after one of our exchanges. "Jeremiah, most people—Christian or not—have very little idea about this. People need to know about the Jesus factor in our world."

The trouble is, it seems more and more people just want Christianity to go away. They say it has no place in modern life. You're probably familiar with the saying "You might get what you want, but you might not want what you get." Prominent atheist Richard Dawkins might even agree with that. Dawkins, who wrote *The God Delusion*, said in a 2010 interview with *The Times* of London: "There are no Christians, as far as I know, blowing up buildings. I am not aware of any Christian suicide bombers. I am not aware of any major Christian denomination that believes the penalty for apostasy is death." Then Dawkins admitted, "I have mixed feelings about the decline of Christianity, insofar as Christianity might be a bulwark against something worse."[2]

I believe the "Jesus factor" is much more than a bulwark against dangerous distortions of theism, such as we see in Islamic violence and extremism. Christianity and a life lived according to the Bible shields us against a host of negative things. The very standard of life we enjoy in the West likely would disappear if Christianity vanished. Without Christians, Christian ethics, and a Christian worldview, how much longer would freedom, liberty, and morality last? Even the concept of truth and absolutes is disappearing in today's highly subjective, postmodern, post-Christian society. Christianity, as expressed in the Old and New

Testaments, is necessary for freedom to flourish. Yet, not until the dawn of the Bible did ideas of universal freedom—that is, freedom as a right for all people—begin to take hold.

Of course, many would probably assert that Christianity—though not nearly as toxic as radical Islam—impedes progress, and that the many positive developments witnessed in history since the rise of the Christian church would simply continue and, indeed, probably accelerate. Assertions like this, however, do not reflect the facts of history and why it is that pagan, primitive, violent Europe was transformed in the early centuries of the Common Era and leapt ahead of the cultures of the East in education, technology, science, and human rights. These beliefs also fail to acknowledge what happened in Germany and Russia, for example, when aggressive anti-Christian leaders gained power and went to work dismantling Christian culture. We actually don't have to imagine the horror of what fills the cultural vacuum when Christianity collapses. There are sobering examples.

Unfortunately, one of the long-term effects of social media is that we are now living in a society that prefers sound bites over substance, which leads to ample confusion and usually a rush to judgment. All this can leave the casual observer feeling overwhelmed or lulled into silence, yet the scales of truth tip in our favor.

In recent years there has been fascination with what is called counterfactual, or alternative, history. That is, attempts to understand how the past and the present would be if a certain event in history had turned out differently. A number of books have explored these possibilities, including an intriguing volume titled *What If?* It features essays from military historians. They explore, for example, the consequences of the defeat of the Greeks at the hands of the Persians in 480 BC, instead of a Greek victory, or the premature death of Alexander the Great, which likely would have meant no dismantling of the Persian Empire and no spread of the Greek language and culture in late antiquity.[3] These two "what ifs" alone would have had huge consequences for the West. It is reasonable to assume that the rise of democracy and the pursuit of science and literacy in the West simply would not have taken place.

Another essay in the book *What If?* raises the question of what might have happened in 1242 if the Mongol invaders of Europe had finished off the last of the Christian armies and reduced the continent to shambles.[4] In actuality, just before the battle for Vienna, the leader of the Mongols, Genghis Khan's son Ogadai, died, and Mongol custom required their fighting men to return home for the election of the new khan. They withdrew from Europe and never returned.

Adolf Hitler ponders counterfactuals in his book *Mein Kampf* (*My Struggle*).[5] In one case, the future *führer* wonders if Germany might have achieved great power without resorting to the Great War (World War I) launched in 1914 if Kaiser Wilhelm II had made different decisions.[6] In another case, after observing how poorly the German government promoted the war effort, Hitler becomes convinced that if he had been in charge of propaganda, Germany may well have won the war.[7]

This book explores what the world would be like had Christianity not emerged and what will happen if Christianity collapses. Some will say this cannot be known; it would require a parallel universe. But I think we can at least get a pretty good idea of a world without Christianity. After all, until Jesus Christ began his ministry in the late twenties of the first century of the Common Era, there was no such thing as Christianity. We can study that world. Also, there are places around the globe today where Christianity has little visible effect. In his famous Sermon on the Mount, Jesus said, "For he makes his sun rise on the evil and on the good, and sends rain on the just and on the unjust."[8] I will also magnify how Christianity has blessed the world to the degree that even if you are a person of no faith, the everyday conveniences and most of the rights you now enjoy would not exist without God working in the world through the faith of his children.

I already mentioned my recent trip to both Santiago and Havana, Cuba, an experience that was both exhilarating and haunting all at once. Outside of a few Catholic cathedrals, Cuba is a modern example of what happens when society pushes God away. The most recent World Watch List from Open Doors USA documents the persecution of more than 215 million Christians living in fifty countries where either Christianity is illegal or Christians are persecuted, attacked, or marginalized.[9] What are those places like? And, of course, there are other examples that serve as stark reminders. We can look at Hitler's Germany and the Communist states of the last century or so, where atheism is or had been the official worldview and Christianity was driven to the margins.

In 2007, the late Christopher Hitchens came out with the book *God Is Not Great*. If his worldview wasn't clear by the title, the book's subtitle left no doubt: *How Religion Poisons Everything*.[10] Many people believe this and, in fact, appeal to this claim as justification for their atheism. But I contend evidence shows that belief in God, specifically as understood in Judeo-Christian theology, has in fact benefited humanity greatly. In fact, this book will show the exceptional Judeo-Christian worldview, which has blessed civilization with inherent values and God-given opportunities for all people.

The poison to which Hitchens refers is not sourced in belief in God but comes from human sin. It is sin that poisons everything, including religion. This is the tragedy of the human condition. The fallen nature of humanity means that love, art, society, politics, education, sports, food, and drink—everything we do and produce—can be and often is corrupted, or poisoned, to one degree or another. But most tragically of all, human sin results in theological corruption, in gross misrepresentation of God, both in reference to his being and nature, as well as in reference to his will for humanity.[11]

After speaking in churches, conferences, and numerous events across North America and the United Kingdom (not to mention my own experiences teaching in a university), what is troubling to me is that in the whole history of the church, the twenty-first century has some of the best-educated people ever to sit in its pews, while also being the most disengaged and biblically illiterate.

When I read Judges 2:10, it is difficult not to be challenged when I think of the unthinking faith represented by so many Christians today: "And there arose another generation after them, who did not know the LORD or the work which he had done for Israel." This passage immediately follows the death of Joshua and the historic miracles of Israel's exodus and inheritance of the promised land. Within just one generation, spiritual decline led Israel and the people of God into complacency, and complacency led to apostasy and eventually rebellion against God. This should cause us to pause and ask, "Where are we in the story? Have we forgotten the works of God? Or are we simply unaware?"

As a professor, I can speak from experience about the modern university classroom. More and more professors are atheists, even *nihilists* (believing that religion is worthless), teaching that life itself is meaningless. Have we so quickly forgotten the message of Jesus from John's gospel? "The thief comes only to steal and kill and destroy; I came that they may have life, and have it abundantly."[12]

It is this sense of an abundant life that we will unlock within the pages of this book. Notice that Jesus did not come that we might simply exist in an ordinary life, but rather we might have an *extraordinary* life. My prayer is that *Unimaginable* will remind us all of the Jesus factor in our world: the way Jesus through his Holy Spirit has worked through his followers to make the world a better place.

Let the evidence speak. Judge for yourself. Are we not better off because Jesus came to earth, died to save us from our sins, and rose from the dead, founding a movement that changed the world?

PART I

THE WORLD **BEFORE** CHRISTIANITY

CHAPTER 1
Our Sense of the Divine

The ancient letter begins on the sweetest of notes.

Hilarion to his sister Alis very many greetings; likewise to my lady Berous and Apollonarion.

Hilarion, the writer of the letter, is a migrant worker in the year 1 BC. He has just addressed his wife, Alis, as *sister*, an expression of endearment suggesting that Hilarion truly loved Alis.[1] (Marriages in antiquity were often arranged and did not always result in love between the spouses.) The "lady Berous" could be Alis's mother or sister, while Apollonarion may be Berous's husband.[2]

Hilarion and others in his work party are in Alexandria, Egypt, about two hundred miles north of his home in Oxyrhynchus. He wants to assure his wife, who is pregnant, that she should not worry about his well-being.

Know that we are still in Alexandria. Do not be anxious when they return and I remain in Alexandria.

At the time, Oxyrhynchus was a prosperous farming community situated adjacent to a canal west of the Nile River. Back then, if you wanted to compose a letter, you hired a scribe, and judging by this letter's unremarkable penmanship, Hilarion likely enlisted a writer who was not highly trained, someone a migrant worker could afford. So Hilarion is not a poor man, but he is not wealthy either, and has taken the opportunity to earn more money on the coast of the Mediterranean.[3]

I ask and entreat you, take care of the child, and as soon as we receive our wages I will send them up to you.

In all probability, Alis was several months pregnant when Hilarion left Oxyrhynchus for work up north in Alexandria. Because of his decision to remain in Alexandria longer than originally planned, he realizes his wife could give birth before his return.

If—may you have good luck![4]*—you should give birth; if it is a boy, keep it; if it is a girl, throw it out.*

Throw it out?! Hilarion's shocking command to his wife, to throw out the newborn if a girl, reflected a common practice of infanticide among Greeks and Romans. Girls, as well as boys, did go to work at young ages and help the family get by. Still, unwanted girls and infants with birth defects and deformities were routinely cast out to die of exposure either to the elements or to wild animals. (In the face of great danger, though, we know that early Christians roamed the streets at night to rescue abandoned children before wild dogs or other animals got to them. More about this later.) In some cases, unwanted children were later sold into slavery or prostitution. The most probable reason for Hilarion's command is that the family could not afford the dowry that would be expected when his daughter was given in marriage. Yet in the first-century Roman world (the world in which Jesus was born), killing an unwanted child was no big deal. Seneca, a philosopher and contemporary of Jesus, described infanticide in his own terms: "Unnatural progeny we destroy; we drown even children who at birth are weak or abnormal." Seneca's Latin is more cryptic (*portentosos fetus exstinguimus . . . debiles, monstrosique*) where children deemed strange or monstrous were terminated.[5] Cicero (106–143 BC) appeals to what The Laws of the Twelve Tables decreed more than three hundred years earlier: "Quickly killed, as The Twelve Tables ordain that a dreadfully deformed child shall be killed."[6]

After all this, Hilarion's letter to Alis closes on a tender note, acknowledging a message evidently conveyed to him by a neighbor or friend.

You have said to Aphrodisias, "Do not forget me." How can I forget you? I beg you then not to be anxious.

There was indeed much to be anxious about in the ancient world. By today's standards, it was hell on earth. Poverty, sickness, premature death, domestic violence, economic injustice, slavery, and political corruption were the givens of life. Absent were any ideas of justice, equality, mercy, democracy (as we know it today), education, and protection of the weak and marginalized. All this started to change when people began living with a sense of the divine, a sense of God's presence.

Spirit World: The Spark That Ignited Civilization

It's a chicken-or-the-egg type question. What came first, civilization or religion?

Anthropologists and historians have long maintained the view that civilization gave birth to religion. The hypothesis is that civilization inevitably led to social hierarchy, whose leadership at the highest level justified its power and affluence by playing a priestly, intercessory role between humanity below and the gods above. Acting as an intercessor, the priest or priest-king could justify the collection of taxes and demands for other forms of support from his subjects. In return, the priest or priest-king provided his subjects with assurance that thanks to his ministrations, the gods were satisfied and would act on behalf of the people.

Organized religion, including a belief in divine power, the argument continues, was nothing more than a by-product of the emergence of civilization many years ago. Once religion had taken hold, it remained a part of human civilization, even as civilization advanced socially and technologically. Its place in the hierarchy of human society was so deeply ingrained it could not be dislodged until relatively modern times.[7]

A discovery in southeastern Turkey, however, has raised serious questions about this long-held view. In a place called Göbekli Tepe, archaeologists uncovered a temple that apparently dates to about 10,000 BC, which is about the time it is believed human civilization began. What has impressed archaeologists, anthropologists, and historians is that there is no evidence that this temple sprang up as a by-product of civilization. In fact, the evidence suggests the reverse. That is, it was the building of the temple that drew people together and in effect sparked civilization. In other words, belief in God or gods preceded the building of the temple, which in turn preceded the emergence of cities and civilization.[8] Belief in God or gods generated a felt need to build the temple as a way to connect with the divine. To build the temple required socialization and cooperation well beyond the demands of farming, herding livestock, and hunting. The building of the temple took human society to a new level and created what today we define as civilization. Religion is not a by-product of primitive society. Rather, religion gave birth to civilization and brought people together.

Most societies in late antiquity, including the Greeks, Romans, and Egyptians, were polytheistic; they believed in more than one god. What is not as well-known is that evidence suggests that in great antiquity—at the very beginning of human civilization—most humans were monotheists and worshiped one God. Polytheism came next, and represents a corruption of monotheism. Even the Jewish people, known throughout their long history for their monotheistic faith, often moved toward polytheism (or at least a form of henotheism, whereby they regarded the Lord as their *principal* god, but not necessarily their *only* god). Again and again, the Jewish prophets of the Old Testament summoned the Jewish people back to their monotheistic faith.[9]

Archaeological work everywhere, in every corner of the world, finds temples in every ancient city. In fact, one can safely say that there was no city or civilization in human history that did not have at least one temple or building whose primary purpose was a religious one.

Today, we may differ as to how to address, understand, and experience this deep sense of the divine, but it's clear that through the years humans have invested a great deal of time and resources into the quest for better understanding and closer connection.

Moral World: What Gave Rise to Law

Humanity's sense of divine reality not only served as an impetus to create civilization but also seems to have led to the creation and articulation of law. And *law* is comprised of morals and ethics.

Law can be understood in purely utilitarian terms in that it is good for us, it protects and promotes justice and fairness. And no doubt utility was a major factor in the creation of law. But law invariably transcends mere utility. Time and again we find in ancient law the belief that law, along with morality, is based in divine truth or divine will. This is why human law and ethics speak of what people *should* do, quite apart from utilitarian factors. We speak of moral obligations, even if the benefit of these obligations, either for ourselves or for others, is not obvious. Why is this so?

The best known and one of the earliest articulations of law is the famous Code of Hammurabi.[10] Hammurabi and his law code are dated to the eighteenth century BC. The code begins with a lengthy preamble, in which it is made clear that the law is rooted in the gods, and expresses their will for humanity. Hammurabi states that he has been ordered by Marduk (one of ancient Babylon's principal deities) to establish law and to rule. Nearly three hundred laws follow the preamble. Many of these laws parallel the better known and somewhat later law of Moses found in the Bible. At the end of his law code, Hammurabi states: "By the command of Shamash, the great judge of heaven and earth, let righteousness go forth in the land."[11]

The law of Moses, part of the covenant that God made with Israel, is also rooted in the divine will, but the preamble in this case is much shorter. In fact, it comprises a single verse. At the foot of Mount Sinai, the God of Israel says to Israel: "I am the LORD your God, who brought you out of the land of Egypt, out of the house of bondage."[12] The well-known Ten Commandments immediately follow.

The point I want to make here is that human civilization, which by its very nature requires law, is not only founded on belief in the divine but was also generated by this belief. Without a sense of the divine, would humans have created civilization? Without a sense of the divine, would humans have created codes of law that give expression to morality and ethics, codes that go beyond mere utilitarian benefits?

These questions are hotly debated today. A number of philosophers and ethicists have pointed out, with good reason in my view, that moral obligations upon which law ultimately rests are "unintelligible apart from the idea of God."[13] I suggest that the ancients understood this very

Our Sense of the Divine

well. Moral laws were not "discovered" and "agreed upon" through discussion. They were not derived democratically. Rather they reflected the divine will. All humans sensed what was right and wrong—whether or not it advanced one's personal interests.

Our sense of divine drove us toward civilization, law, morality, and ethics. But without the impact of Jesus and the church he founded, this sense of the divine could take humanity only so far.

CHAPTER 2
A World of Suffering

I don't subscribe to the notion that the dead can speak to us from beyond the grave. But epitaphs from Greco-Roman times indicate how hopeless many felt as they faced death.[1]

> There is no boat to carry you to Hades, no ferryman Charon, no judge Aeacus, no dog Cerberus. All of us below who are dead have become bones and ashes.[2]

> When I lived the living praised me; but now I am dead. This stone speaks for me![3]

> Your body in its bosom, Callisto, earth has hidden, but memory of your virtue you have left to your friends.[4]

Some epitaphs are philosophical. A dead man asks passersby, with a degree of pomposity:

> What are we or what do we say at last this life is? Just that a man has lived among us and now is no more. Just the stone

and the inscription remain, and no other traces. Now, what is life? It is nothing that you should trouble yourself to inquire about.[5]

> Of his late wife, a grieving husband declares:

Her fair face and figure praised as fair now are an insubstantial shadow, her bones but a bit of ash.[6]

Pain and Sickness

Human sickness and suffering in the ancient world are well attested not only in the surviving literature but in the archaeological record as well. Thanks to the work of archaeologists and curators, modern visitors to places like Epidaurus and Corinth in Greece can observe the remains of temples called the Asclepion, a medical shrine of sorts where the ancients hoped to be healed. The name of these healing centers came from Asclepius, a mythological figure usually thought of as the son of the god Apollo and a mortal mother named Coronis. Asclepius became known as the god of medicine. He achieved this status when he received from the goddess Athena the blood of Medusa, the snake-headed female terror of ancient Greece. The blood drawn from Medusa's veins on her right side contained healing properties.[7] Or so it was widely believed.

Tour Epidaurus today and you'll see numerous sculpted pieces of stone or ceramic that served as testimonials and expressions of gratitude for healing. You can see eyes, ears, hands, feet, genitals, breasts, and so on. Archaeologists and historians rightly infer from these items apparent healing, or at least the hope of healing, of blindness, deafness, weakness or paralysis of the limbs, and sterility. Asclepius was especially looked to for cure of infertility.

Desperate for Healing

The quest for healing of sickness and relief of pain in ancient times bordered on desperation, and it is not difficult to see why. Literary and archaeological remains suggest that on any given day, about one quarter of the population of the Roman Empire was ill, injured, or otherwise in need of medical help.[8] Excavations of tombs where three or four generations of a family have been interred often find that only about one-third of the members of a given family reach adulthood, and many of those who did reach adulthood did not make it to forty years of age. Very few people lived into their sixties and seventies. I should note, too, that here I am describing the skeletal remains of the wealthy, not the poor. If only one-third of the members of an affluent family reached adulthood, we should assume that longevity for the poor was probably much shorter.

It is not surprising that large crowds followed Jesus, sometimes pressing against him in hope of healing. On one occasion Jesus found it necessary to address the crowd by sitting on a boat, pushed away from the shore.[9] The clear implication is that Jesus needed to create a barrier between himself and the crowd if he was to teach without interference. This is illustrated when on another occasion Jesus is pressed by a crowd and a desperate woman grasps his clothing hoping for healing.[10] In yet another case, four men removed a portion of the roof of the house in which Jesus was sitting and teaching, in order to lower their paralyzed friend into the presence of Jesus.[11] With such a big crowd within and around the house, it was the only way they could gain access to Jesus.

Some years ago, a New Testament scholar at Oxford suggested that Jesus drew large crowds not so much because he was a good teacher or his message was provocative, but because he had become known as an effective healer.[12] People both wealthy and poor, desperate for healing, sought Jesus out, even after his death and resurrection. It has been argued that a major reason the Christian church expanded the way it did in the Roman Empire in the first three centuries, despite opposition and at times deadly persecution, was because of amazing healings that took place "in the name of Jesus."[13]

These healings, including exorcisms, were widely regarded as miracles and as evidence of the truth of the Christian message. During the time of Jesus' public activities, we also know of at least one professional exorcist who invoked the name of Jesus.[14] This is remarkable, and to my knowledge unparalleled. Indeed, there is a surprising amount of physical evidence from late antiquity that Jews and pagans invoked the name of Jesus for healing.[15] In other words, Jesus' reputation was such that people from all walks of life and from every religious persuasion appealed to him for healing.

Superstition over Science

Again, none of this is surprising in the least. In late antiquity, medical knowledge was very limited. Illness was often explained in reference to superstition. Moreover, people were convinced that fevers, blindness, and speech impediments were caused by evil spirits.[16] Hippocrates (460–370 BC), after whom was derived the Hippocratic Oath,[17] believed all illness could be traced to one of four causes: heat, cold, phlegm, and bile.[18]

Ceramic medical busts of human torsos produced in late antiquity show that the physicians of the time were not sure where organs were located and were even less sure of their function.[19] Physicians of this era generally did not enjoy favorable reputations. Those familiar with the Christian Gospels will remember the comment with regard to the woman with the hemorrhage, who spent all her money on doctors but only got worse.[20] Pliny the Elder (AD 23–79) warned his son to have nothing to do with physicians.[21] In short, there was almost a complete absence of medical remedies for diseases and illness, most of which today are easily cured.

I recently viewed an exhibit at the Houston Museum of Natural History. On display were many items recovered from ancient Herculaneum and Pompeii, major Roman cities that were buried under volcanic ash when Mount Vesuvius erupted in AD 79. The ash preserved much of the physical culture, including tools, weapons, and medical instruments. The bronze instruments were well-crafted and included scalpels. But even with surprisingly sophisticated tools such as these, the ancients knew little or nothing about the causes of most diseases.

One of the most dreaded diseases was leprosy, which is mentioned in the Bible several times. Jesus is said to have cured, or "cleansed," a few people with leprosy.[22] Some skeptics claim that true leprosy, or Hansen's disease, did not appear in the eastern Mediterranean until early in the Middle Ages. But a recent archaeological discovery settled the debate. In the year 2000, a first-century tomb was discovered in Akeldama in Jerusalem in which the remains of a man were found sealed in a niche. Thanks to the lack of oxygen, the body had not fully decomposed. Part of the man's scalp was recovered, and a subsequent biopsy showed the presence of *Mycobacterium tuberculosis*, which is the cause of tuberculosis, and *Mycobacterium leprae*, the bacterium that causes Hansen's disease.[23] This remarkable discovery proved beyond all doubt that there were indeed lepers in biblical times.

Forensic examination of human skeletal remains from the Greco-Roman world shows that people suffered from various types of parasites and often died from tooth infections. We can infer from references to illnesses in ancient literature the presence of malaria, which caused fever (the probable cause of the death of Alexander the Great), scarlet fever, measles, typhus, diabetes, and perhaps even bubonic plague. In some cases, plagues wiped out as much as one-third of a population (as in fifth-century BC Greece). During the reign of Emperor Titus (AD 39–81), Roman historian Suetonius remarks that a number of disasters took place, including "a plague the like of which had hardly been known before."[24] Alas, one century later, a plague, probably smallpox, wiped out one-third of the population in and around Rome.[25]

Recent work around Israel's famous Sea of Galilee has shown that malaria was in all probability quite common along the southern coastline. All four of the Gospels mention that Jesus healed people afflicted with fever, likely malaria.[26]

In their desperation to find relief from pain, sickness, and death, many people resorted to magic and related rigamarole. Professional magicians required their clients to take certain potions, to do or to avoid certain things, to eat or drink certain concoctions, and then would pronounce over them a charm or incantation. Body parts, locks of hair, nails used in crucifixion, and other grisly specimens collected from cemeteries and places of execution were widely believed to possess curative powers.[27] The ancients did almost anything to find cures and relief from pain and illness.

Death and Hell

Death was the greatest fear of all. Life expectancy then was only twenty years of age, and people's last days often came with a great deal of suffering.[28] Romans also feared death because they were uncertain about the afterlife. Some believed the spiritual essence of human beings simply floated away into the netherworld, or, in the case of very righteous persons, was transported to a place of rest and comfort (variously called the Isles of the Blessed or the Elyusian Fields). Others feared that their destiny was hell (variously called Hades or Tartaros).[29]

Greeks and Romans held out little hope for the afterlife because the idea of resurrection was explicitly denied in their theology. According to Aeschylus (fifth century BC), the god Apollo is emphatic that humans cannot experience resurrection:

> When the dust has soaked up a man's blood,
> Once he is dead, there is no resurrection.[30]

Apollo's position seems clear enough. In *Eumenides*, the son of Zeus explains why resurrection is not possible:

> This is a thing for which my father [Zeus] never made
> Curative spells. All other states, without effort
> Of hard breath, he can completely rearrange.[31]

In the Greco-Roman world, death meant the end. There was no hope, only sorrow. This is why Jesus' ministry was utterly remarkable. He not only predicted his own death and bodily resurrection (Mark 9:31), but he charged his disciples to preach the kingdom of God and to "raise the dead" (Matthew 10:8). No wonder that over thirty times in the Gospels we read about large crowds following Jesus.

The Gospels record that Jesus personally raised three people from the dead. In one case, he raised the daughter of Jairus, the ruler of a synagogue. Arriving at the family home shortly after she had breathed her last, Jesus calls out, *Talitha cum* ("little girl, arise"). We are told she immediately stood, undoubtedly shocking the first-century eyewitnesses.[32]

Jesus also raised the only son of a widow, and in the process, broke cultural barriers. Seeing the boy's funeral processional, he reached out and touched the bier, on which the boy's body lay, and the deceased boy sat up. Touching a corpse or anything related to it would have made Jesus ceremonial unclean. But none of that mattered. Jesus cared about alleviating suffering.[33]

Arguably the most stunning miracle Jesus performed was raising Lazarus. Lazarus had been dead for four days, as dead as one can get. Still, Jesus commands, "Lazarus, come forth!" And Scripture says, "And he who had died came forth, bound hand and foot with wrappings."[34] Remarkable.

It's not hard to imagine why the early Christian movement spread so rapidly around the Mediterranean world. Jesus' disciples were passionate eyewitnesses to the abundant life and resurrected body he promised. "As for us," Peter and John said, "we cannot help speaking about what we have seen and heard."[35]

CHAPTER 3
A World of Fear

I t's a common tendency. When looking at history, we project our own modern ideas into the past. We assume that the way we think was the way our ancestors thought, or at least it was pretty close. But that is rarely the case, especially going back hundreds of years. People of late antiquity understood their world very differently than we do as observers from afar. Nowhere is this difference more obvious than in ideas and assumptions about the gods.

Today, with notable exceptions such as in India, most people speak of only one God—whether they believe in God or not. Most people also think of God as benevolent. If God does exist, likely he is kind and loving. So goes the thinking. Indeed, this very assumption is the reason some people doubt that God exists. They cannot explain evil and suffering in the world if a loving and benevolent God exists.

But people in antiquity did not think this way. The suffering and evil they saw around them was no argument against the existence of the gods. No, most suffering and evil in the world was brought on *by the gods*. Strangely enough (from our modern point of view), suffering and evil were seen as evidence of the existence of the gods and semigods (or "demigods"). Bad things happen *because of the gods*. How could this be?

People thought this way because the gods were not considered benevolent. The Greco-Roman gods were jealous, petty, vengeful, easily offended, and lustful. The essence of these gods was power and immortality.[1] Most were mean-spirited—against one another and against humans in general. People feared that if they enjoyed too much success, it might draw the unwelcome attention of a god eager to keep mortals in their place. Too much success could lead to pride and arrogance. And human arrogance could easily be seen as *hubris*, which could lead to the abuse of power and position and invite disaster at the hands of the gods. In some ways the gods were superhuman more than divine beings. This is why it was so easy for the Greeks and Romans of late antiquity to imagine humans of virtue and achievement being elevated to divine status.

Normally, the Greco-Roman gods had no love for humans. When they did express love, it was usually erotic lust. Several demigods (including Hercules and Dionysus) were the offspring of Zeus (aka Jupiter), who seduced or raped mortal women. The gods cheated on one another, tricked one another, and sometimes injured one another. The marriage between Zeus and Hera, for example, was anything but happy.[2]

People back then normally could not and did not look to the gods for compassion and aid. Through offerings, which were little more than bribery and appeals to a god's vanity, people might secure favors. But in general, they could expect little or no comfort from the gods.

How different this is for followers of the true God. Old Testament sacrifices were made to atone for sin and also to enjoy fellowship with God. But when Jesus came to earth, he became the promised sacrificial lamb. Atonement would not be through the blood of animals but from the "precious blood of Christ."[3] In paganism, sacrifice was primarily intended to influence gods, to appease them or to gain something. In one of the Homeric hymns, we hear that humans suffer, "enduring so much at the hands of the gods . . . heedless and helpless, unable to find for themselves either a cure for death or a bulwark against old age."[4]

Right or Wrong?

For all the religiosity and the great many gods and demigods of late antiquity, there was little morality. That might seem strange. But once again we are letting our modern ideas of God, ideas that are defined by the Judeo-Christian understanding of God, shape our thinking. The gods of that era were not especially moral themselves. They committed crimes, lied to one another, committed adultery, and when it came to humans, they thought nothing of causing harm. Indeed, the gods of the Greeks and Romans seemed to be just as lustful and untrustworthy as humans were.

Recognizing this reality explains what to us seems to be the paradox of so much religion and sexual debauchery side-by-side. The juxta-position was not an uneasy one. No cities from antiquity illustrate this point more graphically than Pompeii and Herculaneum, thanks to the eruption of Vesuvius in the summer of AD 79. At the time of their burial under ash, these cities were filled with temples, altars, shrines, and niches for the display of gods. Almost every public building and private home contained idols and religious utensils. The people of Pompeii and Herculaneum, as did the people of all other cities throughout the Roman Empire, worshiped the major deities (known as the Big Twelve) and a variety of lesser local deities. The gods were worshiped publicly and privately, at work and at home. One might recall Paul's comment in Athens: "I perceive that in every way you are very religious."[5]

However, for all of this interest in the gods—attending to worship, sacrifices, special meals and libations, public and private prayers, building and maintaining countless temples and shrines—the impact on human morality and ethics was negligible. The gods did not expect their devotees to be honest, to be charitable, to be chaste, or to be just. The gods expected their devotees to attend to *the gods*, to show them honor and respect. How humans treated other humans was for the most part of little concern to the gods.[6]

If you visit Pompeii and Herculaneum, you'll see many, many graphic displays of nudity and sexual activity, including every imaginable perversity. These scenes involve the gods as well as humans.[7] In first-century Rome, adultery and pedophilia were not viewed as inconsistent with devotion to the gods. Seemingly rivaling the gods themselves, the phallus appears to have been the primary focus of attention. The male organ is everywhere on display, in art and in various objects and utensils, including religious settings.[8]

A great many graffiti, which number in the tens of thousands (yes, they had graffiti back then), depict crude sexual themes in word or caricature. On the walls of a brothel in Pompeii are erotic paintings whose purpose, like a modern restaurant menu with pictures of food selections, advertised to potential customers what services were provided.

Fear of the Dead

Ancient Greeks and Romans also had a very unhealthy fear of the dead. It was widely believed that persons who died violently or unjustly, or who in life had been evil, could come back as angry spirits and attempt to haunt or even harm the living. In fact, most believed that evil spirits, or demons, that could possess people were none other than spirits of the wicked, restless dead.[9] Several old texts explicitly equate demons with the spirits of the dead (and usually the wicked dead). This was likely assumed by Jesus and the authors of the New Testament.[10]

In AD 41, the cruel and hated emperor Caligula was brutally assassinated and his remains hastily and carelessly burned and buried. The garden where he was buried became disturbed with ghosts and fearful apparitions. The terrors did not cease until the house beside the garden was burned to the ground.[11] Others were haunted by dreams involving Nero, the hated emperor who was condemned by the Senate in AD 68 and subsequently committed suicide.[12] It was even believed by some that the wicked emperor had returned to life and would soon rule over Rome once again.

Greco-Roman literature tells tales of the restless dead who haunt the living and must be appeased one way or another.[13] It is very likely that the demonized man described in the Gospels, who lived among the tombs and called himself *Legion*, would have been understood as possessed by the restless spirits of Roman legionaries whose physical remains lay buried nearby. The possessed boy who was thrown into fire or water provides a vivid example of an evil spirit that wishes to harm, even kill its human host.[14]

The people of late antiquity observed various strange practices in their hopes to pacify the dead. A proper and respectful burial, of course, was standard practice and usually was sufficient to appease the departed. But sometimes more extreme measures were required. In the case of slain combatants, the hands of the dead were cut off and affixed under the arms. This practice, called "armpitting," was thought to weaken the spirit, so that should it make an appearance it would lack the power to do harm. Another common practice was called *os resectum*, the cutting off of a finger of the deceased and placing it in a secure location. It was believed that this practice pacified the dead and assisted in the journey to the next world.[15]

Curses . . . and the Evil Eye

These days, it's easy to laugh about getting an "evil eye" from someone. Certainly, being on the receiving end of a mean glance can be uncomfortable. But more often, an evil eye is an innocent reaction to something irritating. Even dogs and cats are capable of casting an evil eye, judging by photos I've seen online.

In ancient times, however, if someone glanced at you with an "evil eye," it meant they were trying to put a curse on you. People were so concerned about protecting themselves from curses that they would buy "eyes" made of glass, ceramic, or metal designed to ward off negative forces, or they employed experts in magic who claimed to know charms and formulas that would provide protection.[16] In the Sermon on the Mount, Jesus may well have spoken against this practice: "But if thine eye be evil, thy whole body shall be full of darkness. If therefore the light that is in thee be darkness, how great is that darkness!"[17] The implication is that if one "gives the evil eye" to someone else, his own eye will be one of darkness not light.[18] Paul discussed an "evil spell" in Galatians 3:1: "O foolish Galatians! Who has bewitched you?" Paul is stressing the point that the gospel of Jesus Christ brings freedom, freeing people of the fear of evil powers.

A great many magic-related texts have survived from antiquity. On papyri, "magical" bowls, foils (or *lemellae*), and thin tablets (usually made of lead), researchers have found writings intended to protect against evil powers and others for cursing and harming other people.

Spells were inscribed on lead tablets, which were then folded (usually twice), and then, in a hidden place, were fixed by an iron nail. The nail itself was thought to possess a measure of power. The piercing of the tablet with the nail supposedly bound the spell. Hence, these spells were called binding-spells. They were often hidden somewhere in or near the house of the person one wanted to harm or influence through the curse or spell. Of course, there were counter-spells whereby one hopefully could fend off the intended harm and in some cases send the evil spirit back to the sender.[19] Some of these tablets, as well as papyri and foils, contain cartoonish-looking sketches, identifying areas of the body that should be attacked. Archaeologists have also uncovered a number of ceramic figurines that have been pierced with pins and nails through eyes, hands, feet, and genitals.

To protect themselves from these curses, as well as roving evil spirits, people would carry amulets that contained charms and appeals to various deities for protection. Jewish amulets often contain brief passages of Scripture.

Some of the spells were "love charms," but in a most perverse manner. We have found examples where a lovesick, possessive man employs a magician to compose a charm that applies pressure on the desired woman, usually through insomnia. At one point these charms typically read: "Let her, XX whom XX bore, lie awake until she consents."[20]

The Death of Gods and Saviors

The inhabitants of the Roman Empire had much to fear. They feared their gods, they feared the dead, and they feared evil spirits and curses. And their great heroes, their divine emperors, hardly brought comfort, for they, like all mortals, perished and sometimes failed spectacularly.

As *pontifex maximus* (high priest), the emperors were supposed to serve as mediators between mortal humanity below and immortal divinity above. It was believed that in the advent of the emperor, recognized as "son of god" and "savior," the good news or gospel for the world began. Importantly, the opening line of the gospel of Mark, the first gospel written, daringly challenges the emperors' role: "The beginning of the gospel of Jesus Christ, the Son of God."

As daring as this statement is, it would have been appreciated by many. By the 60s, when Mark's gospel likely began its public circulation, the Roman imperial doctrine of the divine Caesar was beginning to look very dubious. Following the deaths of these so-called sons of god, the Roman Senate was supposed to vote for deification. But one emperor after another failed miserably. Postmortem deification of the Caesars had in some circles become a joke. Indeed, not long after the death of Emperor Claudius, Seneca penned a satire he entitled the "Pumpkinification of Claudius."[21]

The growing cynicism is not hard to understand.[22] Julius Caesar (100–44 BC), the founder of the Julio-Claudian line, was power-hungry, arrogant, and completely amoral, yet he was a remarkable leader. After a brief reign as dictator (48–44 BC) and only one month after being awarded absolute power, Caesar was brutally murdered by his colleagues, many of whom had been at one time close friends. After thirteen years of uneasy power-sharing and then open civil war, Caesar's great-nephew Octavian (63 BC–AD 14) emerged as the new emperor, hailed as Augustus.

Caesar Augustus proved to be the greatest of the first twelve emperors of Rome. He persuaded the Senate to deify Julius. After a lengthy and mostly successful reign, Augustus was himself deified shortly after his death. But the great Augustus was hardly a physical specimen. He was small and suffered a variety of health problems. Although publicly moral and devoted to his (third) wife Livia, Augustus was known to be a womanizer and spent time away from Rome so that he might more openly spend time with his mistress.

Tiberius (42 BC–AD 37), son of Livia, succeeded Augustus. Compared to his stepfather, the middle-aged emperor was uninspiring. He resented the fact that his mother was more popular than himself. To hide his pedophilia from Rome, he relocated to the island of Capri. A capable administrator and remarkably successful at enriching Rome's treasury,

Tiberius was nevertheless despised. Those closest to him could hardly wait for the old man to die. In fact, they didn't. On his deathbed the emperor gasped and stopped breathing. All assumed he had died. Then his eyes popped open and breathing resumed. Shocked, Gaius Caligula, his successor, and others piled pillows and blankets atop the gasping Tiberius and smothered him. No one clamored for his deification.

Caligula (AD 12–41) proved to be so wicked and insane that he made Tiberius look like a saint. After a promising start, the young emperor began to behave in monstrous ways, assassinating rivals and imagined plotters and—almost beyond belief—raping the wives of guests at royal banquets. Caligula's mockery of the commander of his bodyguard proved his undoing. One evening in January, while returning from the theater to the palace, Caligula was attacked by his own protectors, with the commander himself striking the first blow. The emperor was hacked to pieces and his body was buried in haste and without ceremony. Needless to say, none called for his deification.

Well-educated and overlooked Claudius (10 BC–AD 54) was hailed as the new emperor. His rule was fair, if not competent, and he was much better liked than his two predecessors. By Roman standards, his physical appearance and quirks were embarrassing. He limped because of a club foot. His nose ran and often drool dripped from his chin. He stuttered. He could not give a speech unless the text was before him. His wife, Agrippina, and stepson, Nero, wickedly murdered Claudius by putting poison in his dinner ("Food of the gods," Nero quipped).

Agrippina may have gotten what she wanted, but in time she did not want what she got. By murdering her husband, she turned loose Nero (AD 37–68) on the world. As a teenager he listened to his advisors, but in his twenties he stopped listening. His acts became as monstrous as those of Caligula. He wanted to build a larger palace and coincidentally, in 64, a fire burned out the very properties he hoped to acquire. Only, the fire burned about half of Rome as well! To quell the rumor that he started the fire, Nero fastened blame on members of a new sect called Christianity and had them tortured and murdered in shocking ways. Neither Rome nor Nero was prepared for the Jewish revolt that broke out in Jerusalem in 66. The emperor brought out of forced retirement Vespasian and sent him and the legions to Judea. But even with a war underway, Nero's support from his subjects continued to plunge, until finally, in 68, the Senate condemned him as an enemy of state. Fearing arrest, torture, and murder, Nero committed suicide. No one suggested that the maniac be deified.

What followed next almost brought the empire to its knees. Galba (3 BC–AD 69) seized power only to be murdered several months later. Otho (AD 32–69), who had backed Galba, seized power, but after three months he saw the writing on the wall and committed suicide. Vitellius (AD 15–69) saw his chance and seized power, but after a brief reign he too was murdered. The imperial doctrine of the divine emperor, the savior of the world, the beginning of the good news, was beginning to sound silly. Needless to say, none of these men were deified.

Finally, after one failed would-be emperor after another, the successful but modest general Vespasian (AD 9–79) was proclaimed emperor. He turned over command of the Roman legions in Judea to his son Titus, who successfully ended the war with the storming of Jerusalem and the fiery destruction of the city's famous temple. Father and son returned to Rome in late 70, and in 71 celebrated a grand triumph, which included parading trophies seized from the Jewish temple. After a relatively uneventful and not particularly glamorous rule, Vespasian took sick and died. It is rumored that as death approached, the emperor—always fond of a good joke—jested: "Dear me, I think I am becoming a god!"[23] With the support of his son and successor Titus and because of his modesty and general likability, the Senate voted for Vespasian's deification. He was only the second emperor to be deified since Augustus and Claudius, and the latter's rites had been suspended by Nero. (It had fallen to Vespasian to revive them.)

Vespasian was succeeded by his sons Titus (AD 39–81) and then Domitian (AD 51–96). The rule of neither was especially successful. This was so in the case of Titus because of his untimely death after a reign of only two years. In his brother's honor, Domitian not only persuaded the Senate to deify Titus, he also built a magnificent arch in the Roman Forum, which stands to this day. Easily offended, Domitian overreacted to criticism and exacted severe retribution for perceived slights. In the end, the Roman elite had had enough. The emperor was murdered after a rule of fifteen years. He was not deified.

Mortal "Gods"

These emperors did not relieve the people of their fears. They brought Romans no assurance of peace with the gods. As "gods," the emperors proved frail and mortal. Of the twelve emperors, six were assassinated, two committed suicide, several of them were likely involved in murder, while only five managed to be elevated to the status of gods (and only on-and off-again in the case of Claudius). This record hardly inspired confidence.

Long ago, philosopher Ludwig Feuerbach (1804–1872) famously claimed that "God did not, as the Bible says, make man in His image; on the contrary man . . . made God in his image."[24] There is little doubt that many in the ancient world—not only Greeks and Romans—did just that. The world before and without Christianity was suffused with gods and religion. But the gods were products of human invention that reflected the values and morals of those who made them. These gods brought little comfort. Often they only added to human fear and misery.

In the next chapter we shall consider the misery humans brought upon one another.

CHAPTER 4
A World of Inequality

'll never forget my journeys to see the grand ancient ruins of Ephesus. A port-city with a heaving population of 250,000 in its day, it was home to one of the seven wonders of the ancient world, the Temple of Artemis, featuring 127 columns towering 60 feet high.[1] My university students always enjoy seeing the picture slide of Audrey and me posing with Nikê, the Greek goddess of victory, which oddly enough resembles the Nike swoosh.

The city of Ephesus looms large in the book of Acts and was a prominent destination on Paul's second and third missionary journeys. In fact, so important was this location that Paul not only spent over three years preaching in Ephesus, but Luke records in Acts 19:10 that "All who lived in Asia heard the word of the Lord, both Jews and Greeks" (NASB). For all of its splendor and ancient glory, there is a detestable side to the city of Ephesus: the slave market. For two hundred years (100 BC–AD 100), Ephesus was the headquarters of the Roman slave trade and as such, was the largest slave market in the empire. A modern individual would find the market horrifying. Would-be buyers were able to inspect the "stock" (individuals). Often they were nude. Slaves were valued by appearance, age, physique, education, skill-set and, yes, the condition of their teeth. The price of a slave could be bullish or bearish depending on the market, which was dictated by supply and demand. The pricing not only fluctuated, but much like purchasing a vehicle today, the prices varied. Attractive girls were sold for 2,000 to 6,000 denarii in the Republic, and later on in the empire, 25,000 to 50,000 denarii were paid for boys.[2] These are massive sums of money when one considers that a year's wages for a skilled worker was around 360 denarii.

This evil practice was and is astonishing. Audrey and I knelt and prayed in the Great Theater in Ephesus, and the Lord brought to my mind the statement of Paul the apostle. In one of the boldest, most revolutionary utterances in the first-century Roman Empire, Saul of Tarsus, better known as the apostle Paul, declared: "There is neither Jew nor Greek, there is neither slave nor free, there is neither male nor female; for you are all one in Christ Jesus."[3] From Roman and Jewish perspectives, every part of this astonishing declaration is problematic.

In Paul's time, people were divided by race, by free or slave status, and by gender. What Paul says in his letter that circulated among the churches he founded in the region of Galatia in Asia Minor (today's Turkey) would have been flatly rejected by the vast majority of the inhabitants of the Roman Empire, including the Jewish people. Many would have thought Paul's ideas laughable.

Slave or Free?

In ancient Greece, wealthy and powerful people owned slaves. Even the not-so-wealthy owned slaves (and sometimes complained it was difficult to feed them).[4] Slaves could be beaten, humiliated in public, sexually exploited, and sold or traded.[5] Aristotle, the great philosopher, regarded a slave as "living property."[6] Elsewhere he wrote: "The slave is a living tool and the tool a lifeless slave."[7] Of course, the main function of the slave was to work the farm and assist with the chores around the house or shop.[8]

The Roman world, much more than its older Greek counterpart to the east, came to depend heavily on slave labor. Slaves were used in every part of the empire, including Italy, and outside the boundaries of the empire. Slaves were homegrown and imported. Some children were sold into slavery by impoverished, desperate parents. Many were taken captive in war, as part of the spoils. Julius Caesar's seven-year campaign in Gaul alone created over one million slaves for the empire.[9]

Although the demographics of antiquity are hard to estimate, some think that in the first century BC, as much as 40 percent of the population in the Roman Empire was slaves or servants. By the second and third centuries AD, the percentage may have decreased to as low as 15 percent. Even so, if the population of the empire in the second century AD was about 50 million, there may well have been as many as 7.5 million slaves.[10]

The garments of slaves were distinctive so that in public their status was instantly recognized. Slaves often ran businesses for their masters, including tanneries, shops, bakeries, and brothels, where managers, pimps, and prostitutes alike were slaves.[11] Sexual exploitation of slaves—both male and female—was both legal and commonplace.[12] No owner could legally be charged with the rape of his or her slave.[13] The law required runaway slaves to be pursued, captured, and returned to their owners.[14]

There is no question that the sexual exploitation, including forced prostitution, was one of the most appalling aspects of slavery in the Roman Empire. For this very reason, no Jewish priest, no matter how eminent, could serve as high priest if one of his female ancestors had ever been a slave. The implication is that if the priest's female ancestor had been a slave, it would be assumed that she had been raped and that the priest's line of descent might not be purely Jewish and Levitical, thus disqualifying service as high priest.[15]

At its worst, the Roman Empire was not only a slave economy—it was a slave machine that ground up its human labor. Roman historian Diodorus (first century BC) wrote that slaves who worked in mines were "all in chains, all kept at work continuously day and night . . . there is no indulgence, no respite . . . [they are] kept at their labor by the lash, until overcome by hardships, they die in torment."[16]

The reality of slavery in the world of late antiquity is reflected in some of Jesus' parables. Slaves labored in the fields, served their masters, and could be punished. The apostle Paul's assertion that in Christ Jesus there is "neither slave nor free" would have struck Romans of his time as both foolish and dangerously subversive. The vast inequalities involved in slavery were right and natural, they believed, and nothing would ever change them.

Wealthy or Poor?

The gulf between rich and poor in the Greco-Roman world was very wide. Very few were wealthy. There was a middle class of sorts, but it was small. Most people scraped by in agriculture, and many congregated in cities looking for daywork or charity. Poor women, especially women who had been abandoned as infants or young girls, often supported themselves as prostitutes.

In the Greek world, wealth was celebrated and there was little sympathy for the poor. Even the poets, surprisingly, gave expression to these values.[17] "'Money's the man.' It's true. There's no poor man who's known as good or valued much," declared Alcaeus of Mytilene.[18] In step with this philosophy, Theognis of Megara wrote, "For the multitude of humankind there is only one virtue: money."[19]

A few poets and playwrights, however, were willing to concede that money corrupts. In his play entitled *Wealth*, Aristophanes has a character confess: "There is nothing sound or honest in the world, the love of money overcomes us all."[20] Readers of the Bible will immediately recall the warning: "For the love of money is the root of all evils."[21] The verse is often misquoted as "money is the root of all evils," but even misquoted, the verse has clear, timeless application.

Romans sometimes made no distinction between the poor and slaves, regarding both with contempt. Cicero (first century BC) gives eloquent expression to this thinking: "Unbecoming to a gentleman, too, and vulgar are the means of livelihood of all hired workmen whom we pay for mere manual labor, not for artistic skill; for in their case the very wage they receive is a pledge of their slavery."[22]

In a world of rampant poverty, it is not surprising that beggars were everywhere. But beggars found little sympathy from the wealthy and powerful. Seneca (c. 4 BC–AD 65) declared in reference to beggars: "[T]o some I shall not give although they are in need, because, even if I should give, they would still be in need."[23] Accordingly, Greek historian Polybius (c. 200–118 BC), who greatly admired Rome, bluntly stated: "No Roman will give anything to anyone."[24] There was no such thing as charity or social justice among the Greeks and Romans. Some pagans did humanitarian acts, but this was an exception, certainly not the rule.

Jesus encountered beggars in his public activities. Some of them were impoverished, ill, or disabled. In his parables, Jesus spoke of a dishonest manager who had lost his position and was "ashamed to beg."[25] Jesus' parable of the rich and poor man provides a graphic picture of the extreme contrast between wealth and poverty. Whereas the rich man wears finery and feasts daily, his poor neighbor is covered with ulcers and shares with dogs the food cast out.[26] Juvenal (second century AD) expresses horror at begging, describing a hungry beggar as "munching dirty scraps of dog's bread."[27]

The prevalence of poverty and its attendant ills, such as prostitution, was almost beyond imagination in the world of late antiquity. Yet the affluent Greeks and Romans did not seem too bothered by it. Most believed poverty was the fault of the poor.

Male or Female?

In a play Sophocles published sometime in the fifth century BC, a character affirms: "O woman, woman's best jewel is silence! For as leaves decorate trees, wool is the beauty of the sheep, the mane the glory of horses, and the beard the pride of man, so silence is the jewel of women!"[28] To be sure, it is a fictional character who utters this cluster of similes, but we have every reason to assume that he was expressing a widely held view that women were not equal to men. A similar sentiment, in harsher tones, is found in a fragment of a lost work by fifth-century BC contemporary Democritus: "A woman must not practice argument; this is dreadful. To be ruled by a woman is the ultimate outrage for a man."[29] Few, perhaps none, would have disagreed at the time.

And what of the Jewish world? The second-century BC sage Yeshua ben Sira seems to be largely in agreement with the sentiments of the Greco-Roman world. He wrote that a "silent wife is a gift of the Lord."[30] Although he acknowledged that a faithful and industrious wife is a blessing, the sage missed no opportunity to describe and decry the cranky, evil, and drunken wives of his imagination.[31]

Some of the later Jewish sages, known as the Rabbis, also reveal their chauvinism. In an early commentary on the book of Deuteronomy, an authority is remembered to have said, "A woman may not speak in a man's stead."[32] Rabbi Judah, under whose authority the Mishnah was compiled in the early third century AD, was remembered to have said, "There are three Benedictions which one must say every day: 'Blessed be

He who did not make me a Gentile; blessed be He who did not make me an uneducated man; blessed be He who did not make me a woman.'"[33] Perhaps even more egregiously, a later rabbi opined, "Better to burn the Torah than to teach it to a woman!"[34]

Nowhere did the gender gap express itself in late antiquity more starkly than in what might be called "family planning." Early in this book, I presented a letter from migrant worker Hilarion, telling his pregnant wife that if she has a girl, the baby should be abandoned, or exposed, to likely die. In a legal document that dates to 8 BC, a recently widowed but pregnant woman asserts that she "retains the right to expose the infant [that she is carrying] and to unite herself to another man."[35] The implication is that the infant, whether male or female, may be a hindrance to her remarriage. If it is, she will expose the baby, regardless of gender. In cases such as this, even male infants were in danger. But most of the time it was the female infant who was cast out to die.

For Aristotle, exposing deformed children was not an option but a requirement. He was not alone in his opinion. The Roman Law of the Twelve Tables (*Leges Duodecim Tabularum*), which may date in its earliest form to the fifth century BC, required fathers to put to death any child who was deformed. One of these laws reads: "A notably deformed child shall be killed immediately."[36]

The widespread practice of infant exposure is also attested by explicit condemnation of the practice in early Christian texts. According to the *Didache* (early second century): "Do not murder a child by abortion, nor kill it at birth."[37] The same proscription is found in the *Epistle of Barnabas* (mid-second century): "Do not murder a child by abortion, nor, again, destroy that which is born."[38] The *Didache* also speaks of those "who persecute the good, who hate truth, who love falsehood . . . who do not show mercy to a poor person, who are not distressed by [the plight of] the oppressed, who do not know him who made them, [who are] child murderers, who destroy what God has formed."[39] The clear implication is that because the wicked do not know God, who created humanity in his own image, they think nothing of murdering children and destroying what God forms in the womb.

These harsh criticisms may reflect the older expression found in the Wisdom of Solomon, which condemns the "ruthless slayers of their own children."[40] In the ostensible literary setting of this apocryphal work, it is King Solomon who speaks, and so perhaps would be understood as referring to the pagan practice of child-sacrifice that took place in the ancient Near East. But in the time of the writing of the Wisdom of Solomon (first century BC), child sacrifice was rare.[41] It may be that the author was alluding to abortion and infant exposure as practiced by contemporary Greeks and Romans.

We find that in the Greco-Roman world of late antiquity women were at a great disadvantage. As infants they were far more likely to be cast out as unwanted. As young girls or teenagers they faced the risk of sexual abuse, if not outright prostitution; as grown women they were under the control of their husbands, who might abuse them, neglect them, or even abandon them; and in their older years, especially if widowed, they faced the prospects of poverty.

Theist or Atheist?

Was there religious freedom in the Greco-Roman world? Yes and no. There were indeed a number of gods to choose from and a number of cults as well. With the exception of the Jewish people who enjoyed exemption thanks to alliance with Rome dating back to the second century BC, all people in the Roman Empire were expected to worship at least some of the gods, and some of these gods had to be worshiped, at least now and then. In short, atheism was not an option—at least not a safe one.

A few philosophers and writers in the Greco-Roman world questioned the existence of the traditional gods, that is, the gods of Olympus (Zeus, Hera, et al.). It was rumored that Epicurus (fourth century BC), who publicly taught that the gods existed but took no notice of human affairs, was really an atheist but kept this opinion private out of fear of the public.[42] His caution was well placed. After all, Socrates (fifth century BC) was forced to drink hemlock, having been convicted of teaching atheism to the youth of Athens.[43] A colleague of Socrates, Theodorus, acquired the sobriquet "the Atheist" after his banishment from Athens, "for atheism and for corrupting the youth."[44] Not surprisingly, Plato, the famous pupil of Socrates, discussed the question of the existence of the gods in an academic setting.[45] It was alleged that Critias was the author of a play in which a character asserts that the gods are an invention designed to deter crime that otherwise would go undetected and therefore unpunished.[46] Whether or not Critias wrote this play, he got himself into a lot of trouble.

By the turn of the era, little had changed. Judging from the comments of Philo of Alexandria (c. 20 BC–AD 50), there must have been a few atheists in his time.[47] But whoever they were, they were discreet and for the most part apparently tried to remain anonymous.[48] Their caution is not surprising, considering the persecution Christians endured for their refusal to acknowledge the existence of the Greco-Roman gods.

In the first three centuries of the Christian church, Christians were routinely accused of atheism, for they did not acknowledge the existence of the Greco-Roman gods and refused to worship the emperor as "son of god."[49] Early Christian martyrs included Ignatius (died c. 110), Polycarp (died c. 155), and Justin Martyr (died c. 165).

In Polycarp's case, the mid-second-century bishop of Smyrna in Asia Minor (Izmir in modern Turkey) was charged with "atheism" for refusing to confess the divinity of the emperor or worship the gods of the

Greeks and Romans. According to the *Martyrdom of Polycarp*, written not long after his death, the pagan multitude shouted against the Christians, "Away with the atheists! Find Polycarp!"[50] When Polycarp is brought before the Roman proconsul, the latter demands, "Swear by the divinity of Caesar."[51] Polycarp of course refuses. The proconsul demands that Polycarp swear the oath to Caesar and revile Christ. His refusal to swear by the divinity of Caesar would have been interpreted as proof of the charge of atheism. In the trial that follows, the crowds shout, "This is the teacher of Asia, the father of the Christians, the destroyer of our gods, who teaches many not to sacrifice or worship."[52] The bishop continues to refuse and so is executed.

During the administration of Pliny the Younger (c. 110–112) over Bithynia and Pontus in Asia Minor, Christians were arrested, interrogated, tortured, and in some cases executed.[53] From the mid-second-century on, pagans regularly accused Christians of atheism. In his *First Apology* (c. 155), Justin Martyr replies to this charge: "[W]e are called atheists," though at the same time conceding and explaining, that "we are atheists, so far as gods of [the pagans] are concerned, but not with respect to the most true God."[54] "What sober-minded man," Justin further argues, "will not acknowledge that we are not atheists, worshiping as we do the Maker of this universe . . ."[55] He adds further that "those who lived reasonably are Christians, even though they have been thought atheists."[56] In his *Second Apology* (c. 161), Justin complains that Crescens, the pagan philosopher, unfairly describes Christians as "atheistic and impious."[57] Tatian complains too that the Greeks exclude Christians "from civic rights as if we were the most godless of men."[58] Athenagoras devotes several chapters of his apology to counter the charge that Christians are atheists.[59]

The charge that Christians were atheists reaches back to the first century and is even attested in the book of Acts. One will recall the accusation that Demetrius the silversmith, who specialized in figurines of the goddess Artemis, made against Paul: "[No]t only at Ephesus but almost throughout all Asia this Paul has persuaded and turned away a considerable company of people, saying that gods made with hands are not gods." Demetrius goes on to warn that Paul's preaching could bring their trade to an end and bring the temple of Artemis into disrepute.[60] A riot ensues and Christians are arrested.

What we find is that for all the claims of religious tolerance and inclusivity, it turns out that the Greco-Roman world was not so tolerant after all. In effect, the policy was something like this: "You may worship any gods you wish, but you must revere and support our gods as well." Religious rights and equality were extended to those who followed the party line. Christians, along with atheists, did not and so were persecuted.

A New Understanding of God

The Greco-Roman world of late antiquity was a world of inequality. It was a world of oppressive slavery, grinding poverty and economic exploitation, callous mistreatment of females, and superstitious, intolerant zealots. Navigating such a world was not easy. Most faced lives of hardship—and rather brief lives at that. It was a world desperate for change, a world that needed a new message and a new vision.

One of Polycarp's curious declarations in the face of his martyrdom is that Christ has done him "no harm" and in fact has saved him.[61] At first blush the statement seems strange, at least to us moderns. But when it is remembered that in late antiquity the Greco-Roman gods were widely regarded as capricious, unloving, and at times jealous and vindictive, Polycarp's confession would have struck his accusers as startling and even suggestive. Underlying his confession was a whole new understanding of divinity: God loves and cares for all people.

CHAPTER 5
A World of Bondage: Racism

As a devout Pharisee, Saul of Tarsus was no egalitarian. He did not believe in the equality of Jews and Gentiles (non-Jews). He did not believe in the equality of the sexes, and he had no problem with some people being slaves while others were free. As discussed earlier, most Romans held these same beliefs, so Saul, a Jew and Roman citizen, fit right in. But after he encountered the risen Jesus Christ, the real Son of God, his thinking was radically changed. His name was changed, too, and he became *Paul* the apostle.

One of Paul's greatest discoveries in his new faith was that in Jesus Christ there is equality and brotherhood. This is why he boldly affirmed, "There is neither Jew nor Greek, there is neither slave nor free, there is neither male nor female; for you are all one in Christ Jesus."[1] In the redemption that Christ brings, the human family is restored. All are brothers and sisters. Accordingly, racism and sexism and anything else that divides are excluded. We are "all one in Christ Jesus."

This Christian principle was very strange teaching in the ears of the people of the Roman Empire. As mentioned earlier, slavery was widely accepted. As many as one-quarter of all who lived in the empire were slaves. Remarkably, some historians contend that there was no racism in ancient times.[2] But not only is there abundant evidence of it, it matches modern racism in several ways.[3]

From Stereotypes to Racism

It has been said that the eyes are a window to the soul. I can't argue against this adage, especially knowing it is rooted in something Jesus said: "The eye is the lamp of the body."[4] However, I believe that just as well as our eyes, what comes out of our mouth—our words—reveals what is in our heart and soul.

For ancient Greeks, a single word in surviving records may be the oldest evidence of racism: the word *barbarian*, which they used regularly when referring to non-Greeks. The Greek word *barbaroi* (plural) mimics how other languages sounded to the Greek ear—a babbling sound, something like "bar-bar."[5] The word *barbaros* (singular) came to mean a person who not only spoke oddly and unintelligibly, but who was not "civilized" in the eyes of Greeks.[6]

Another example of racist language comes from a third century BC writer pretending to be Aristotle the great philosopher, who asserted that "those living in the north are brave and stiff-haired, and those in the south are cowardly and have soft hair."[7] Ptolemy (active c. AD 146–170) elaborated still further, explaining that foreign lands were guided by different astral constellations, with the result that some people are "more unscrupulous, despicable cowards, treacherous, servile, and in general fickle," while other people—like Jews and others in the Middle East—who are born and live under other stars, "are in general bold, godless, and scheming."[8]

Physiognomy, trying to deduce a person's character on the basis of certain physical features (their skin color, shape of head, facial features, and the like), was a common form of racism in late antiquity. For example, it was written that "curly hair indicates a man who is very deceitful, greedy," while the blond hair of the Germans "indicates wild and savage customs."[9] Further, Egyptians were considered cunning, Celts ignorant, and Thracians, a group of Indo-European tribes, were lazy drunkards.

Ideas relating to eugenics were discussed as early as Plato (c. 429–347 BC) and Aristotle (384–322 BC). Plato spoke metaphorically of the need to keep the precious "metal" of Greece "pure."[10] And Aristotle recommended abortion and infant exposure, lest the quality of the Greek population decline.[11] Also ominous was Aristotle's justification for slavery: "Slaves are subhuman or lesser men, while masters are superior."[12]

At first blush, many of the prophets and contributors to Israel's ancient writings seem to be as racist as their contemporaries. In the books of Moses, which describe the founding of the people of Israel and their special covenant with God, we repeatedly hear of nations being driven out of the promised land (the land of Canaan, which in time became Israel).[13] Over and over again we read how Israel, though not a mighty or an especially deserving people, is God's chosen people.[14]

But is Israel's tradition of being a "chosen" people an example of racism? I say no. God chose the Israelites not because they are special or better than others.[15] What makes the Israelites (the Jewish people) distinct is not themselves but their God.[16] In the famous scene on Mount Sinai where God forgives Israel and renews his covenant with the people, God says to Moses, "I will be gracious to whom I will be gracious, and will show mercy on whom I will show mercy."[17] Election is all about God, not Israel.

Egypt and other nations were condemned for enslaving or attacking Israel. But the criticism directed against them was not racially based.

They were not judged because they were inferior, or because their skin color was different, or they spoke a foreign language, and so forth. Nations, including Israel itself, were criticized and judged for their behavior, for acting unjustly. But Israel's prophets spoke of the redemption of the nations, including Egypt. According to Isaiah, after Egypt was punished, the nation "will return to the LORD, and he will heed their supplications and heal them."[18] Isaiah pronounced a blessing on Assyria also. This is remarkable when it is remembered that at the time the prophet Isaiah was speaking, Israel's greatest threats were Assyria to the north and Egypt to the south. Yet Isaiah declares the word of the Lord: "Blessed be Egypt my people, and Assyria the work of my hands, and Israel my heritage."[19]

Israel's wise and famous King Solomon, son of David, built the first temple in Jerusalem. Upon its completion, Solomon utters a prayer of dedication, in which he asks God to hear the prayers of Gentiles who come to the temple: "Likewise when a foreigner, who is not of thy people Israel, comes from a far country . . . and prays toward this house, hear thou in heaven thy dwelling place, and do according to all for which the foreigner calls to thee."[20] The ecumenical spirit of this prayer is amazing. This is hardly the ideology of racism.

There is no question that deeply ingrained in Israel's national consciousness is the conviction that they are special people, a chosen people, a people with a future. In some of the later rabbinic interpretation and theology, racist ideology does find expression, but this is hardly true to the original vision and teaching of the writers of Scripture. The kind of crude racism that we detect in the literature of classical antiquity is not present in Israel's ancient Scripture.

This Scripture, reinforced by the teaching of Jesus and his disciples, quashed the racist ideas of classical antiquity. For centuries no one of influence argued for racism. No one, that is, until the Enlightenment.

Then racism staged a comeback with a vengeance and set the stage for other very negative developments.

Racism Disappears . . . Reappears

The revolutionary Christian message of brotherhood swept the Roman world and all of the West. The Greek and Roman Empires were Christianized, as was Europe. Over the next millennium, there were no great philosophers or Christian theologians arguing for racism, providing justifications for it, or advocating slavery. There were no medieval "Aristotles," promoting eugenics or infanticide. The apostle Paul's message of "neither Jew nor Greek" had taken hold, and widespread racism receded.

Then there were the eighteenth and nineteenth centuries. Scientific knowledge accelerated at an unprecedented speed, leading to the industrial revolution and advances in medicine (for example, the discovery of microbes) and inventions, including the steam engine, the electric light, the telegraph, the telephone, and so much more. The era also saw a rise of anti-Christian philosophy and its attendant rejection of Christian ethics and the authority of the church. Sparked by misguided yet influential writers and philosophers, racism reappeared.[21]

Among the first of the proponents of "scientific" racism was Georges-Louis Leclerc, Count of Buffon (1707–1788).[22] A prolific writer, Buffon believed that Caucasians represent the apex of human evolution, but because of migration to tropical climes, some humans devolved into an inferior race. Buffon was certain that if blacks moved to the North, they would become white. To support this "degeneration" argument, the count tried to point to examples among animals, such as donkeys, which he said were at one time horses, and apes, which at one time were humans. Accordingly, he argued that some human races were closer to the most advanced humans (Caucasians), while others were closer to animals.[23] Regrettably, this pseudoscience was very influential throughout the eighteenth and nineteenth centuries.

David Hume, a famous Scottish philosopher and atheist (1711–1776), asserted that "Negroes, and in general all the other species of man (for there are four or five different kinds), [are] naturally inferior to the whites." Hume also wrote: "You may obtain anything of the Negroes by offering them strong drink; and may easily prevail with them to sell, not only their children, but their wives and mistresses, for a cask of brandy."[24]

French philosopher and writer Voltaire (1694–1778) wrote, "Negro men and Negro women, transported to the coldest countries, still produce there animals of their own species."[25] Voltaire believed in polygenesis, the theory that maintains that humans originated from multiple ancestors. Such an idea, which of course has no scientific foundation whatsoever, was adopted by racists.[26] Voltaire, moreover, was a deist who mocked Christianity.[27] In a letter to Frederick II, King of Prussia, Voltaire asserted that Christianity "is assuredly the most ridiculous, the most absurd and the most bloody religion [that] has ever infected this world. Your majesty will do the human race an eternal service by extirpating this infamous superstition."[28] Voltaire was convinced that the rise of Christianity and the collapse of paganism brought about the fall of the Roman Empire.[29] His writings also contained expressions of anti-Semitism.[30]

Immanuel Kant (1724–1804), the German philosopher famous for his *Critique of Pure Reason*, believed that blacks had accomplished nothing of importance: "The Negroes of Africa have by nature no feeling that rises above the trifling."[31]

Perhaps the most influential of the lot was Auguste Comte (1798–1857), a "militant atheist," who may be regarded as the founder of Humanism. His views influenced Karl Marx, founder of Communism, and the English writer George Eliot (aka Mary Ann Evans), who translated several radical works. Comte was a troubled soul who got along with almost no one (including John Stuart Mill, one of Comte's closest disciples). His wife left him in 1842. After publishing his signature work *Discours sur l'Esprit positif* ("Treatise on Positivism"), he went on to develop strange ideas about secular, atheistic religion, in which certain rituals were to be practiced, a female saint to be venerated, and Comte himself recognized in the role of high priest. Today most think he was insane.

The idea of the human being as a soulless machine caught on in Germany. It is not surprising, for the diminished view of humanity cohered with the new views of materialism, which many philosophers and scientists were embracing with enthusiasm in the nineteenth century. Among these scientists was Karl Vogt (1817–1895), who grew up in Germany and later emigrated to Switzerland. Vogt took the idea of "man as machine" to an extreme, believing that what humans eat not only affects them physically, but even determines their thoughts.[32] He once quipped, "Tell me what you eat, and I will tell you who you are."[33] An atheist, Vogt believed all morality was relative, differing from society to society. He noted, for example, that in some places the murder of the elderly and infirm was acceptable.[34]

The new materialism was also enthusiastically advanced by German philosopher and physician Ludwig Büchner (1824–1899) in several publications. Among his most influential was *Force and Matter* (1855), in which he argued that humanity is made up of nothing more than the matter and energy of the universe. More than twenty-five years later, he wrote *The Power of Heredity and Its Influence on the Moral and Mental Progress of Humanity*, and argued that vice and virtue are purely the results of heredity.[35] In keeping with this hypothesis, he argued that the various human races inherit different abilities and tendencies. This pseudoscience led him to assert, for example, that Jews are by nature merchants. Büchner was an energetic defender of scientific materialism.[36] Thus, the universe has no purpose and no ultimate meaning. And because there is no God, there is no universal morality, no universal right and wrong.

More examples could be reviewed, but I think we have seen enough to this point. The odd ideas, the pseudoscience, and the grotesque racism we see in these influential philosophers and writers, all of whom rejected most or all of Christianity, resurrected the racism of the classical philosophers and writers of late antiquity. This was not a coincidence, for Plato, Aristotle, and others were widely read among the educated in Europe in the eighteenth and nineteenth centuries. The resurrection of these bad ideas, which Christian theology and behavior had for more than a millennium sidelined, created an intellectual atmosphere in which a new science of body and mind could blossom and set the stage for the horrors of the twentieth century.

PART II

THE WORLD **WITHOUT** CHRISTIANITY

CHAPTER 6
A Slippery Slope

I n the United Kingdom, the only estate called a palace but not belonging to the Royal family is the sprawling 2,700-acre Blenheim Palace in Oxfordshire, which belonged to the Churchill family. My wife, Audrey, our young daughter, Lily Faith, and I made the short eight-mile trip via taxi from our residence in the city center of Oxford because I had to see Sir Winston's home. Soon we were standing in the small room off the Great Hall where he was born on November 30, 1874. We remembered the fact that Winston was once called "that troublesome boy," and that his father, Lord Randolph, wrote him a letter shortly before Randolph's death, telling Winston he was a major disappointment and would never amount to anything.

So the story begins of Churchill's life. A difficult beginning is no guarantee of an obscure life. Thank God for Mrs. Everest, Winston's nanny, who not only reared him but also was a key Christian influence in his early life.

Churchill, of course, would go on to be that great defender and protector of *Christian civilization*, a term he used with confidence. A political rival, Clement Atlee, upon Churchill's death in 1965, called him the greatest leader and Englishman of the twentieth century. When Churchill died, the British historian Sir Arthur Bryant wrote, "The day of giants is gone forever."[1] Churchill's life proves that history is made by dynamic individuals who achieve the extraordinary. History is not made by detached occurrences or anonymous entities.

Churchill, like Abraham Lincoln, became famous first for his oratory skills. History remembers him as the man who hated surrender. Following the battle of Britain and during the evil days of the Nazi blitz, Churchill spoke to the male students of Harrow (a boarding school he attended) and said, "Never give in, never give in, never, never, never—in nothing, great or small, large or petty—never give in except to convictions of honour and good sense. Never yield to force; never yield to the apparently overwhelming might of the enemy."[2]

It was on June 4, 1940, however, that Churchill truly established himself as the greatest statesman of the twentieth century. Over 300,000 troops had successfully been evacuated from Dunkirk, but morale was terribly low. Many were calling for British leaders to negotiate with Hitler and leave the continent for the Nazis. It was in this moment that Churchill addressed Parliament and rallied a nation to stand against evil:

> We shall not flag or fail. We shall go on to the end, we shall fight in France, we shall fight on the seas and oceans, we shall fight with growing confidence and growing strength in the air, we shall defend our Island, whatever the cost may be; we shall fight on the beaches, we shall fight on the landing grounds, we shall fight in the fields and in the streets, we shall fight in the hills; we shall never surrender, and even if, which I do not for a moment believe, this Island or a large part of it were subjugated and starving, then our Empire beyond the seas, armed and guarded by the British Fleet, would carry on the struggle, until, in God's good time,

the New World, with all its power and might, steps forth to the rescue and the liberation of the old.[3]

I start this part of the book with these stories because they reflect a recent, almost unimaginable time when a large part of the world turned its back to Christianity. It's a slippery slope when God is sidelined and Christianity is marginalized; evil reigns. Unfortunately, cultural forces are now moving in such a way that we may be doomed to see history repeat itself if we do not wake up. And as the saying goes, "Each time history repeats itself, we pay a higher price."

Without God, Something Always Fills the Void

The rediscovery of early paganism and its ill-conceived ideas of racism bore some very evil fruit in the nineteenth century. These bad ideas were advanced by some articulate, passionate men:

Ludwig Feuerbach (1804–1872)

Charles Darwin (1809–1882)

Karl Marx (1818–1883)

Friedrich Nietzsche (1844–1900)

Sigmund Freud (1856–1939)

These men could be regarded as the Big Five in terms of significantly moving the world away from a Judeo-Christian worldview, and by doing so, opening the door for the hell that would descend upon humanity in the twentieth century. I do not mean to imply that these men should be held responsible for the Holocaust or for the World Wars. My point is that bad ideas can and often do lead to horrifying consequences. In this chapter, I will discuss the first three men: Feuerbach, Darwin, and Marx.

Ludwig Feuerbach

Ludwig Andreas von Feuerbach was born in Landshut, Bavaria (Germany) in 1804.[4] He studied at the universities of Heidelberg, Berlin, and Erlangen, where he earned his doctoral degrees. In 1839, he published *Philosophie und Christentum* ("Philosophy and Christianity"), in which he claimed that he had shown that Christianity had vanished as a real force in humanity. In 1841, Feuerbach published *Das Wesen des Christentums* ("The Essence of Christianity"), which was translated into English by the aforementioned Mary Ann Evans, who became well known under the pen name George Eliot. Writing about Christian theology, or "Revelation" as he put it, Feuerbach asserted, "The belief in Revelation not only injures the moral sense and taste—the aesthetics of virtue; it poisons, nay, it destroys, the divinest feeling in man—the sense of truth, the perception and sentiment of truth."[5]

Following the publication of this book, Feuerbach became increasingly critical of Christianity, continuing to argue that religion was a matter of subjectivity, not objective revelation, a matter of feeling and fancy, not fact. Looking back on his work, Feuerbach famously claimed that he had shown that *God* had not made man in his image (as declared in the Bible); rather, *man* had made God in his image.[6]

In my opinion, the philosophy of Feuerbach helped lay an intellectual foundation on which Marx, Nietszche, Freud, and others in the nineteenth century would build. The dismissal of revelation and the corresponding reduction of religion to nothing more than subjective emotions and preferences cleared the way for the far more destructive philosophies.

I should mention that Feuerbach and his family were scandalized in 1813 (when Feuerbach was only nine years old) when his father, Anselm, left his mother and became involved with the wife of one of his friends. The adulterous affair lasted nine years. During this time

Anselm had a son and named him after himself. When his mistress died, he returned to his family. The experience of rejection of this nature and the disgraceful behavior of his father may well have contributed to Feuerbach's cynicism and atheism, which he adopted not long after leaving home for university.

Charles Darwin

Charles Darwin was born in 1809 in Shrewsbury, Shropshire (England). His grandfather and father were medical doctors with keen interest in new philosophical ideas. His father was also interested in some of the new ideas emerging in science. Darwin studied medicine at the University of Edinburgh, though he completed his degree in divinity at Christ's College, Cambridge. At Cambridge he became interested in aspects of natural science. He joined a club that was keenly interested in the new materialistic philosophies that challenged traditional Christian theology. In December 1831, Darwin set sail with Captain Robert FitzRoy on the *HMS Beagle*. The voyage was to take Darwin around the world. The Galápagos Archipelago in the Pacific, west of northwest South America, was probably the most important area of study. While on the voyage, Darwin read Charles Lyell's *Principles of Geology*, a massive three-volume work that discussed the appearance and disappearance of various species of fauna.[7] After the voyage Darwin became acquainted with Lyell.[8]

The voyage lasted nearly five years, though Darwin spent most of his time on land exploring, observing the native flora and fauna, and collecting specimens. Based on his observations and later conversations with scientists, Darwin concluded that species evolve into new species through natural selection and adaptation to environmental conditions. In 1859, he published *On the Origin of Species*,[9] a work that rocked the scientific community and was an instant bestseller. Darwin became a celebrity and was in demand as a speaker.

Although Darwin himself avoided speaking directly about the evolution of humankind in *On the Origin of Species*, he did state near the end of his epic-making book: "Light will be thrown on the origin of man and his history."[10] Years later Darwin published *The Descent of Man*, in which he openly spoke of the evolution of the human species, explicitly stating that humans descended from "Old World monkeys."[11]

Historians and scientists today debate aspects of Darwin's theism. He was raised in Unitarianism, which from the point of view of orthodoxy is regarded as heresy. However, while at Cambridge, Darwin was ordained as an Anglican. In the 1830s and 1840s, he regarded himself as a Christian, though his faith in God was beginning to falter. When his ten-year-old daughter, Annie, died in 1851, Darwin began struggling with the question of evil and suffering in the world. It was at this time that he no longer attended church. In his old age he expressed the view that one could not be both a theist and an evolutionist.[12] Only a few years before his death, Darwin denied that he had ever been an atheist, explaining that "an agnostic would be the most correct description of my mind."[13]

Darwin's theories were debated by philosophers and theologians. Many of the former readily accepted the new science, and, surprisingly, a number of the latter did too. Some philosophers and theologians saw in evolution evidence of God's design. Of course, many theologians were strongly opposed to Darwinism (as it came to be called), thinking that evolution supported atheism and robbed humanity of its special status among all living species. Others believed that Darwin's research provided a firm foundation for scientific atheism.

Still, Darwin's ideas were eagerly adopted by many philosophers and scientists, especially in Germany.[14] The worst by-product of Darwinism was that it created the context for new ideas about racism, which could now be considered "scientific." As mentioned earlier, Darwin himself believed that humanity evolved into races or subspecies.[15] Evolution opened up the possibility that not all human tribes were as advanced as others. Some went so far as to opine that the *races* or *subspecies* of humankind evolved from different primates (that is, polygenesis), in different times and places, again suggesting that some races are more evolved and advanced than others.[16] Some suggested that lesser-evolved human races were closer to apes than to the more fully developed humans who lived in Europe.[17] Not only did this understanding of humanity accommodate racist ideology, but it provided a theoretical foundation and justification for slavery itself.

Before moving on, it is important to note a few things in defense of Darwin. In this chapter I am describing the philosophies of men whose views laid the foundation for the evil that was unleashed on the world in the twentieth century. Darwin himself should not be painted with this brush. There was nothing evil or dehumanizing about the man.[18] He was a faithful husband and a loving father. The death of his daughter, as well as his own ill health, troubled him greatly. And although many theologians and church leaders were initially skeptical and in some instances sharply opposed to his views, in time, many Christians who were themselves leading scientists in paleontology, geology, biology, and zoology accepted, corrected, and improved upon Darwin's work.

Today, there are many Christians who are leaders in various fields of science who speak of evolution and creation. Among these is Francis Collins, who headed up the Human Genome Project.[19] Books like *The Privileged Planet*, in which strong arguments are made for divine creation, the great age of the universe, and the evolution of life on earth, have been written by devout Christians.[20] Readers should know that the gulf between science and faith has long been bridged. Christian scholars and scientists recognize how Scripture and science, in fact, complement one another.

But in the nineteenth century, when Darwin published his influential books, the new science was understood by some to mean that it was no longer necessary to reference God. For them, there was no bridge between science and belief in God. The new science meant the end of God. The age of the earth (millions of years, instead of thousands) was seen as a conflict with the Bible.[21] Biological evolution was seen as a natural explanation that precluded the actions of a divine Creator. The mind itself, as we shall soon see, was understood in a new light that some thought negated spirituality and perhaps even morality. In short, God was seen as simply unnecessary—little more than a relic of a superstitious past. Darwin unwittingly contributed to an emerging worldview that suited the likes of men like Ludwig Feuerbach and Karl Marx.

Karl Marx

Karl Marx was born into a Jewish family in 1818 in Trier, Prussia (German Confederation). He studied political economy and Hegelian philosophy at the universities of Bonn, Berlin, and Jena. Deeply influenced by Feuerbach,[22] Marx embraced materialist philosophy and developed a materialist understanding of history, with a focus on economics and class struggle. For Marx, the whole of human history revolved around class struggle, a struggle largely provoked by economic inequities. Hegel's deterministic understanding of history provided Marx with a framework for his later views.[23]

Marx's father, Heinrich, nominally converted to Lutheranism in order to avoid anti-Semitic prejudice, which unfortunately existed in nineteenth-century German society. Heinrich's children, including Karl, were baptized, though the family was not active in the church. As a teenager Marx became involved in a radical political group. He also joined a drinking club. Marx sometimes got into trouble, including participating in a duel on one occasion, and because of academic problems was forced to transfer from the University of Bonn to the University of Berlin. In Berlin, Marx studied law, but he was more interested in philosophy. In 1840, the twenty-two-year-old, a committed atheist, began working with Bruno Bauer, himself an atheist and radical historian who promoted the eccentric view that Jesus of Nazareth was not a historical person.[24] For a time, Marx and the older Bauer were close friends, sometimes laughing and talking loudly in church services, in order to be disrespectful, or getting drunk in public.[25] Later the two fell out of friendship.

In 1843, Marx and his wife moved to Paris, where he became involved in a group of writers and activists who wanted to unite German and French radicals. The following year Marx met Friedrich Engels. The two became friends and worked closely together to the end of Marx's life. While in Paris, Marx began studying political economy. In 1845, Marx and Engels relocated to Brussels. There they published their pamphlet *Manifest der kommunistischen Partei* ("Manifesto of the Communist Party," later known as the "Communist Manifesto"), whose appearance in 1848 immediately created controversy and even incited a plot to overthrow the French monarch King Louis Philippe.

Marx left Brussels and lived for about one year in Cologne. Then in 1849, he moved to London, where he would remain for the rest of his life. To support his family, Marx wrote columns for various newspapers, including the *New York Tribune*. He and his family were often in poverty. Only three of his children reached adulthood. Marx himself was troubled with poor health. He died at the age of sixty-four. It is widely acknowledged that his personal poverty and ill health very likely influenced his ideas. During his London years, Marx produced his most important work: *Das Kapital: Kritik der politischen Ökonomie* ("Capital: Criticism of Political Economy").[26]

Assessing Marx's thought is mixed but not especially difficult. Some of his observations were sound and most of his concerns were just, even if in a very abstract, hypothetical sense. After all, in his lifetime the industrial revolution created thousands of new jobs, but many of them exploited workers and subjected them to unhealthy and dangerous working conditions (none of which Marx himself ever personally observed). Marx rightly believed that this would lead to conflict. Marx was also correct in seeing a general progression in human history toward socialism, in which people increasingly pooled resources for the common good.

But much of Marx's analysis was faulty, naïve, and at times downright dishonest.[27] It has been said that Marx "was not interested in finding the truth but in proclaiming it."[28] Indeed, Marx himself had no sense of finance or economy. He borrowed money from family and friends, rarely expressing thanks. For years he received a stipend from Engels.

Marx's understanding of humanity was limited, largely due to his materialist commitments and utter rejection of the spiritual dimension of individuals. "We are the apes of a cold God," he once asserted.[29] Marx viewed humanity through an apocalyptic lens. His interpretation of history was in reality a form of eschatology. He knew what was coming; he spoke of "the Day of Judgment" and the fiery destruction of cities.[30] There was no science or scholarship here; it was little more than wild poetry. Had Marx believed in God, most would probably have written him off as a religious kook. All of this eschatology was ultimately rooted in what Marx perceived as economic injustice.

Contrary to Marx's thinking, however, not everything people do or think is guided by economic interests. Some people make decisions based on altruistic motives or religious commitments. Marx, of course, viewed religiously inspired motives as wrong-headed. For him, religion and its promise of heavenly rewards numbed people to the realities of economic injustice in the here and now. Belief in God, Marx thought, blinded people to oppression, in effect drugging them, so that they were unable to see clearly the reality in which they lived and the urgent need for change.

It is in this connection that Marx infamously stated that religion "is the opium of the people."[31] It is worth quoting the passage in full, in which this remarkable assertion occurs:

> *Religious* suffering is, at one and the same time, the *expression* of real suffering and a *protest* against real suffering. Religion is the sigh of the oppressed creature, the heart of a heartless world, and the soul of soulless conditions. It is the *opium* of the people. The abolition of religion as the illusory happiness of the people is the demand for their real happiness. To call on them to give up their illusions about their condition is to call on them to give up a condition that requires illusions.[32]

This statement is hardly more than tautology: A is B because B is A, or something to that effect. Marx assumed a host of things, for which little or no evidence was provided. His statement was also condescending, for he apparently believed he knew better than others what they experienced in religious faith and why they sought it. Marx, of course, was a committed atheist and so could not imagine any connection with God or any real spirituality. He asserted that the world is "heartless" and "soulless." Why would that be so, and how did he come to that conclusion? For Marx, it was because people worked hard and were paid little. Surely there is more to the human condition. Given his commitment to materialism, however, Marx could shed no further light on humanity's problem.[33]

What is ironic is that his understanding of the world and of the human condition was in itself nothing less than a form of religion, even if in secular and atheistic dress. Within his understanding of materialist history was eschatology, a goal, an end, toward which human history inexorably moves. How did Marx know this? By faith, of course! How else? Marx piously believed that heaven would be achieved on earth. It would be a new garden of Eden, a new paradise—a utopia in which all humans would live together in peace and harmony, a society in which there would be no selfishness, no greed, and no desire for power.

The eschatology of Marx hardly differs from the eschatology of Judaism and Christianity. The only difference is that Marx thought economic revolution and the empowerment of the working class would bring about this remarkable act of salvation. But that is exactly where Marxism is weak: It naïvely misdiagnoses the human condition, believing that replacing white-collar power with blue-collar power will solve humanity's problems.

I might add that although many of the architects of Communism had good intentions—they truly hoped that under extreme socialism the human condition would improve—their ideas and practices failed, sometimes spectacularly. Communist Russia and the Soviet Union, formed through military force, collapsed in 1990. Communist China, though still a one-party tyranny, now openly embraces free enterprise, big business, and trade. As a result, its once stagnant, backward economy is booming and there is a growing middle class. The late Hugo Chavez, dictator of Venezuela, wrecked what had been a relatively prosperous, oil-driven economy with his Marxist economic policies. Now the dictator is dead and the country is dead broke. About the only traditional Communist country left is Cuba, whose economy is on life-support and its people impoverished. Of course, with the fading away of the Castro regime, Communism in Cuba may soon disappear.

During my recent visit to Cuba, I learned the average family lives on twenty to thirty dollars per month (not per day). For many families, it is not uncommon for money and food to run out before the end of the month and the next government check. All that keeps many of these poor people from starving to death are the bananas, mangos, guavas, and papayas that grow everywhere. If ever there was a "Banana Republic," it is Cuba. But it is not food that the people crave; Cubans are hungry for the Christian message. Atheist Communism has left Cubans spiritually starved. Even Raúl Castro, Cuba's current dictator and brother of the late Fidel Castro, not long ago spoke of his openness to personally return to the church.[34] Small house churches are springing up everywhere, a sign that major changes in Cuba are sure to come.

In the next chapter, we will consider the last of the Big Five intellectuals who set the stage for the great battles between good and evil in the twentieth century.

CHAPTER 7
Dehumanizing Humanity

It's the second greatest commandment—a foundation of the Christian faith: Love thy neighbor as thyself. But if Sigmund Freud had his way, the command would be vastly different: "Love thy neighbor as thy neighbor loves thee."[1] Freud, the father of psychoanalysis, pointedly disagreed with Christian ethics, especially the idea that all of humanity should be loved. "Not all men are worthy of love," Freud wrote in 1930. "If I love someone, he must deserve it in some way. . . . He deserves it if he is like me in important ways that I can love myself in him . . . that I can love my ideal of my own self in him."[2]

Freud and Friedrich Nietzsche profoundly influenced Western culture. Nietzsche laid the groundwork for destroying a nation's soul. Freud discovered ways of destroying the individual's soul. Without a doubt, the worst of the nineteenth century's Big Five was Friedrich Wilhelm Nietzsche.

Friedrich Wilhelm Nietzsche

Nietzsche was born in 1844 in a small town near Leipzig in Saxony (Prussia). His father, a Lutheran pastor, died a few months before young

Friedrich's fifth birthday. He had been very close to his father and the loss was a serious blow to which Nietzsche would refer in later life. His widowed mother received a pension that allowed Nietzsche to enroll at a prestigious prep school. His academic work was at best modest; his taste in subjects and recreation eccentric, if not unsavory. Because of drunkenness, Nietzsche was demoted in class rank.

In 1864, Nietzsche enrolled at the University of Bonn and began studies in theology and classical philosophy. This is difficult to explain, for two years earlier Nietzsche had written a paper in which he opined that critical scholarship had cast doubt on the most important elements of Christian faith.[3] After one year of study at Bonn, Nietzsche lost interest in preparing for the Lutheran ministry; he also lost his faith.

Nietzsche returned to Leipzig where he studied the writings of Arthur Schopenhauer, an atheist and an advocate of philosophical pessimism, which supposedly "faces up" to the negative realities of the world, refusing to indulge in hope or faith. His work deeply influenced Nietzsche. In 1866, Nietzsche read an influential work on materialism by Albert Lange, who was also an atheist.[4] This work also had a major influence on the young Nietzsche.[5] After a brief stint in the military, Nietzsche was appointed professor of philology at the University of Basel in Switzerland. He was only twenty-four and had not yet received either his doctorate or his habilitation.

During the Franco-Prussian War (1870–1871), Nietzsche served as a medical orderly. He suffered various illnesses, including syphilis. After the war, he returned to Basel, but his publications were met with little enthusiasm. Because of declining health, Nietzsche was forced to retire in 1878. During the 1880s he was surprisingly productive given his poor health and increasing dependence on opium. In his 1882 book *The Gay Science*, Nietzsche wrote perhaps the most well-known phrase in philosophy, "God is dead," and a year later he completed the first part of *Thus Spoke Zarathustra*. Near the end of his life he wrote polemical works that attacked Christianity or Christian values either overtly or implicitly. These included *Beyond Good and Evil* (1886), *On the Genealogy of Morals* (1887), *Twilight of the Idols* (1888), and *The Antichrist* (1895).[6] He began an autobiography that he planned to call *Ecce Homo* ("Behold the Man!"), a clear allusion to Pilate's reference to Jesus when the latter stood before the crowd calling for his crucifixion.[7] The themes of some of these books focused on the death of God, moral relativism, Aryan racism, and the coming of an *Übermensch*, variously translated as "Overman," "Overhuman," or "Superman." The latter will be discussed in more detail.

In January 1889, while visiting Turin, Italy, Nietzsche developed a severe psychological disorder.[8] He never recovered. Before dying he wrote a number of strange letters, in which he spoke of Caiaphas (the Jewish high priest who condemned Jesus), of being crucified by German physicians, and a number of other incoherent instructions and opinions, touching politics and religion (including a letter to the Pope). Nietzsche was placed in the care of family and friends, spent time in clinics, and finally, suffering from dementia and at least one stroke, died in August of 1900 at the age of fifty-five. Historians continue to debate the actual cause of death.[9] Another lingering question centers on whether Nietzsche was entirely sane while writing in the 1880s.[10]

Superman?

Nietzsche's best known concept is his idea of the Superman.[11] But Nietzsche's Superman bears little resemblance to the comic book figure of the same name that appeared in the 1930s and became a big hit on television and in movies. The latter is a benevolent being from another world; the former is a monster from our world. Superman and his alter ego Clark Kent strive to serve and protect humanity. He is a savior figure.

Nietzsche's Superman wishes to dominate humanity and, as necessary, cull the human "herd." A savior figure he is not.

Perhaps you have heard Nietzsche and his Superman fantasy presented in a more positive, innocuous light. There are university professors of philosophy, literature, and political theory who sing the praises of this demented man. But when you read his work, not the abridged and sanitized "CliffsNotes" versions, you will find little that is positive and nothing that is innocuous about Nietzsche's understanding of existentialism and how the authentic, self-asserting person ought to live. Indeed, Nietzsche could be fairly described as the godfather of Nazism and Fascism.

Historian Richard Weikart rightly points out that Nietzsche's commitment to atheism led him to dehumanize humanity. Nietzsche rejected the idea that man was made in the image of God. Man is no more than a two-legged animal, Nietzsche believed. Indeed, Nietzsche said, speaking to all of us, "You have made your way from worm to man, and much in you is still worm. Once you were apes, and even now, man is more ape than any ape."[12]

Nietzsche not only did not believe in God, he hated Christianity. In his eyes, following the crucified Jesus meant the refusal of life.

Nietzsche also did not believe in equality. Some men were superior to others (and men were superior to women). The most advanced humans, he said, should breed in such a way as to advance humanity still further, while less advanced humans should be forced into slavery.[13]

"The great majority of men have no right to existence, but are a misfortune to higher men,"[14] Nietzsche said. The highest of these men, he argued, is the Superman himself. Nietzsche was not speaking in metaphors; he meant what he said, explaining that the destruction of most of humanity in order to benefit the superior "human species, would indeed constitute progress."[15] Those to be destroyed included the physically and mentally handicapped.

In some ways, Nietzsche proclaimed the unvarnished reality of atheism, in which there really is no morality, only a sort of law of the jungle, a survival of the strong and aggressive. He called Christian morality "slave morality," for it is weak and protects the weak[16] and "preserves what is ripe for destruction."[17] We live in a highly competitive society, but as followers of Jesus we must reject the "get ahead at any cost" notion and replace it with the example of servant leadership we find in the life of Jesus.

Nietzsche recommended suicide and infanticide, urging physicians to snuff out the handicapped and encourage the elderly and infirm to end their lives "after the meaning of life, the right to life, has been lost."[18] That Nietzsche could say this was quite remarkable, when we recall that he had been infirm for years and needed daily care himself. Particularly troubling is the ease with which Nietzsche could speak of the loss of "the right to life." Of course, in the world of Nietzsche, there were no inalienable rights, as proclaimed in the American Declaration of Independence. To him, the weak and infirm have no right to life; rather, they must be culled from the "herd" of humanity.

Had these ravings been ignored, little harm would have been done. Regrettably and unbelievably, many people read Nietzsche and found in these words of hatred and extreme bigotry inspiration and dreams of a new world. In the aftermath of Hitler and Mussolini, some apologists have tried to sanitize the insanity and to downplay the depravity, all in an effort to depict Nietzsche in a more humane and even benign light. These efforts, however, are disinguous and unpersuasive.[19] As one critic has rightly underscored, Nietzsche's "philosophy licenses the atrocities of a Hitler."[20]

Nietzsche influenced plenty of people, some of whom were in positions of power and therefore able to implement the insane man's philosophy. One of these was Benito Mussolini, the Italian dictator before and during World War II. Another disciple of Nietzsche was Adolf Hitler. Yet another was Josef Stalin. As we shall see, practitioners of brute force gladly draw upon philosophical justifications, whatever their political leanings, left or right.

There were many others in the early twentieth century who drank deeply from the well of Nietzsche, including the likes of Martin Heidegger, Jean-Paul Sartre, and Michel Foucault. The actions and beliefs of these men were appalling, and surprisingly many in today's universities and entertainment media give them a pass. Their Nietzschean philosophies are deserving of trenchant criticism.[21]

Sigmund Freud

Sigismund Schlomo Freud, or Sigmund Freud as he is better known, was born into a Jewish family in 1856 in Freiberg in Mähren, Moravia, of the Austrian Empire (now Příbor, Czech Republic).[22] In 1881, he received his doctor of medicine degree at the University of Vienna. A few years later he established his practice in Vienna. In 1902, he was appointed as an adjunct professor at the University of Vienna. Freud remained in Vienna until he had to flee Austria in 1938, in the aftermath of the Nazi takeover. He died in England the following year.

In his early years, Freud was influenced by Schopenhauer, Darwin, and Nietzsche. As an atheist he interpreted the human mind in materialist terms. Freud became well-known for his development and practice of psychoanalysis, especially for his theory that human psychology is driven by sexuality or, more specifically, an Oedipus complex (in which children are sexually attracted to the parent of the opposite gender). Freud believed that boys and girls experience the complex differently, with the former fearing castration and the latter envying the former's genitalia. Failure to resolve the complex can lead, Freud believed, to pedophilia and/or homosexuality. Without necessarily endorsing Freud's theory, modern research has shown that sexually abused children are far more likely to engage in rape and pedophilia or adopt a homosexual or transgendered lifestyle.[23] Although the medical value of Freud's legacy is disputed, there is little doubt with regard to his influence in popular culture.

Freud regarded belief in God as illusory. He viewed it as satisfying the need of a child to have a father figure on whom he could rely and in whom he could trust. Religion, he maintained, is little more than a psychological crutch.[24] Indeed, said Freud, religion could be described as "the universal obsessional neurosis of humanity."[25] Belief in God is "patently infantile" and amounts to "mass-delusion."[26] In expressing this view, Freud anticipated by about eighty years Richard Dawkins's poorly researched but bestselling *The God Delusion*. Given that fewer than 5 percent of the world's population is committed atheist, this amounts to a rather dismal assessment of *most of humanity*.

Although Freud conceded that in early human civilization, belief in God was useful as a way of curbing humanity's violent tendencies, in modern times it no longer serves a useful purpose. Belief in God should be replaced by science and reason, Freud said.[27] It is, of course, ironic that the worst violence in human history has taken place fairly recently, brought on by atheists supposedly guided by science and reason. I will say more about this later, but for now, it should not go unobserved that Freud assumed that belief in God and science were at odds and always will be.[28] Indeed, it was as an atheist that Freud developed his theory and practice of psychoanalysis.[29]

A major support for Freud's proposed Oedipus complex was the idea that primitive societies were totem cultures in which the father was eaten. Not long after Freud advanced his hypothesis it was destroyed by ethnologist Wilhelm Schmidt. He showed that ancient cultures and contemporary primitive cultures simply did not exhibit the characteristics suggested by Freud. Of note, most primitive cultures were monotheistic. Monotheism seems to be the original form of theism, with polytheism representing departures from and distortions of the older monotheism. Freud never abandoned his anthropological foundation, despite its fundamental flaws.[30]

Freud saw love not only as reciprocal but—very importantly—as narcissistic; love of others is in reality love of ourselves, or at least it should be. Contrary to the Christian emphasis on *agape* (selfless love), Freud said an ethic of love should be based on *eros* (sexual love).[31] Grace finds no place in Freud. One suspects that Freud's critique may reveal more of Freud himself than a sound ethic that can be universally applied.

One also cannot help but wonder if Freud's preoccupation with sex had more to do with his own problems than with objective study of the science of mind and soul. Freud famously blamed his tobacco addiction as a substitute for masturbation.[32] Moreover, there is compelling evidence that Freud had an affair with his sister-in-law.[33] Freud regularly used cocaine, writing a number of papers extolling its values, including alleviating and even curing mental problems.[34] Notoriously, Freud encouraged his friend Ernst von Fleischl-Marxow to use cocaine as a way of ending his addiction to morphine, which he had been taking to deal with chronic pain. However, his use of cocaine led to serious mental problems. Fleischl-Marxow returned to using morphine and not long after died.[35] Freud no longer publicly recommended using the narcotic.[36]

Professionally, Freud's most embarrassing misadventure involved longtime friend and colleague Wilhelm Fliess, an ear, nose, and throat specialist. Freud and Fliess found common ground in their radical ideas relating to sexuality. Fliess promoted the pseudo-scientific idea of biorhythms, in which he believed men and women went through fixed cycles, and a dubious concept he called "nasal reflex neurosis."[37] In reference to the latter, Fliess believed that the nose and genitals were related, convinced that treatment of the one could help the other. Freud accepted this odd idea, allowing Fliess to operate on his nose and sinuses, supposedly to cure Freud's own neurosis.

On Freud's advice, one Emma Eckstein, who suffered from premenstrual depression and (according to Freud) engaged in "excessive masturbation," allowed Fliess to surgically remove a bone from her nose. Following surgery, Eckstein almost bled to death. In the days and weeks that followed, she developed a serious infection. This too almost killed her. (The infection ended after another surgeon removed a half-meter length of gauze that Fliess had left in the woman's sinus!) The twenty-seven-year-old Eckstein was left horribly disfigured, with the left side of her face sunken. Freud blamed Eckstein, stating that her hemorrhaging constituted psychological "wish-bleedings," which in turn were caused by desire for affection.[38] Evidently Freud failed to perceive the utter quackery of the theory and the procedure. Freud later distanced himself from Fliess, completely breaking with him in 1906. Eckstein became a psychiatrist.

Freud's death was due to a doctor-assisted overdose of morphine. For several years he had suffered from a cancerous tumor in his mouth, which migrated to his jaw. Surgery and medical treatments slowed the spread of the cancer, but when the pain and discomfort were more than he could bear, Freud called on his medical friend and colleague Max Schur to assist him in administering a fatal dose of morphine. Schur did so, and Freud died in September 1939.[39]

Recent research into Freud's personal life has raised serious questions about the integrity and validity of his work and theories about human psychology. Freud's personal correspondence, taken with what is already known, strongly suggests that Freud was sexually involved with his sister-in-law Minna Bernays.[40] This incestuous affair, along with Freud's hatred of his father, probably explains Freud's advocacy of his Oedipus complex, in which the son destroys his father and has sex with his mother. Freud feared that if this illicit affair became public, he and his theory would lose all credibility.[41] The affair is now widely acknowledged and, as Freud feared, his credibility is seriously undermined. Freud's unprofessional and immoral behavior certainly damaged his reputation. But not all of his insights are without merit. His idea that one's faith in God may be in some way related to one's relationship with one's father is suggestive, though not exactly the way Freud proposed. The psychological link between faith and father will be explored in the next chapter.

CHAPTER 8
Atheism and the Broken Soul

So why did Nietzsche, Freud, and the other Big Five thinkers behave so badly and go on to promote bad ideas that hurt and marginalize individuals still today?

This topic is addressed in *Intellectuals*, a well-researched book by Paul Johnson about influential thinkers in the West. From Karl Marx and Percy Shelley to Victor Gollancz and Lillian Hellman, Johnson shows how prominent men and women allowed their personal corruption to corrupt their research, thinking, and writing. The record is so dismal that Johnson worries the general public no longer trusts intellectuals. And in this day and age of the internet, where anyone can access in an instant any assertion and any theory, no matter how crazy or evil, Johnson's worry seems well founded. "One of the principal lessons of our tragic century," he writes, "is—beware the intellectuals." What makes them so dangerous, says Johnson, is their ability "to create climates of opinion and prevailing orthodoxies, which themselves often generate irrational and destructive courses of action."[1]

History bears witness to this grim truth. The theories and doctrines of many of these intellectuals are ultimately dehumanizing, which is not hard to fathom, given the nihilism that underlies their worldview.

Bad behavior and the bad ideas grow out of spiritual corruption and collapse. Michael Jones, author of *Degenerate Moderns*,[2] sees the problem sourced in the decision to turn away from God and the Judeo-Christian worldview that grows out of belief in God. When the intellectual abandons morals—almost always involving sex—trouble begins. If a theory can be found or an argument made that explains away or, better, justifies the behavior, then well and good. One's theory alleviates the sense of guilt. Sin is absolved, not through repentance but through subverting or outright destroying the moral code. Of course, to get rid of the moral code almost always requires getting rid of God. It is no wonder that almost all of the intellectual bad actors are atheists.

One of the most intriguing aspects of Sigmund Freud's work was his proposed link between human psychology and belief in God. In an oft-quoted and much-discussed passage, Freud states, "Psychoanalysis has taught us the intimate connection between the father complex and belief in God, and daily demonstrates to us how youthful persons lose their religious belief as soon as the authority of the father breaks down."[3] Freud suggests that belief in God fulfilled a desire for a close relationship with a parent.

But the idea of wish-fulfilling cuts both ways. Atheism, the rejection of God, can just as readily be explained as due to a child's loss of respect for a parent, especially for his father. Rejection of one's earthly father (for whatever reason) provides motivation for rejecting one's heavenly Father.

A link between relationship with one's father—whether healthy or unhealthy, encouraging or discouraging belief in God—does not prove or disprove the existence of God. But it is a possible explanation for much of the angry atheism that has been expressed in modern times. It also may explain how the world itself can be viewed in such radically different ways.

Look at the contrasting reactions to nature expressed by the English poet William Wordsworth in 1798 and German skeptic Arthur Schopenhauer in 1818. Wordsworth saw beauty throughout the world and believed it testified to the goodness of God. Schopenhauer could only see suffering and pain and so concluded there could be no God.[4] Whose inferences reflect the truth? Is the world good, or is the world evil? Does the world have a purpose? Or is it without purpose?

Today, two centuries after Wordsworth and Schopenhauer, we can compare theist C. S. Lewis, who spoke of being "surprised by joy,"[5] with atheist Richard Dawkins, who has spoken of nature's "pitiless indifference."[6] The contrast of perspectives is stark.

Why People Reject God

People turn their backs to God for any number of reasons, but it is especially troubling when they adopt atheism to justify arguments against Christian ethics and morals related to sexual behavior. In short, atheism is far more accommodating to a lifestyle of sexual promiscuity.[7] This is the background of several prominent atheists, including Jean Jacques Rousseau, who fathered five children out of wedlock and abandoned all of them; Percy Bysshe Shelley, a cheat and an adulterer; Karl Marx, an adulterer and racist; Leo Tolstoy, an adulterer and gambler who showed his wife no respect; Bertrand Russell, a serial adulterer and seducer of female students; and Jean-Paul Sartre, also a seducer of female students.[8] The actions of Russell and Sartre were especially egregious. Today, these men would be dismissed from their academic posts and in all likelihood would be prosecuted. Indeed, you can't have your cake and eat it too. Atheism is very elitist, which is ironic because it presents itself as the religion of the common man. Truth is, in its elitism it acts as if the traditions, laws, and contstraints that humans have almost universally embraced don't apply to atheists.

What should deeply concern us all is that several of these atheist intellectuals were not honest with their research. In effect, the methods and the results of their "research" were rigged to reach preferred conclusions. In the following paragraphs I briefly describe a few of the most notorious examples. I begin with Aldous Huxley because he openly confessed this tendency on his part and on the part of other like-minded intellectuals.

Aldous Huxley

Prominent atheist Aldous Huxley (1894–1963) made no attempt to hide the motives behind his atheism and the atheism of some of his counterparts.

> For myself as, no doubt, for most of my contemporaries, the philosophy of meaninglessness was essentially an instrument of liberation. The liberation we desired was simultaneously liberation from a certain political and economic system and liberation from a certain system of morality. *We objected to the morality because it interfered with our sexual freedom.*[9]

Not only does Huxley acknowledge that his and fellow atheists' choice of ethical nihilism (that is, the "philosophy of meaninglessness") is motivated by a desire to remove anything that "interfered with [their] sexual freedom," he even admits that the preference for nihilism placed limits on their academic integrity. He informs his readers: "We don't know *because we don't want to know*. . . . Those who detect no meaning in the world generally do so because . . . *it suits their books that the world should be meaningless.*"[10] This is a remarkable confession, not least for its candor. One must wonder if, as had Schopenhauer long ago, the atheist sees only horror and meaninglessness in the world because that is what he or she prefers to see. The atheist is simply unwilling to see more, to see the goodness and purpose of life, and the divine power behind it.

Margaret Mead

A notorious example of misrepresenting research so that the results would agree with one's sexual ethics is seen in the work of Margaret Mead (1901–1978), the celebrated anthropologist. After six weeks of language study and a few months of personal observation and study in Samoa, Mead published her bestseller *Coming of Age in Samoa* in 1928. She claimed that the Samoans practiced very open sexuality and, in fact, did not reserve sexual intimacy for marriage.[11] As it turned out, Mead's assertions were false, as a later study showed.[12] What eventually came to light was that the sexual liberality that Mead claimed existed among Samoan youth reflected her own sexual proclivities, including adulterous relationships with men and women. In reality, the sexual mores of the Samoans were very much Judeo-Christian. In Samoan culture, sexual intimacy was reserved for marriage. Mead's otherwise sympathetic biographers have admitted that she read her own views into the data. Mead simply did not report her findings truthfully but shaped them according to her personal preferences and practices.[13]

Alfred Kinsey

Another example of rigging research so that it would lend support to one's moral preferences, as opposed to Judeo-Christian norms, is seen in the publications of Alfred Kinsey (1894–1956), the entomologist who became a self-taught sexologist. His so-called *Kinsey Reports* deeply influenced Americans and set the stage for the 1960s sexual revolution, suggesting that there really were no sexual or moral norms.[14] Once again, it turns out that the researcher was neither objective nor honest in his analysis and conclusions. Kinsey's assertions reflected his own ideas of moral relativity.[15] Later it came to light that Kinsey himself engaged in masochistic activities and even encouraged his students to engage in orgies. Kinsey even filmed some of these activities. Today, this kind of behavior on the part of faculty would result in dismissal and charges.[16] But in his time, Kinsey got away with it under the guise of "research."[17]

Bertrand Russell

Sometimes the atheist intellectual doesn't bother with research; he or she simply pontificates on a variety of topics, including morals. It makes no difference if he or she possesses any expertise whatsoever. Bertrand Russell (1872–1970) is a classic case in point. He was brilliant in math, placing seventh in Cambridge's highly competitive exams in 1893, but largely unstudied in all else. (Of note, that same year G. T. Manley, a Christian scholar who later wrote *In Understanding Be Men* and chaired the committee that founded Tyndale House at Cambridge, came first in the math exams.)[18] Nevertheless, Russell had plenty of advice on world politics, philosophy, and morals. He was also an accomplished philanderer.[19]

Russell was two when his mother died and four when his father died. Russell was then taken in by his paternal grandparents, but his grandfather died when he was six. His grandmother, Lady Russell, known as "Deadly Nightshade," continued to raise the lad.

Russell found comfort in nature, not in people. Relatives insist that throughout his life Russell searched for God, could not find him, and so rejected him. At an early age Russell adopted atheism, though it seems this did not preclude an ongoing search for God. The ethical and philosophical positions he took often were contradictory.

Russell's treatment of women was simply appalling. He cheated on all of his wives, and he went from mistress to mistress. It was said that Russell "had no scruples about seducing any woman who fell in his way," including servant girls.[20] His shabby treatment of his wives and mistresses often involved deception and lying. He was an arrogant, opinionated academic elitist who despised the general public. Russell was a chauvinist; he did not think women were intelligent, certainly not on the level of men.

Russell's principal criticism of Christian theism was not especially profound: he didn't like it, above all, the ethics that go along with it. Some atheists still appeal to his book *Why I Am Not a Christian*,[21] but there is nothing in it that is penetrating or persuasive. Russell claims the idea of God is not coherent, but he cannot really say why that is so. Why some academics today think highly of this man is hard to say.

Jean-Paul Sartre

Jean-Paul Sartre (1905–1980) grew up as an only child. Fatherless, he was nevertheless surrounded by women who made him feel like the center of the world. Sartre recalled that at a young age he was quite precocious, though apparently adults who knew him as a child don't remember it that way.[22] In any case, Sartre grew up with the conviction that he was brilliant and of great importance. Since anybody with any sense wanted to hear what Sartre said (or so he thought), Sartre talked on and on. He also wrote millions of words. Like Bertrand Russell, Sartre had a number of mistresses. Best known was Simone de Beauvoir, a noted philosopher and feminist.[23]

When France was overrun by Germany at the beginning of World War II, Sartre had no difficulty getting along with the Nazis. He wrote and directed plays throughout the occupation. After the war, Sartre identified with Marxism. In 1960, he visited Cuba, meeting with Fidel

Castro and Ernesto "Che" Guevara, the former dentist who became the iconic Communist guerrilla. Sartre regarded Guevara as a great intellectual and "the most complete human being of our age."[24] Untroubled by Guevara's bloody violence or Communism's grim record of suppression, Sartre joined Bertrand Russell in a campaign against US involvement in Vietnam. However, for all his Marxist bravado, Sartre was better known as an existentialist and armchair revolutionist.

Sartre not only supported Josef Stalin, whose policies resulted in the deaths of millions, he also supported Mao Zedong of China, whose policies also resulted in the deaths of millions, many through starvation; and as already mentioned, he supported Fidel Castro as well.[25] Sartre is also said to have inspired Pol Pot and the Khmer Rouge of Cambodia in the 1970s, which resulted in millions of deaths.[26] But for all his bold talk about taking action and being willing to die, Sartre was careful never to put himself in harm's way.[27]

Sartre was an intellectual snob and an academic elitist who viewed women as conquests. When Sartre ended a relationship with yet another mistress in 1966, and the distraught woman committed suicide, Sartre expressed no remorse. "When I was told she had killed herself, I had a short asthma attack, but then nothing," he explained. "Since I am absolutely certain that after one's death there's nothing, I cannot grieve. . . . For me, it's simple: death is nothingness, hence not part of life, so I do not think of death."[28] Even Sartre's admirers were put off by their idol's callous indifference, which is a bit surprising given their chosen worldview: if there is no God—if human life is nothing more than a cosmic accident—then life ultimately has no purpose or value.

As he aged, Sartre faded from the scene. He made attempts to recapture the public attention to which he was so accustomed. He tried to incite demonstrations at factories. He called workers to action. But apart from a few colleagues, no one took notice anymore. No one knew who he was. Sartre apparently didn't realize that the workers had good paying jobs with good benefits. Why would they protest or riot? Who was this odd-looking little man? In his late sixties, "Sartre was an increasingly pathetic figure, prematurely aged, virtually blind, often drunk, worried about money, uncertain about his views."[29] In his attempts to gain attention, Sartre became a parody of himself. He wandered from mistress to mistress, but soon money and health deserted him. Confused and babbling nonsense, Sartre died in a hospital in 1980.

The New Atheists

The latest generation of atheists, dubbed New Atheists, is led by the "Four Horsemen": Richard Dawkins, Daniel Dennett, Christopher Hitchens, and Sam Harris.

Richard Dawkins (1941–), the suave and well-spoken biologist of Oxford, gained notoriety in 2006, when he published *The God Delusion*.[30] He is separated from his third wife, Lalla Ward, and has a daughter by his second wife.[31] An only child, Dawkins was born in Kenya, where he spent his early years. As a young lad he was sent off to an Anglican boarding school, where at the age of nine he was sexually molested. This experience led to very negative feelings about Christianity, which, as psychology professor Paul Vitz points out, would have primed Dawkins for his later "atheist conversion."[32]

Daniel Dennett (1942–) is an award-winning philosopher and cognitive scientist. His much-discussed book *Breaking the Spell: Religion as a Natural Phenomenon*[33] attempts to explain widespread belief in God in terms of psychology and brain science. Born in Boston, Dennett's parents relocated to Lebanon during World War II. When he was five, his father died in a plane crash, the cause of which was never disclosed. Dennett and his mother returned to Massachusetts. Writing years later, Dennett expressed relief that he, unlike his friends, did not have to live up to the high expectations of an accomplished father. Dr. Vitz finds this view odd, commenting that Dennett strangely expressed "no sense of positive loss." Rather, Dennett congratulates himself on being fatherless and "'shudders' at what would have happened if he had had a father."

Christopher Hitchens (1949–2011) was an English journalist who made himself well-known for bashing theism and Christianity. His best known work on atheism is his book *God Is Not Great: How Religion Poisons Everything*.[34] As in the case of Dawkins, Hitchens simply did not like God. He found God authoritarian and oppressive. But once again, one cannot help but wonder if the adults in Hitchens' life, especially the male figures, played a decisive role in steering the teen toward atheism. Hitchens' father was weak and unsuccessful. His parents' marriage was not happy. In his late teens, Hitchens discovered that his mother had become involved with an ex-Anglican priest who had become a devotee of the Maharishi Mahesh Yogi—widely known in the West because of his association with the Beatles. Hitchens' mother and the ex-priest ran off and were later found dead in a hotel in Athens, apparently the result of a suicide pact. A weak father, a faithless mother, and an immoral, lapsed clergyman primed Hitchens to reject God and gratuitously claim that religious faith "poisons everything." Hitchens died of cancer at the age of sixty-two.

The fourth member of the "Four Horsemen" is Sam Harris (1967–). Harris is an accomplished neuroscientist. There is not a great deal of biographical information about him. As far as we know, he enjoyed a stable, healthy upbringing, with no difficulty between himself and his father. Dr. Vitz suggests that unless new information comes to light to suggest otherwise, Harris should be regarded as an exception to the common backgrounds of outspoken atheists.[35] But I am not so sure.

By his own admission, Harris states that his upbringing was quite secular (which in all probability pointed him in an atheist direction). While pursuing his bachelor's degree at Stanford University, Harris experimented with MDMA,[36] a powerful psychoactive drug, which supposedly resulted in profound insights. The drug, widely known as ecstasy, can also damage the brain. Harris dropped out of school, experimented with other drugs, and traveled to India, where he studied with various Hindu and Buddhist teachers. He eventually returned to Stanford, where he received his degree in philosophy in 2000 at the age of thirty-three. Nine years later he received his PhD in cognitive neuroscience from UCLA. His research interest focused on how the brain is related to belief, disbelief, certainty, and uncertainty. Although critical of Judaism and Christianity, Harris, who sees himself as a secular Jew (as is his mother), is especially critical of Islam because of its tendency toward coercion and violence. The Islamic terrorist attacks in 2001 triggered his interest. Harris has written several books critical of Judaism, Christianity, and Islam.[37]

Harris cuts an interesting figure. His atheism in some ways is not typical. For example, he sees nothing wrong in looking for metaphysical insight and spiritual states of mind. Harris believes that a universal, benevolent morality for humanity can be found, even without reference to God.[38] But his critics—theists and atheists alike—aren't buying it.[39]

In my view, Harris is not a true atheist (most are not); he is agnostic and a seeker. Indeed, he seems to be a lifelong seeker. Contrary to Harris, classical atheists of the type described previously, rightly infer and vigorously argue that if there is no God, there really are no moral absolutes, at least no legitimate grounds for them. Humans must make it all up as they go. Morality can never be more than a matter of personal preference and utilitarian function.[40] Interestingly, the disasters that befell the twentieth century have motivated the New Atheists, at least a few of them, to find the basis for a humane morality.

The Making of an Atheist

In *The Making of an Atheist*, James Spiegel points out that the vast majority of humanity believes in God, and that has been the case, so far as we know, since the emergence of human civilization thousands of years ago. Belief in God is almost universal in young children, yet some abandon this belief as teens or young adults. Drawing on the work of Dr. Vitz and others, Spiegel finds that broken relationships with fathers and/or sexual immorality go hand in hand with the making of an atheist.[41]

There are, of course, exceptions in both directions. There are devout believers who were raised without a father or were abused by their father. Other people raised in homes with very positive father relationships nevertheless embrace atheism, or at least abandon theism. But the statistics, such as we know them, are very suggestive. Belief in God is not, as Freud claimed, the result of a psychologically hurting person, longing for a healthy father figure. Belief in God is the orientation and conviction of a psychologically healthy person. It is atheism that suggests that something is wrong. It is the lack of a positive father figure that can damage the soul of a human and leads one to believe (wrongly, in my view, of course) that there is no God, at least not one worthy of our attention or respect.

In the next chapter, we turn our attention to the most notorious practitioner of Nietzsche's dehumanizing philosophy and a time when the unimaginable happened.

CHAPTER 9
"Superman" Arrives

The nineteenth century produced a particularly toxic brew of worldviews, and Adolf Hitler became its incarnation—Nietzsche's Superman—a madman determined to destroy most of humanity to benefit a "superior" race.

From previous chapters, we can see that Hitler was not some sort of "one-off," an extremist who came out of nowhere. Far from it. Hitler was the end-product of the West's determination to move away from its Christian heritage. In rejecting Christianity, the radical atheism of the twentieth century did not take humanity forward into some enlightened post-Christian utopia; it took humanity back into pre-Christian barbarism. According to noted historian J. Rufus Fears, "Before 1914, a perverted science of racism was popular. In England, some believed that the Anglo-Saxon and Germanic races were superior to all others. Many of the best minds of the day taught this reprehensible doctrine, and Hitler absorbed it."[1]

What Hitler and the Nazis put into practice was the philosophy of the pre-Christian world, with all of its racism, hatred, eugenics, and justification of slavery. Theistic-based ethics were swept aside and replaced by a new "scientific" ethics that had no problem with supposedly superior humans enslaving and murdering supposedly inferior humans. The main difference between pre-Christian antiquity and post-Christian totalitarian governments is that the latter possesses far greater zeal and far more dangerous tools.

A Bright But Lazy Student

Adolf Hiedler was born in April 1889 in Braunau am Inn (Braunau on the river Inn), Austria. He was the fourth son of Alois Hiedler (whose birth name was actually Schicklgruber) and his third wife, Klara Pölzl, a devout Roman Catholic. Young Adolf had a number of siblings through his father's previous marriages and dalliances. Alois Hiedler (1837–1903) was almost fifty-two when Adolf was born.

Alois himself had been born out of wedlock. His mother was an Austrian peasant named Maria Anna Schicklgruber. It is speculated that the man who got her pregnant was Jewish.[2] If so, one of Adolf's grandparents was Jewish. The irony of this can hardly be missed. But the evidence is far from conclusive (though as it turns out, DNA tests still leave the matter open); the father may have been the man who eventually married Maria.

Four years after the birth of Alois, his mother married a man named Johann Georg Hiedler. Thirty-five years later, Hiedler forced Alois to drop the name Schicklgruber and adopt the Hiedler name. He may have done this to hide the fact that his son (whether natural or adopted) had been born out of wedlock. In any case, Alois was no longer Schicklgruber; he was now Hiedler.

For unknown reasons, Alois Hiedler, or perhaps his son Adolf, finally settled on spelling the family name as *Hitler*. In German, the pronunciation of *Hiedler* and *Hitler* would be almost identical. (From this point on, I will refer to Hitler by his widely recognized name.)[3]

Alois and Klara had six children, but only two—Adolf and his sister Paula—lived beyond childhood. Alois Hiedler held a position in the Austrian customs bureau. After he retired, his family moved to Leonding near Linz, Austria. Alois was hot-tempered and Klara was passive. There is evidence that Alois beat Klara and Adolf. Adolf was an average student, bright but lazy. His grades were mediocre. Alois died when Adolf was fourteen. One year later, Hitler dropped out of school. Historians think that Dr. Pötsch, Hitler's history teacher and vehement nationalist, may have inspired the young Hitler toward nationalism. This could be true, for years later Hitler presented two copies of *Mein Kampf* to his former teacher. In 1907, Klara died of breast cancer, leaving Adolf devastated and grieving.

Supported by the state's orphan's stipend, Hitler lived in Vienna, where he pursued his interests in art. After his mother's death, Hitler's finances were so limited that he found it necessary to live in hostels and shelters for the homeless. While in Vienna Hitler was exposed to anti-Semitic rhetoric, but it probably was not until after World War I that he became a confirmed anti-Semite, believing that Germany's defeat and other ills were due to the Jewish people.[4] In 1913, Hitler inherited his father's estate but left Austria for Munich, Germany, perhaps to avoid the Austrian draft. Hitler seemed eager to serve in the military, but not in the Austrian military, which he apparently regarded as weak and poorly led. When World War I broke out, he quickly volunteered for service in Germany.[5]

Hitler joined the Bavarian Army and served until his discharge in 1920. He served with enthusiasm throughout the war, suffering injuries and receiving two Iron Crosses. Hitler returned to Munich where he became involved with nationalist extremist groups and became acquainted with men who later would become part of the inner core of the Nazi Party. During this time, Hitler improved his rhetorical skills, becoming a popular speaker, especially in the beer halls of Munich.

Rise to Power

In 1923, Hitler and his followers attempted to overthrow the struggling Weimar Republic, which had been formed after the war and the abdication of Kaiser Wilhelm. Hitler was convicted of treason, and in April 1924, was sentenced to five years in the Landsberg prison (where he was well treated and served only seven months). There he began writing *Mein Kampf,*[6] about which much more will be said later. After his release from prison, he formed the Nazi Party. His speeches, in which he denounced Jews, Marxists, and especially the hated Treaty of Versailles, gained an ever-increasing following. It was this treaty, which blamed Germany for the Great War (1914–1918) and placed on Germany heavy reparations, that above all else attracted a hurting and resentful German public to Hitler. Against the backdrop of Germany's serious post-war economic depression and social unrest, which included fear of a Bolshevik-style revolution, Hitler's message despite its savagery and incoherence appealed to many.

In 1932, Hitler became a German citizen and was elected to the German Reichstag (or Parliament). The next year he was appointed Chancellor of Germany. Soon after, Hitler and the Nazi Party seized complete control of the German government, and in 1934 Hitler was proclaimed führer (leader) of Germany. The newly minted führer immediately began preparing for war.

There is no need here to recount World War II, which began in 1939 and ended in 1945. There is no need to go into the details, some of them murky, surrounding Hitler's final days in his Berlin bunker that ended with his suicide. It is enough at this point simply to tally up the horrific body count. It is estimated that between 5.5 and 6 million Jews died, mostly in the death camps; more than 19 million civilians and prisoners of war died; and 29 million soldiers and civilians died in military action. In all, somewhere between 53 and 54 million human beings perished during Hitler's brutal rule over Germany and large parts of Europe. Hitler has good claim to being one of the most evil and murderous men who ever lived. We shall see, however, that there were two or three others in his time who worked hard to win second place.

Hitler's "Religion"

A much-debated question today centers on Hitler's religion. Was he religious, and if so, in what way? At one time it was fashionable to claim that Hitler was a Christian.[7] After all, shortly after his birth he was baptized as a Catholic. The claim that Hitler was a Christian and that his murder of six million Jews was an example of Christian anti-Semitism has frequently been made, especially by some Jewish historians. Superficially, one can see how some scholars might assume this. But the accumulated evidence seems to show that Hitler was no Christian. In fact, as we shall see, Hitler did not believe in God in any conventional sense. His was a strange, incoherent, mystical religion that had its roots in paganism more than anything else. Today, most historians and theologians see Hitler as a pantheist of sorts—someone who equated God with nature.

The evidence against Hitler as a Christian is substantial, but there is also some counter evidence, which is why some writers today continue to insist that Hitler really was a Christian. It is not hard to see what motivates some to argue this. Hitler was, as we have mentioned, baptized as a Catholic and was raised by a very devout Catholic mother (though his father, Alois, was very irreligious). Moreover, Hitler was part of a society that was largely Christian, whether devout or nominal. On top of this, Hitler did claim in public settings that he was a Christian. Atheists, of course, don't want to include Hitler in their number. Communist atheists have already racked up a high enough body count, without adding Hitler's fifty-plus million to it. So was or wasn't Hitler a Christian?[8]

In a speech before a crowd in Munich, in 1920, Hitler spoke of the Nazi Party's Twenty-Five Point program. The twenty-fourth point contained the assurance that the party "stands for a positive Christianity, without binding itself denominationally to a particular confession."[9] The qualification about not being bound to a particular confession is in reference to Roman Catholicism and Protestantism (which in Germany mostly meant Lutheran). Throughout his speeches and in many places in Mein Kampf, Hitler spoke of the "two denominations" that waste the energies of their followers in endless squabbles. In many of his speeches Hitler referenced "positive Christianity"[10] (German: Positives Christentum). But in time it became clear that Hitler's Positive Christianity bore little resemblance to historic Christianity and certainly not to the Christianity practiced by Catholics and Protestants.

There is ample evidence for this claim. Hanns Kerrl was appointed by Hitler to form a Reich Church (Reichkirche) under the banner of Hitler's Positive Christianity. It was expected that all clergymen would swear allegiance to Hitler. According to Kerrl, Positive Christianity had nothing to do with the Apostle's Creed, nor would its adherents place their faith in Jesus Christ.[11] Alfred Rosenberg, an outspoken anti-Semite, one of Hitler's trusted lieutenants and founder of the Militant League for German Culture, planned to eliminate the "foreign Christian faiths" (that is, Roman Catholicism and all Protestant denominations) and replace them with Positive Christianity. Rosenberg hoped Hitler's Mein Kampf would replace the Bible and the Swastika would replace the cross.[12] What Rosenberg envisioned was replacing Christianity with Germanic paganism, in which there would be no more talk of the Ten Commandments and redemption through Christ.[13] The new religion would be based on racial purity and conquest, not turning the other cheek and praying for one's enemies. There would be nothing Christian about the new Positive Christianity.[14]

Heinrich Himmler, commander of the SS (*Schutzstaffel*, the "Protection Squadron"), strongly supported Rosenberg's ideas and plans to such an extent that he even began developing rituals that aped Christian practices.[15] Himmler had rejected historic Christianity and had become intrigued with mysticism and the occult. According to historian Ian Kershaw, "The assault on the practices and institutions of the Christian churches was deeply embedded in the psyche of National Socialism."[16]

Hitler's talk about Positive Christianity was nothing more than a ruse. A number of perceptive contemporary critics saw right through him and spoke out (though in exile).[17] Hitler knew perfectly well that if he openly condemned Christianity or declared himself an atheist, he would have almost no following among the German people. So cautious was Hitler on this point that even as late as 1941 he did not permit Joseph Goebbels, his minister of public enlightenment and propaganda, to withdraw from the church. This was "for tactical reasons," Goebbels wrote in his diary.[18] Hitler knew that he could not advance an anti-Christian agenda at the beginning of his rule. He hoped to gain Christian support by presenting himself as an opponent of Russian Bolshevik Communism and atheism.[19] By sounding like a defender of a new, vigorous form of Christianity, Hitler believed he could keep Catholics and Protestants in line. After winning the war, Hitler planned to purge Germany of Christianity. The evidence is clear on this point. Like Nietzsche before him, whom he admired,[20] Hitler hated Christianity.

Much of this evidence derives from private remarks Hitler made to his closest associates.[21] By 1937, Hitler "was declaring that 'Christianity was ripe for destruction,' and that the churches must yield to the 'primacy of the state,' railing against any compromise with 'the most horrible institution imaginable.'"[22]

Even more ominous was the language Hitler used. He not only spoke of the "destruction" (*Untergang*) of the church, but often spoke of the "church question," much as he would speak of the "Jewish question," terminology used by Hitler at least as far back as 1919.[23] We all know how Hitler answered the "Jewish question." There is no reason to doubt that Hitler planned the same for the Christian church.[24] Other historians have reached the same conclusion: for all his quasi-religious talk,[25] Hitler was not only *not* a Christian and *not* a theist in any Judeo-Christian sense, he planned to destroy Christianity *and* wipe out the Jewish people.

Hitler was convinced that Christianity was doomed and deservedly so because of science. Like Nietzsche before him, Hitler's worldview had been definitively shaped by the scientism of the nineteenth century. Historian Alan Bullock suggests that Hitler, Stalin, and Napoleon were materialists who embraced "the nineteenth-century rationalists' certainty that the progress of science would destroy all myths and had already proved Christian doctrine to be an absurdity."[26] In Hitler's thinking, shared by many of his contemporaries, science had brought an end to God and to the Christian faith.[27] It was destiny, his calling to usher in the new era—the era of science, eugenics, and German (Aryan) mastery over the world. This so-called science will be treated shortly.

By the late 1930s, Hitler had no more use for Positive Christianity or a Reich church. At this stage in his administration, Hitler would no longer meet with Hanns Kerrl, the director of the Reich Church. In fact, when Kerrl died in 1941, Hitler did not bother to replace him.

The shift in Hitler's strategy, that is, from pretending to be a Christian to dropping the pretense, is well illustrated in Heinrich Hoffmann's picture book *Hitler As No One Knows Him*, published in support of Hitler.[28] The intention of the book was to present the human side of the führer. In the first edition, which appeared in 1935, a photo of Hitler exiting the *Marienkirche* (Marien Church) in Wilhelmshaven shows a cross on the door immediately above Hitler's head, providing something akin to a halo effect. The caption that accompanies the photograph reads: "A photographic chance event becomes a symbol: Adolf Hitler, the supposed 'heretic,' leaving the Marienkirche in Wilhelmshaven."[29] Richard Weikart suspects that the photograph was hardly a "chance event." It was almost certainly staged.[30] In any event, the whole point was to convince Germans that Hitler truly was a Christian and supported the church, even if some of his ideas were unorthodox. In the 1938 edition of the book, the cross over Hitler's head no longer appears. The caption now reads: "Adolf Hitler after sightseeing at the historic Marienkirche in Wilhelmshaven."[31] The ruse had been abandoned; Hitler had not attended a religious service, as the 1935 caption implied; he was only sightseeing.

That Hitler and his closest supporters intended to bring about the end of Christianity in Germany (and in Europe) is revealed in the Hitler Youth song sung at the 1934 Nuremberg Party Rally. The anti-Christian sentiment is blunt and shocking:

> We are the joyful Hitler Youth
> We need no Christian virtue
> For our Führer Adolf Hitler
> Is ever our Mediator.
> No Pastor, no evil one, can hinder
> Us from feeling as Hitler's children.
> We follow not Christ but Horst Wessel,
> Away with incense and holy water.
> The Church can be taken away from me,
> The swastika is redemption on the earth,
> It will I follow everywhere,
> Baldur von Schirach, take me along![32]

In their wretched song, the Hitler Youth asserted that they "need no Christian virtue." Their leader is Adolf Hitler, their "mediator," an unmistakable allusion to Jesus Christ, who according to Christian faith is the true mediator between God and humankind. In the thinking of the Hitler Youth, the führer has taken on this role.[33] The song goes on to say that no one, not even one's pastor, can stop the youth from thinking of themselves as "Hitler's children." These children no longer follow Christ; they instead follow (the example of) Horst Wessel, that is, Horst Ludwig Georg Erich Wessel (1907–1930), a young Brownshirt who was murdered by Communist sympathizers and came to be regarded as a martyr and hero.[34] The Hitler Youth are ready to dispense with "incense and holy water," which allude to Catholic liturgy. Indeed, the Youth are happy to have the church "taken away." Who needs the church? After all, the "swastika is redemption." The Hitler Youth will follow it, not (it is implied) the cross of Christ. The Youth concluded their song by calling on Baldur von Schirach, the leader of the Hitler Youth, to take them where they need to go. Unfortunately, he did. Many of the Hitler Youth went to war and died. At the end of the war, Baldur himself went to prison. Whatever one's religious commitments (even if none at all), the sentiment of this song is as disgusting as it is frightening.

If Hitler was not a Christian, what was he? Most agree that Hitler was not exactly an atheist, at least not in the conventional sense. In 1941, Hitler asserted that through the observation of nature "people discovered the wonderful concept of the Almighty, whose rule they venerate. We do not want to train people in atheism."[35] But was Hitler once again being disingenuous? In this case probably not.

Hitler did not have any interest in the occult, mysticism, or astrology (in fact, he spoke out against astrology and the occult). Instead, he held to a vague idea of a higher power (*Gewalt*), a creative force (*Kraft*), fate (*Schicksal*), or providence (*Vorsehung*). Hitler sometimes even spoke of "the Almighty" (*der Allmächtige*), as in the quotation above. Some think that Hitler's idea of God ultimately derived not from the Bible but from the ancient Greek idea of fate.[36] Hitler often linked God and the German people (i.e., the Aryans). From this kind of talk, Max Domarus, who edited four volumes of Hitler's speeches, concluded that the God of Hitler was a "peculiarly German God."[37] But from all the evidence, Weikart concludes that "Hitler's position was closest to pantheism."[38]

However we nuance Hitler's peculiar religious ideas, his rejection of Judeo-Christian theism and his new ideas created in Germans a theological and spiritual confusion. Hitler did as much spiritual damage to Germany and Europe as he did physical damage.

CHAPTER 10
Hitler's Hell on Earth

Nietzsche's dark vision was realized thirty-three years after his death, when Adolf Hitler gained power over Germany and the march toward World War II began. In the previous chapter, we considered Hitler's life and his strange, quasi-religious ideas. Here we will look at his infamous book *Mein Kampf* and the nightmarish impact it had on Germany and Europe. You will also read accounts of two men who survived the concentration camps. These are dark topics, but they reflect what life is like without Christianity. Thankfully, a brighter viewpoint is possible when we look at the contributions of Winston Churchill, the British prime minister who withstood Hitler.

Mein Kampf and the "Science" of Racial Purity

It was in 1924, while in prison, that Hitler dictated most of *Mein Kampf* to his deputy Rudolf Hess and Emil Maurice, who would assume a position of leadership with the Brownshirts. The long, rambling book originally appeared in two volumes.

Hitler had difficulty deciding on a title. He called the first volume *Eine Abrechnung* (A Reckoning) and the second volume *Die Nationalsozialistische Bewegung* (The Nazi Movement). But what should the main title be? Hitler proposed *A Four and Half Year Struggle against Lies, Stupidity, and Cowardice: A Reckoning with the Destroyers of the Nazi Party Movement*. Max Amann, who helped Hitler publish his book, suggested the simple title *Mein Kampf* (My Struggle).

The book is simply abominable. On the back cover of a reprint edition I own, it reads: "*Mein Kampf* is an evil book, but it remains necessary reading for those who seek to understand the Holocaust, for students of totalitarian psychology, and for all who care to safeguard democracy."[1] I completely agree. But I would add a fourth reason to read it: *Mein Kampf* testifies to the moral and spiritual bankruptcy of a man who has replaced God with a Nietzschean cult of racism and the law of the jungle.

If Nietzsche was right in his view of the world and humanity, and if the majority of a nation wishes to embrace the hateful vision of a man like Adolf Hitler, in what sense is that wrong or evil? According to Richard Dawkins and other atheists, there are no moral absolutes. The natural world is utterly indifferent to right and wrong, to our survival or to our destruction. If Nietzsche and Dawkins are correct, then human ethics can never rise above democratic utilitarianism. In short, the majority decides what is best.

But why a majority? According to the law of the jungle, it is the smartest, fastest, and strongest (not the majority) that determine who lives and who dies. So even democratic utilitarianism rests on a shaky foundation. And this is my point: once God is pushed out of the picture, moral absolutes are very much in doubt. Eugenics, mass murder, slavery, and tyranny are not necessarily wrong; *perhaps* they are necessary; *perhaps* they can be justified.

This perspective is very evident in *Mein Kampf*. Hitler's overriding concern in his dreadful book is with the racial purity of the Aryan race. Hitler rails against the Jews, saying they are an inferior but clever race, bent on world domination. He also rails against blacks (referred to as *Negroes*), asserting, for example, that "it is Jews who bring the Negroes into the Rhineland."[2] For a pure-blooded Aryan, whose home is the Rhineland, nothing could be more disgusting. But a greater sin, Hitler said, is to allow nature's "most gifted beings by the hundreds and thousands . . . to degenerate" through interracial marriage.[3]

It is hard to believe that anyone could think and talk this way in the twentieth century. But for Hitler and a great many of his inner circle, such thinking logically followed the science of the nineteenth century. Darwin and others had supposedly proven that humanity descended from lower creatures. Some anthropologists also argued that humanity originated from different species (polygenesis) and so human races, or subspecies, are clearly not equal; some are obviously more advanced, others less so.

Hitler was especially fond of this bogus science and did not want the Aryan race to intermarry with "lower" forms of humans: blacks, aboriginals, Jews, and others he considered closer to apes and monkeys.[4] Aryan nation-states, Hitler said, were "based on work and culture"; other states, to their detriment, permitted the existence of "Jewish colonies of parasites."[5] If Germany, if the Aryan race, was to be saved, Europe had to be purged of the lower forms of "human organisms."[6]

Jesus and his teaching hardly appear in *Mein Kampf*. The teaching of Jesus is echoed when Hitler solemnly states, "Verily a man cannot serve two masters."[7] But Hitler's point is completely different.[8] In one place, Hitler does allude to Jesus in a significant way, but at the expense of the Jewish people.[9] The passage is found in the context of what Hitler thinks is an important discussion of Jewish religion. Critical studies, he writes, "make this kind of religion seem positively monstrous according to Aryan conceptions." Jesus recognized this in his time, Hitler assures us. Jesus, who really was not Jewish but was himself an Aryan, "made no secret of his attitude toward the Jewish people, and when necessary he even took to the whip to drive from the temple of the Lord this adversary of all humanity, who then as always saw in religion nothing but an instrument for his business existence. In return, Christ was nailed to the cross." Hitler is referring to the passage in the Gospels that has been traditionally called the cleansing or clearing of the temple.[10]

In reality, Jesus did not view the Jewish people or the Jewish religion as monstrous. Quite the contrary. The action Jesus took in the temple precincts in Jerusalem, which no doubt contributed to his arrest and crucifixion, was directed against the ruling priesthood, which had become corrupt and oppressive. Jesus acted on behalf of the Jewish people, much as Israel's great prophets had in earlier times. Many of his contemporaries agreed with Jesus, which is why the temple authorities were unable to seize Jesus on the spot. Jesus deeply loved his people and shared their ancient faith in the God of Abraham. Hitler's misuse of this passage was cynical and served his own purpose, which was to denigrate the Jewish people as nothing more than merchants and lenders.[11]

The worst part of Hitler's call for racial purity, attested throughout *Mein Kampf*, was that it was taken seriously and put into effect. The result was the Holocaust. Although various groups and individuals fell victim to this travesty, none suffered more than the Jewish people. But extermination of the Jewish people was not enough.

With several hundred thousand Jews imprisoned at any given time in the concentration camps, it was convenient for Hitler's doctors and scientists to conduct experiments to prove the "truth" of the führer's theories of eugenics. The most notorious of Hitler's doctors was Josef Mengele. Known as the "Angel of Death," Mengele was especially interested in dwarfs, twins, and people whose eyes were two different colors. Ultimately, the point of his research was to show that the non-Aryan races were in various ways inferior and that because of interracial breeding were in genetic decline. Survivors of the war described Mengele as unfeeling, sadistic, and virulently anti-Semitic. His experiments included injecting his living subjects with bacteria or various toxins. He also amputated limbs and had healthy teeth extracted. One of the camp inmate doctors, forced to work as his assistant, was a Hungarian Jew named Miklós Nyiszli, who survived his time in the camps and wrote a graphic account of Mengele's activities.

Nyiszli recounts how Mengele enjoyed the comforts of an office and lab next to the crematoriums "where my soft-brained superior really felt at home: the blazing glow of the pyres and the spiraling smoke of the crematorium stacks; the air heavy with the odor of burning bodies; the walls resounding with the screams of the damned and the metallic rattle of machine guns fired pointblank; it was to this that the demented doctor came for rest and relaxation."[12] Following one gruesome experiment, which supposedly lent support to Mengele's eugenic pseudoscience, Nyiszli remarks that "Nazi propaganda never hesitated to clothe its monstrous lies in scientific apparel."[13] Nyiszli survived the war and was reunited with his wife and daughter who had been held at Bergen-Belsen concentration camp.

Mengele fled Germany after the war, managing to elude capture for the rest of his life, residing mostly in South America. Shortly before his sixty-eighth birthday, he suffered a stroke while swimming and drowned. Although buried under a false name, his remains were identified in 1985, with DNA confirmation following in 1992. Ironically, his bones are today in the custody of the São Paulo Institute for Forensic Medicine, where they are studied by students.[14] In life a collector of specimens, in death Mengele himself became a specimen.

From Eugen Kogon, who spent six years in the Buchenwald concentration camp, we have another eyewitness account of the horrors the Nazis inflicted on Jews and others held in the camps. Kogon was the son of a poor, unmarried Jewish Russian woman. Kogon was raised by a Catholic family but he also spent time in the care of the church. Although he was Jewish, Kogon became a devout Catholic.

In 1927, he received his doctorate and went to work as an editor for the Catholic magazine *Brighter Future* (German: *Schönere Zukunft*). Kogon wrote against the Nazis in the 1930s, and in 1937 and 1938 he was arrested three times. The third time he was arrested he remained in custody. When the war began in September 1939, Kogon was sent to the Buchenwald concentration camp where he remained until liberated by the American Army.

During his time in Buchenwald, Kogon's faith in God grew. The difference between good and evil, between God and atheism, became crystal clear. Gaining the trust of the camp doctor, under whom he served, Kogon was able to save several lives. After his release in 1945, Kogon testified at the war crimes trials and became well-known for his gripping account of what took place in the Buchenwald camp. American officials asked Kogon to write an account of his experience, which in a matter of months was book-length. It was published in 1946 under the title *Der SS-Staat: Das System der deutschen Konzentrationslager* (The SS State: The System of the German Concentration Camps), though it is better known to English readers as *The Theory and Practice of Hell.*

The German version went through more than forty editions and became a bestseller.[15] For the rest of his life, Kogon spoke out on the importance of truth, justice, and morality, and received many honors and awards.[16]

Two things strike me above all else in the accounts of Nyiszli and Kogon: Nazi *brutality* and *deceit*. The brutality comes as no surprise; it is fully in keeping with the whole purpose of the camps.[17] But what really stands out is the systemic deceit. It seems the camp guards never told the truth. Much of the deceit was for the purpose of getting the inmates to cooperate, to go to this area or to that room, and so forth. Inmates undressed and stepped into "showers" only to be gassed, or lined up for roll call only to be gunned down.

Like their führer, the Nazis were pathological liars. Usually mounted above the gates to concentration camps were spurious mottos. A well-known one read: *Arbeit macht frei*, which means, literally, "Work makes free," or in more idiomatic English, "Work sets (you) free." This motto was posted at some of the most notorious concentration camps, including Auschwitz and Dachau. Of course, this was a lie told to deceive the unfortunate concentration camp inmates. One could work until he faints, but there would be no freedom.

I wonder how many concentration camp inmates thought of the similar-sounding words, *Wahrheit macht frei*, or "Truth makes/sets (you) free"? I am reminded of what Jesus once said to his critics, "You will know the truth and the truth will set you free";[18] or when Jesus stood before Pilate, the Roman governor of Judea, and said, "I was born and came into the world to testify to the truth. All who love the truth recognize that what I say is true," to which Pilate replied cynically, "What is truth?"[19] The Nazis had no more idea of truth than did the Roman governor.

Nazi philosophy and militarism posed a grave threat to free societies. When Germany invaded Poland, Britain and France declared war on Germany. (At the beginning of the war, Russia was actually on Germany's side and took part in the invasion of Poland.) Months later, Germany invaded France, and in a couple of weeks France surrendered. Britain alone stood against Hitler. Many thought there was no hope; German victory was inevitable. But one man thought otherwise.

In Defense of Christian Civilization

Winston Churchill, the British bulldog, as he was sometimes known, stood up to Hitler and his war machine. Churchill was made prime minister in May of 1940, only one month or so before France surrendered, leaving much of the British Army stranded at Dunkirk. Churchill's heroic leadership and ultimate victory, when all seemed hopeless, are well-known and do not need to be rehearsed here. What is of particular interest is Churchill's reason for fighting Hitler to the death: to preserve Christian civilization.

A recent study explored the role of faith in the thought and life of Britain's greatest prime minister.[20] Writers Jonathan Sandys, Churchill's great-grandson, and Wallace Henley agree that Churchill was not especially religious and did not regularly attend church services, but they find substantial and compelling evidence that Churchill believed in God and embraced the Christian faith. He frequently made reference to "Christian civilization" and the need to protect it.[21]

In a speech given to the British House of Commons in 1938, at a time when the government of Neville Chamberlain was pursuing peace with Hitler through appeasement, Churchill told his colleagues: "There can never be friendship between the British democracy and the Nazi power, that power which spurns Christian ethics, which cheers its onward course by a barbarous paganism."[22] That Churchill early on recognized the pagan character of Hitler and the anti-Christian character of the Nazis was truly insightful, for the Nazis at that time were still speaking of a quasi-religious piety and Positive Christianity. Many of Churchill's contemporaries had been deceived by Hitler's phony rhetoric. Churchill saw it for what it was and spoke out against it.

In 1940, three days after Churchill was made prime minister, he stood up in the House of Commons and gave his famous speech, which began with the words: "I have nothing to offer but blood, toil, tears, and sweat."[23] Britain's policy, Churchill warned his colleagues, would be "to wage war, by sea, land, and air, with all our might and with all the strength that God can give us: to wage war against a monstrous tyranny." The following month, France surrendered to the German Army and formed the Vichy government, which governed southern France and functioned as an ally of Germany. Britain stood alone. On June 4, Churchill stood in Parliament and delivered his famous speech about never giving up.[24] He was confident, come what may, that "in God's good time" victory would come. Later, in June, Churchill again delivered a speech to the House of Commons, in which he conceded that the Battle of France was over and the Battle of Britain was about to begin. Churchill declared, "Upon this battle depends the survival of Christian civilization."[25]

During the Battle of Britain (July–October 1940), when German bombers pounded the city of London and Britain's airstrips, Churchill referred to the English capital as "this strong City of Refuge, which enshrines the title deeds of human progress and is of deep consequence to Christian civilization."[26] Britain held on, and Germany finally had to break off the operation. Churchill rightly recognized the fearful consequences should Germany overpower Britain and destroy the "City of Refuge." In using this expression, one cannot help but wonder if Churchill was referring to the Bible, which often speaks of God offering a place of safety and refuge for his people.[27]

More than his political colleagues, Churchill rightly saw in Hitler and Nazi Germany the potential end of all the mercies and benefits Christianity had bestowed on the West. Churchill rightly saw in the Nazi movement the destruction of what made Western civilization benevolent and wholesome.[28] "If we fail," Churchill rightly predicted, "then the whole world . . . will sink into the abyss of a new Dark Age made more sinister, and perhaps more protracted, by the lights of perverted science."[29] Through his wise and resolute leadership, Churchill defeated Hitler and preserved the Christian civilization that he so dearly loved.[30] The perverted science of which Hitler was so fond did not become the new standard for the world.

Churchill also found very personal relevance in the Christian faith. When he was twenty-five and taken prisoner during the Second Boer War (1899–1902), he managed a daring escape from the prison where he and other British officers were housed. Wandering in the dark, lost and uncertain, three hundred miles from friendly forces, Churchill gave careful thought to his desperate situation. Years later he related:

> I realized with awful force that no exercise of my own feeble wit and strength could save me from my enemies and that without the assistance of that Higher Power which interferes in the eternal sequence of causes and effects more often than we are always prone to admit, I could never succeed. I prayed long and earnestly for help and guidance. My prayer, it seems to me, was swiftly and wonderfully answered.[31]

Churchill's prayer was indeed answered. He not only succeeded in getting back to the British lines safely, he rode ahead of the army and liberated the men held in the very prison from which he had escaped. In the eyes of the British, Churchill was a hero.

Winston Churchill faced Hitler with a faith and a resolve that led to success and made him famous. But Hitler was not Churchill's only enemy. There were other monsters on the loose, threatening Christianity.

CHAPTER 11
When Truth Is What You Want It to Be

Unfortunately, Hitler wasn't Nietzsche's only heir. Others in the twentieth century accepted the demented man's philosophy of racial supremacy and the need to reform the world through coercion and violence—and with no God and no morality to get in the way.

In this chapter, we will look at Italy's "emperor" Benito Mussolini, who in some ways mentored Hitler in Hitler's early days. We will also look at Josef "the man of steel" Stalin, who gained power over the Soviet Union and seized as much of Europe as possible. We will also look at the Asian dictators Mao Zedong, Ho Chi Minh, Pol Pot, and North Korea's three Little Kims. The theme that runs throughout the leadership of these men is their utter disregard for human life. For them, there are no morals, and truth is what you want it to be.

Benito Mussolini: Little Caesar

Benito Mussolini (1883–1945) served in the Italian Army during World War I. After the war, Mussolini was a supporter of the Italian Socialist

Party. Later, he denounced the socialists and founded the Fascist Party. In 1922, he became Italy's prime minister. Mussolini had grand plans, thinking that through his charismatic leadership the Roman Empire of old could be reestablished (which was part of the justification for the invasion of Ethiopia in 1935). Like Hitler, Mussolini was addressed as *Il Duce* ("the Leader"). His Blackshirts and secret police (which also had their counterparts in Nazi Germany) terrorized the public and clamped down on dissent. In 1943, after a series of military reversals, the Allied invasion of southern Italy, and the thousands of Italian soldiers who died fighting on the Russian front, Mussolini was ousted and imprisoned. He was rescued by German Special Forces, and then German troops occupied most of Italy. When the Allies overran Italy, Mussolini attempted to escape but was captured by Italian Communists, who shot him and his mistress and then trucked their bodies to Milan and had them hung upside down in public view.

Although raised by a devout Catholic mother, Mussolini embraced atheism and became a sharp critic of the Catholic Church. He justified his brutal actions on the basis of his understanding of Darwin and Nietzsche, especially the latter, whose notions of "will to power" and the "Superman" fascinated the Italian dictator.[1] Mussolini wanted to destroy Christianity, but like Hitler, he knew that he could not openly attack the church until he had won the war and consolidated his power.[2] How many people died because of Mussolini's brutal rule is hard to tell. It is estimated to be around 400,000, military and civilian. However, that number may underestimate how many died in Ethiopia.[3] Had Mussolini's military been more efficient, the death toll in all probability would have been much higher.

Mussolini desired to portray himself as a new Caesar who would restore Italy and the Roman Empire and reestablish the Romanità, or "the spirit of Romanness," of the Italian people, according to Jan Nelis.[4]

His idea was somewhat akin to Hitler's ideas about advancing Aryan supremacy (though Mussolini was irked with Hitler's emphasis on the *northern* aspects of his racialism), in which the Third Reich would embody the pre-Christian classical world.[5] The Italian leader compared himself to Julius Caesar, the true founder of Rome, and to Caesar Augustus, the builder of the empire and the bringer of the Augustan peace (the *Pax Romana*).[6] Fascists even spoke of the "apotheosis of living man," that is, the divinization of Mussolini, like the ancient Roman senate divinized Julius Caesar and later Augustus.[7] Nelis describes Mussolini's obsession with this idea of Romanità as almost cultic.[8]

Mussolini further believed that the "history of Rome would teach Italy how to become a great nation."[9] The dictator was opposed to the church because "Christianity was a disease, which turned out to be fatal for the ancient Roman gods."[10] The implication was that Christianity would get in the way of the reemergence of the new Rome and the new Italian empire. Mussolini was not alone in thinking this. The influential Italian fascist philosopher Giovanni Gentile "voiced an intention to subordinate the Catholic faith to his ideal state."[11] Reminding Italians of the Punic Wars, where Rome fought for its life in its struggle with Carthage, Mussolini argued that war would lead to Italy's "regeneration," as it did for ancient Rome.[12] The New Rome would create a "New Italian people," which would be superior to all others.[13] And like Nazi Germany, the regeneration of the "new" people required limiting contact with Jews and other inferior peoples.[14]

I bring up Mussolini's delusions to underscore the intentional thinking of both the Nazis and the Italian fascists. Both regimes saw themselves not simply as anti-Christian, but as those making efforts to take their respective countries back to some imagined golden era that pre-dated Christianity. Christianity was seen as a disease that weakened the classical world and the Roman Empire. Further, Christianity's foolish belief in egalitarianism and its illogical compassion for the disabled invariably led to racial impurity and the nation's loss of "will to power." Hitler and Mussolini sought in their respective ways to take their countries back to the glories and greatness of the pre-Christian world. Both Hitler and Mussolini envisioned a world without Christianity. They believed it would be a better world. In their eyes, millions might have to die to create this world, but to them it would be worth it.

Josef Stalin: The Man of Steel

In 1878, Vissariaon Djugashuli and his wife, Ekaterina Geladze, who lived in the small city of Gori, Georgia, welcomed a son into their family. They named him Josef. In later life, Josef Vissariaon Djugashuli gave himself the name *Stalin*, which in Russian means "steel." Of his many nicknames, *Stalin* proved his favorite, especially during the Russian Revolution.[15]

Stalin's father was a violent drunk who beat Stalin and his mother. They left him, but then faced financial hardship. An orthodox priest welcomed the mother and son into his home and cared for them. Through the clergyman's influence, Stalin was allowed to enroll in the Gori Church School. Although the youthful Stalin was a good student, he often quarreled and fought with other boys. In 1894, he enrolled in the Tiflis (or Tbilisi) Seminary, a Russian Orthodox school that trained men for the Christian ministry. There, Stalin became fluent in the Russian language. However, he was expelled five years later after failing to take his final exams.[16] Stalin embraced atheism (possibly something like Hitler's vague ideas about nature) and joined the Communist Party, which was officially atheist and anti-Christian.

During the Bolshevik Revolution, Stalin quickly rose to prominence, taking part in the war with Poland from 1919 to 1921 and playing an important role in the invasion of Georgia in 1921. Stalin rose to secretary general of the Communist Party, and when Vladimir Lenin died in 1924, Stalin achieved absolute power, driving Leon Trotsky and rivals into exile. In the years that followed, Stalin ordered massive purges and relocations, mostly to Siberia. Countless millions died, either worked to death in the camps or as a result of execution, starvation, or exposure to cold.[17] Even Stalin's second wife, Nadezhda, was victimized. She dared speak up to her husband about the starved Russian populace and was harsly rebuked and driven to suicide by her own husband.[18] Stalin died in 1953 at the age of seventy-four. Nikita Khrushchev, a war hero who succeeded Stalin, denounced Stalin and Stalinism.

Josef Stalin was another man who wanted to create a new and better world, at least for committed Communists. He embraced the utopian vision of Karl Marx and Friedrich Engels, as modified and adapted by Vladimir Lenin and modified still further by himself. Stalin envisioned a world without God and without Christianity, a world in which the State would determine morals and control families, education, the economy, and the culture itself. Millions died and millions more suffered.

Mao Zedong: The Green-Toothed Tiger

Mao Zedong (1893–1976) was raised by a stern father who beat Mao and his brothers. For a time Mao flirted with Buddhism. Soon he became interested in politics and took up the Chinese nationalist cause. Shortly after moving to Beijing in 1917, Mao was introduced to Communism, reading Marx and following with great interest the Bolshevik Revolution in Russia. Mao joined the Communist Party and took part in the Chinese Civil War that broke out in 1927 and in the resistance against the Japanese invaders. When World War II finally ended, the Civil War in China continued, with Mao and the Communists capturing the mainland in 1949 and establishing the People's Republic of China. In 1950, Mao sent Chinese troops into North Korea.

Although Mao was able to consolidate his power over mainland China and protect China against foreign aggression, many of his social and economical policies were failures, some disastrous. The Great Leap Forward of 1958 resulted in famine and the death of millions. At least thirty million peasants died between 1959 and 1962.[19] Believing that the problems were brought on by thievery and hoarding, Mao launched purges, which only resulted in more deaths, some by suicide; others were beaten to death.[20]

More chaos and economic hardships ensued when China broke with Russia and then launched the Cultural Revolution. The result was the death of millions more, many at the hands of the notorious Red Guard, and the destruction of irreplaceable cultural artifacts. Mao's government experienced more turbulence thanks to the so-called Gang of Four, which included Jiang Qing, his last wife. Mao died, and the revolution ended.

The latter years of Mao's life were marked with personal and health problems. Mao may have suffered from dementia. On one occasion, his physician timidly suggested that Chairman Mao brush his teeth. Mao loved drinking strong green tea but he did not brush his teeth, and they had become yellow with a noticeable green tinge. Mao would have none of it. "A tiger never brushes his teeth," the chairman scowled.[21] It's hard to imagine the doctor ever brought up the subject again.

Mao was married four times, and the last of his wives, as already mentioned, created havoc in the Gang of Four controversy. After Mao's death in 1976, there was no one to protect Jiang Qing. She was put on trial and condemned to death, but her sentence was commuted to life in prison. She was released in 1991 and shortly thereafter committed suicide.

Like contemporaries Hitler, Mussolini, and Stalin, Mao strongly opposed Christianity in China, which has roots to the seventh century.

Christians in China built clinics, hospitals, schools, and orphanages. They also opposed the opium trade. After Mao's takeover, Christian missionaries were expelled and the Christian church went underground. It was especially difficult for Chinese Christians during the Cultural Revolution. Christians were imprisoned, some were tortured, and churches and homes were looted and vandalized.[22] Nevertheless, the church continued to grow. Christianity is now legal, though there are restrictions in place. It is estimated today that there are between 70 and 85 million Christians in China, and they certainly outnumber Communist members in the country—the legacy of Jesus endures.[23]

Ho Chi Minh: "Uncle Ho"

Born Nguyen Sinh Cung, Ho Chi Minh (1890–1969) was one of the better educated of the Communist leaders in the twentieth century.[24] Ho attended university and lived in exile for some thirty years, which enabled him to become functional, if not fluent, in French, English, Russian, Cantonese, and Mandarin, as well as his native Vietnamese. Ho entered political life in order to work for Vietnam's independence from France. This effort was delayed thanks to the Japanese invasion of Indo-China during World War II. Following the war, Ho, affectionately known as "Uncle Ho," petitioned US President Harry Truman (as he had President Woodrow Wilson prior to the war), but received no reply. It is likely that Ho's Communist leanings and adoption of violent tactics, including murderous purges against those critical of his leadership, explain Truman's reluctance to support him. In any case, civil war broke out. When the French withdrew, US advisors, and eventually half a million troops, entered Vietnam.

Ho died in 1969 and was succeeded by the Vietnamese Communist Politburo. The war ended in 1974 with a treaty, recognizing two Vietnams, North and South. After the US withdrew all military, the North invaded and overran the South, massacring at least one million, mostly in Saigon, the capital city of South Vietnam. The terms of the peace treaty obviously meant nothing to the Communist regime.

Pol Pot: "Oh Brother!"

Saloth Sar, better known by his *nom de guerre* Pol Pot (1925–1998), grew up on a rice farm in Cambodia. After failing in school, he became active in politics in the 1950s. Pot led the Khmer Rouge from 1963 to 1979. In the spirit of Communism, Pot liked to refer to himself as "Brother Number One." His alleged goal was to establish an agrarian socialist utopia. To do this, he banned all religions, massacred an estimated 25,000 Buddhist monks, crushed the educated—especially if educated according to Western thinking—and imprisoned and tortured all suspected of dissent. In the end, Pot and his paranoid government, supplied with weapons from Communist China, murdered more than one-fourth of Cambodia's population. Ironically, the leaders in the Cambodian massacres were trained in Paris, where they came under the influence of existentialist and Nietzschean philosopher Jean-Paul Sartre.[25]

Pot's downfall came when he attacked Vietnam. His forces defeated, Pot fled to Thailand. In hiding, he remained leader of the Khmer Rouge, even though he resigned in 1985 due to ill health. In 1995, Pot suffered a stroke. Three years later he died. It is suspected that he committed suicide when he heard that his party had agreed to surrender him to an international tribunal to face charges for war crimes.

The Three Little Kims: The Dearest Leaders of Them All

Kim Il-sung (1912–1994), born Kim Song-ju, became the leader of the Korean Communist Party and gained control of part of Korea in 1948.

Backed by China and Russia, Kim attempted to conquer South Korea and unite the peninsula under his rule. UN forces, led by the United States, fought against Kim and his allies, forcing a stalemate that ended the war in 1953. Kim ruled North Korea until his death in 1994. It is estimated that his government killed at least one million people. How many more died of starvation and malnutrition will likely never be known.

Kim was succeeded by his son Kim Jong-il (1941–2011). Kim number two took the cult of the leader to new levels. He was officially referred to as "Dear Leader" and "The Great Leader." After his death, the government declared that he would become known as the "Eternal General Secretary" of the Worker's Party of Korea.

Kim number two was succeeded by Kim number three, or Kim Jong-un (1984–), the current Chairman of the Worker's Party of Korea and Supreme Leader of the Democratic People's Republic of Korea. It is typically Communist to use language such as *workers, people's republic,* and *democratic.* None of it is accurate, of course. The workers of North Korea have no say in anything, political or otherwise. There is no democracy ("rule by the people"), and the Republic of Korea is governed not by the people who form a republic but by a small number of the elite, backed by the military.

North Korea is a secretive, paranoid country. The public is almost never told the truth. Because of shortages of food, medicine, and fuel, hunger and malnutrition are widespread. North Korea adults are on average two inches shorter than South Korean adults. How many starve to death each year is unknown. Concerned South Koreans, many of whom are Christians, from time to time send truckloads of food, clothing, and medicine to their impoverished cousins.

The over-fed and pampered Kim number three has had a number of family members and political rivals murdered. How stable his government is at this time is unclear. He continues to engage in threatening military moves against South Korea and US interests in the region. Kim number three is also enlarging his family's personality cult tradition. On a hillside in Ryanggang Province these words have been carved: "Long Live General Kim Jong-un, the Shining Sun!" The carving runs about 1,600 feet and can be seen from space.[26]

Nazism, Fascism, and Communism: The Cult of Death

Atheism, from the time of Marx and his earliest followers, stands at the very center of Communism. There is no need to infer this; the Communists themselves proclaim it. Hitler's Nazi ideology is far more complicated, because lying behind it is not atheism exactly but some form of neopagan pantheism. Whatever it was and however it should be described, one thing is clear: Hitler's ideology rejected Christianity and Judeo-Christian theism.

The record of Communism in the twentieth century is appalling. Why left-leaning academic elites in the West remain mesmerized by Communism and continue to promote it or make excuses for it is puzzling. After all, left-leaning academic elitists have traditionally called for openness and critical inquiry. Yet they seem strangely blind to the sins of Communism and the grievous record of experiments in atheistic governance. Why is this? Why the reluctance to face up to the grim facts?

Stéphane Courtois and colleagues decided to confront the public and the academic elitists with the grim record of Communism. In 1997, they published the results of their work under the title *Le livre noir du Communisme: Crimes, terreur, répression*, or in English: "The Black Book of Communism: Crimes, Terror, Repression."[27] The assembled facts are staggering. Courtois conservatively estimates that as many as 100 million people have died under Communist regimes (as of 1997, when their book appeared; in the ensuing years, the number has likely grown).

Courtois and most of the contributors find that morally, Communism was no better than Nazism. I suspect if the full data were known, and it never will be, we would find that Communism was far worse than Hitler and company. Because of their naïve commitment to collective farming and industry, Communist governments rarely met quotas, resulting in shortages of necessities, which in turn led to starvation, want, unrest, and repression. Communist governments, it seems, were better at killing people than at governing. The class genocide perpetrated by the Communists, Courtois concludes, was comparable to the racial genocide of the Nazis.

Several Communist East Bloc European dictators added to the suffering. They make up a veritable rogues' gallery. We can start with Erich Honecker (1912–1994) of Communist East Germany, or the German Democratic Republic. It was not a democracy, of course; none of the Communist "Democratic Republics" were. Honecker ruled East Germany from 1971 until its collapse and reunion with the Federal Republic of Germany in 1989. Honecker was arrested and put on trial for using his hated Stasi secret police to intimidate, torture, murder, and falsely imprison thousands of East Germans. Many will recall that on Honecker's orders, many Germans were shot trying to go over the infamous Berlin Wall and escape to freedom. He was convicted, but because of ill health he was granted clemency, something he did not extend to others. A serial adulterer, Honecker was married three times and had at least one child out of wedlock. In the aftermath of the collapse of Communist East Germany, a series of investigations were launched as anxious and angry parents demanded to see the official records relating to their children, who had been taken away to be trained in Communist orthodoxy.

Strong man Marshal Josip Broz Tito (1892–1980) ruled over Yugoslavia after World War II until his death. His was an oppressive regime, which suppressed human rights and mismanaged the economy. After Tito's death, it was clear that the economy was in deep trouble. His abrasive ethnic policies paved the way for the violent breakup that convulsed Yugoslavia throughout the 1990s.

Todor Hristov Zhivkov (1911–1998) was the nepotistic ruler of Communist Bulgaria. He too was intolerant of dissent, ordering the murder of leading dissenters. He was probably involved in the infamous and unsuccessful plot to assassinate Pope John Paul II in 1981.

It would be hard to beat Nicolae Ceauşescu (1918–1989) of Romania. He ruled his country with a heavy hand from 1965 to 1989. He mishandled the economy, creating shortages of food, fuel, and medical supplies. He suppressed dissent ruthlessly. When his people discovered that he had ordered troops to fire on unarmed demonstrators, they were outraged and stormed the presidential palace. His bodyguards—Iranian mercenaries, not ethnic Romanians—shot at the protestors but were themselves picked off by the Romanian Olympic rifle team. Ceauşescu and his wife fled but were captured. After a brief trial, they were executed by firing squad. Volunteers for this task were solicited. Hundreds volunteered. It seems everyone was willing to shoot the hated president.

There is a positive note to add to the Romanian story. Twenty-five years after the death of Ceauşescu and the end of Communist rule, the Romanian government conducted an investigation into the abuses of the former Communist government. In 2006, President Traian Băsescu publicly issued the following apology:

> As Head of the Romanian State, I expressly and categorically condemn the communist system in Romania, from its foundation . . . to its collapse in December 1989. Being aware of the evidence presented in the Report, I affirm with full responsibility: the communist regime in Romania was illegitimate and criminal. . . . In the name of the Romanian State, I express my regret and compassion for the victims of the communist

dictatorship. In the name of the Romanian State, I ask forgiveness from those who suffered, their families, all those who, in one way or another, saw their lives ruined by the abuses of dictatorship.[28]

Atheist regimes, whether fascist or socialist, whether Nazi or Communist, are morally blind.[29] This hardly occasions surprise. After all, once God has been removed, all that is left is the law of the jungle. Ethical philosopher Zev Friedman rightly asserts: "Without religion the coherence of an ethic of compassion cannot be established. The principle of respect for persons and the principle of the survival of the fittest are mutually exclusive."[30] Ethicist Richard Taylor agrees, affirming: "The concept of moral obligation [is] unintelligible apart from the idea of God. The words remain, but their meaning is gone."[31]

Christian philosopher William Lane Craig drives home the same point. In a debate with atheist Paul Kurtz, he asked, "Why think that if God does not exist, we would have any moral obligations to do anything? Who or what imposes these moral duties upon us?"[32] Without God, there is no ultimate authority that provides direction. Answering his own questions, Craig said, "Thus, if atheism is true, it becomes impossible to condemn war, oppression, or crime as evil. Nor can one praise brotherhood, equality, or love as good. It doesn't matter *what* you do—for there is no right and wrong; good and evil do not exist."[33]

Well-known atheist Richard Dawkins has said basically the same thing: "The universe we observe has precisely the properties we should expect if there is, at bottom, no design, no purpose, no evil and no good, nothing but blind, pitiless indifference."[34] Dawkins is wrong, of course, but at least at this point he is consistent. He does not address how it is that a universe without purpose, without pity, and utterly indifferent to pain and suffering, somehow managed to produce sentient beings who seek purpose in everything and are not indifferent or without pity.

In his reply to Craig, Kurtz spoke of "ethical intelligence" and learning "to reason together and find common moral principles." He added, "Can we find such common ground?"[35]

How can there be? Without God, ethics can take any form, even exceedingly wicked forms, as we saw in the atheist and anti-Christian regimes of the twentieth century. I am not speaking theory; this is not opinion. The dreadful facts of the atheist regimes, whose morality was not tethered to God, speak for themselves.

Those who are eager to jump on the New Atheism bandwagon should think again. The atheist legacy is littered with death and destruction. There are many atheists who are good people, who recoil at the crimes committed by atheist regimes. But I worry that these decent people do not fully grasp the potential for harm that the atheist worldview can bring about. If atheism is harmless; if it is, in fact, enlightened and positive, *then why is its track record so appalling*? And if it is so attractive, why are the people of the former atheist societies returning to God?

The Plot to Kill God and the Legacy of Christ

When the Bolsheviks captured Russia for Communism and set up the Soviet Union, they set out to eradicate Christianity. Atheist Communism had no use for the church or for Christian faith. The Communists believed that people needed to be reprogrammed and reeducated. Belief in God was passé; the New Science had arrived. It was assumed that within a generation, Russia and the other members of the USSR would be almost entirely atheist and religion-free. Only it didn't turn out that way.

Communist theorists assumed that everything centered on economy— if the people were better off economically, then the need for religious pie in the sky, or what Karl Marx had called the "opiate of the people," would disappear. Thinking as a Marxist, if the State "had total control of the means of cultural production, [it] could control the ideology of a population."[36] Or so the materialist social and cultural engineers of the Kremlin thought. They were wrong; it simply failed. It failed because Communist anthropology is deeply flawed; it views the human as physical and as nothing more.

After almost seventy years of coercive Communist rule, with complete control over education and culture, the percentage of the population that embraced atheism did not increase. The Soviet plot to kill God failed. In a recent study, Paul Froese sums up the evidence, remarking that "the most generous estimates of atheistic belief show that less than one-fifth of Soviet citizens were atheists at the height of Communism, and this number drops to less than 4 percent of the population immediately following the fall of Soviet Union."[37] The Communist plot to stamp out God and the Christ of Christian faith did not work. God didn't go away.

Even some of the committed Communist leaders themselves had a change of heart. One thinks of Gustáv Husák of Communist Czechoslovakia, a comparatively moderate leader by Communist standards.[38] Husák resigned in 1989, four days before the collapse of the Communist regime. Days before his death in 1991, the longtime Communist and atheist renounced atheism and in the presence of a Catholic priest repented and confessed his faith in Jesus Christ. Likewise, Poland's General Wojciech Jaruzelski, the last of Poland's Communist leaders (1981–1989), converted to Christianity shortly before his death in 2014.

Perhaps the most dramatic conversion of all involved Wilhelm Keitel, high commander of the armed forces in Nazi Germany, second only to Adolf Hitler himself. Sentenced to death at the Nuremberg war crimes tribunal, Keitel faced execution in October 1946. US Army Chaplain and Lutheran minister Captain Henry Gerecke, who could speak fluent German, entered Keitel's cell and offered to pray with Keitel. Gerecke had visited Keitel often and a rapport between the two men had developed.

> The two men went to their knees, and Gerecke . . . prayed in German. Suddenly, it seemed to hit Keitel that he was really about to die. He trembled and "wept uncontrollably" as he "gasped for air." Just before he was hanged, Keitel received Communion, served by Gerecke. As the chaplain later recalled, Keitel, "with tears in his voice," said, "You have helped me more than you know. May Christ, my Savior, stand by me all the way. I shall need Him so much."[39]

I should also mention the remarkable story of Monsignor Hugh O'Flaherty, who served a diplomatic function in the Vatican from 1943 to 1945. The monsignor set up an underground network that hid downed allied pilots, members of the Italian resistance, military escapees, and Jews and helped them make their way to Switzerland. SS Col. Herbert Kappler, who acted as Chief of Police in Rome, suspected what the monsignor was up to, but could not prove it. He threatened O'Flaherty and even tried to assassinate the annoying priest, but the Allies arrived before he could. As the American and British Armies approached, Kappler begged O'Flaherty to help his family escape. Initially, the monsignor was angry and refused to help the Nazi. After all, because of Kappler, at least twenty-three hundred innocent people had died. Tearfully, Kappler asked O'Flaherty, "Is there no God? Is there no humanity?" Shortly thereafter Kappler was in the custody of the British Army. Later he learned that his family had been safely taken to Switzerland.

At the war crimes tribunal in Italy, Kappler was sentenced to life in prison and was placed in the Gaeta military prison. His wife divorced him and his family disowned him. They never visited him in prison. But one man did visit regularly: Monsignor O'Flaherty.

Kappler repented, abandoned his atheism and Nazi beliefs, and placed his faith in Christ.[40]

The questions the desperate Kappler put to Monsignor O'Flaherty rightly linked God and humanity: If there is no God (as atheism asserts and Nietzsche proclaimed), there really is no humanity. Humans are nothing more than two-legged animals, and morality is nothing more than the survival of the fittest. We humans have no purpose; we have no meaning. We are nothing more than the chance product of a pitiless, indifferent universe. But is this true? On the contrary! We humans know deep in our souls that this is not true. We do, in fact, have meaning; we do have purpose.

The repentance of former Communist and Nazi leaders is surely encouraging. Of course, it would have been much better had they seen the light sooner, before doing so much harm. There are signs, too, that in the countries where once atheism was enforced, the general population is finding God and returning to faith. It is estimated today, for example, that Chinese Christians now outnumber Chinese Communists. For this reason, some anticipate that in the not-too-distant future China will be the largest Christian nation.[41] The same seems to be happening in Russia, as the number of atheists in that country continues to shrink.[42]

Will We Forget?

Have we in the twenty-first century forgotten the hard lessons of the twentieth century? I wonder. Many college students today seem to know almost no history. Some aren't sure what World War II was about. Other people haven't a clue about the appalling record of Communism. The ghost of Nietzsche seems to be making a comeback, and he is looking for new disciples.

The evidence for the Nietzschean revival is seen in the arguments of the New Atheists and in the emerging "culture of death," as some call it.[43] The Hippocratic Oath, "Do no harm," is no longer widely accepted. Abortion on demand, at any time of the pregnancy, including partial-birth abortions, seems perfectly acceptable to many people today.[44] So also is assisted suicide, at any age and for any reason.

The New Atheism and its enthusiastic reception in some circles concern me. I worry that in embracing the new secularism and its moral relativity our society will throw away a precious spiritual and cultural heritage, the very foundation on which Western society was built. Why embrace the philosophy of Nietzsche and his ilk, which inspired men like Hitler, Mussolini, and Stalin? Rather, why not embrace the philosophy of Jesus, whose followers made the world better? Join the ranks of men like William Wilberforce, who labored long and hard to end slavery in the West, and the many men and women who fought for democracy, for education, for literacy, for science, for medicine, for the arts, for equal rights, and for justice.

In the chapters that follow we will explore how Jesus changed the world and how his church has created one institution after another and makes the world a better place for everyone.

PART III

THE WORLD **WITH**
CHRISTIANITY

CHAPTER 12
Jesus' Tour de Force:
Good News for All People

Did you know there are 7,487 promises from God to us in the Bible?

The 1956 Christmas Eve issue of *Time* magazine highlighted Canadian schoolteacher Everek Storms of Kitchener, who during his twenty-seventh reading of the Bible, took the time to count each and every promise. It took him eighteen months![1] Actually, he found a grand total of 8,810 promises in the Bible, including 290 promises by men or women to God, 28 promises from angels, and even 9 promises made by Satan.

Promises are important to God, and likely, they are important to you. We thank God for those trusted people in life who keep promises, and it is often hard to forget those who break them.

Of all the 7,487 promises God made to his creation, one stands like a mountain peak, because even though God made it to a pagan man named Abram some four thousand years ago, that promise still stands for us today.

Genesis 12 recounts the gripping story of when Yahweh (often translated *Adonai* or Lord—meaning the "One Who Is") appeared to Abram in what is now modern-day Iraq. God promised Abram, "I will bless those who bless you, and the one who curses you I will curse. *And in you all the families of the earth will be blessed.*"[2]

This promise—that through Abraham (God's new name for him, meaning "father of multitudes") everyone on earth will be blessed—was so weighty that God repeatedly made the same promise. In Genesis 22:18, we hear more details: "*In your seed* all the nations of the earth shall be blessed."[3] Then God repeats the promise to Isaac, Abraham's son: "I will multiply your offspring as the stars of heaven and will give to your offspring all these lands. And in your offspring all the nations of the earth shall be blessed."[4] Finally, Isaac's son Jacob (whose name changes to Israel when God left him with a limp) was given this promise in a dream: "And in you and your offspring shall all the families of the earth be blessed. Behold, I am with you and will keep you wherever you go."[5]

Turning to the New Testament, we see this promise in a central place in the preaching of both Peter and Paul. Early in the book of Acts, Peter is preaching on the eastern side of the temple in Solomon's Portico, and he reminds his Jewish audience of God's promise to Abraham: "You are the sons of the prophets and of the covenant that God made with your fathers, saying to Abraham, 'And in your offspring shall all the families of the earth be blessed.'"[6] Peter declares the offspring and blessing promised about by the God of Abraham, Isaac, and Jacob was indeed "Jesus, whom you delivered over and denied. . . . You killed the Author of life, whom God raised from the dead."[7]

For Paul, the significance of the Abrahamic blessing can hardly be overstated. The incarnation, suffering, death, and resurrection of Jesus had both holistic and global implications for *all* people: "And the scripture, foreseeing that God would justify the Gentiles by faith, preached the gospel beforehand to Abraham, saying, 'In you shall all the nations be blessed.'"[8] Similarly, in the nativity announcement, the angel (likely Gabriel) pronounced to the shepherds in the fields near Bethlehem that the presence of Jesus was "good news of a great joy which will come to all the people."[9]

Certainly today, like in those early days of the Roman Empire, we need this good news.

The Value of Life and Human Dignity

Sadly, there are people who don't see the good news of Christianity and wish for the day that America (and other countries) are completely secularized. A Pew Research study revealed that 63 percent of atheists and agnostics think houses of worship "contribute not much or nothing at all to solving important social problems."[10]

So would doing away with Christianity and churches make society better? The clear answer is *no*.

My friend Byron Johnson is distinguished professor of the social sciences at Baylor University and directs its Institute for Studies of Religion (ISR). The institute studies how religion (all religions) intersects culture and society. I had the honor of participating in a recent ISR roundtable at Baylor related to the creation of this book, and learned of a fascinating report they contributed to for the Republican Study Committee: "What Would America Look Like If We Were a Nation Without Faith?" Another noteworthy study in the *Interdisciplinary Journal of Research on Religion*, this one from Brian Grim and Melissa Grim, a father–daughter research team, makes further compelling points about the impact of faith in America.

There are an estimated 350,000 religious congregations in the United States, and a "vast majority . . . serve in some capacity as a community safety net for those in need."[11] Together with faith-based organizations, congregations help over 70 million Americans each year, fueled by a staggering $20 billion in donations.[12] One key service is feeding the millions who are struggling with poverty and limited access to food. Over 60 percent of the 46,000 agencies working with food banks nationwide are faith-based organizations. Simply put, America would starve if the church vanished.

Churches and faith-based organizations are also vital in disasters. Hurricane Katrina took more than 1,400 lives and caused more than $15 billion in damage. In the midst of the devastation and after many sought escape from New Orleans (and understandably so), a committed group of local church pastors remained in New Orleans, "scouring housing complexes for survivors, running shelters out of their churches, helping residents rebuild. One group run by ministers in Louisiana used its network of more than fifty churches to distribute 62 million pounds of resources through the storm-stricken region."[13] A majority of the organizations (59 percent) providing relief services to the devastated areas were churches or faith-based organizations.[14]

What about the economic impact of faith in America? According to the Grim study, religion's $1.2 trillion impact is more than the global annual earnings of Apple and Microsoft combined.[15] Congregational spending on social programs continues to increase, with over $9.24 billion contributed in 2012 (compared with $3.17 billion in 2006 and $2.37 billion in 1998).[16] A survey of the fifty largest US charities reveals that twenty are faith-based and receive $45 billion in annual donations.[17]

One section of the Baylor ISR study focused on the city of Philadelphia, which has "one of the densest concentrations of houses of worship in urban America, with an estimated 2,095 congregations." Researchers found that the economic valuation of these voluntary and religiously motivated services in the City of Brotherly Love amounted to a replacement value of $247 million per year. What is remarkable is that when compared with corporations that on average donate just 1 percent of their pretax income for charity, the congregations in Philadelphia outpace the for-profit world by designating up to 40 percent of their annual budget to serve their community.[18] Rodney Stark of Baylor University has ample evidence to persuasively conclude that "the total current savings to US society from America's religiousness is $2,660,430,000,000—that is, $2.67 trillion per year."[19]

The church is also filling a major gap in serving families with mental health challenges. People are often surprised when they learn that more US citizens kill themselves than kill one another each year. That's stark evidence that we are more dangerous to ourselves than we are to other people. Globally, one person dies *every forty seconds* by his or her own hand. The CDC's National Center for Health Statistics recently released a study documenting the surge in suicide rates in the United States—increasing at an epidemic level from 1999 to 2014 to a nearly thirty-year high of 42,773 completed suicides in 2014. Yet optimism should abound because the church is not ignoring the suicide epidemic.

Twin Lakes Church in Santa Cruz, California, for example, recently hosted a well-attended community gathering on mental health. I was honored to serve as one of the speakers. The goal for the event was not Christian conversion or proselytization, but rather to provide a forum for education and collaboration among community leaders to remove the stigma often associated with mental illness. (Speakers and participants included police officers, a former California secretary of state, the president of the National Alliance of Mental Illness (NAMI), school principals, spiritual leaders, parents of children struggling with mental illness, and a university professor.) The event was not faith-based, but it was faith-inspired. Again, it was the church that spearheaded this forum for community, civil, and political leaders to have open dialogue on the serious issues of mental illness in their community.

With nearly ninety million Americans living in areas where there is a federally recognized shortage of mental health professionals,[20] the Baylor ISR study quantified the vital role of the church in helping those afflicted with or affected by mental illness:

> With approximately 353,000 clergy serving their communities in the United States, they dedicate roughly 10–20 percent of their work week to counseling individuals suffering from emotional or marital problems. This amounts to roughly 138 million hours of mental health services per year; services provided at little to no cost to those who seek them.[21]

The mental health crisis in America is grim, to be sure, but in less-religious countries, suicide rates soar. For example, while America has a suicide rate of 11 per 100,000 people, in Russia (where in earlier chapters we covered the impact of atheism) the suicide rate is 34.3 per 100,000.[22] Clearly, a society that lacks faith also lacks hope. Commenting on this correlation, Baylor's Rodney Stark estimates that "should all Americans become non-attenders [of church], mental health costs could increase by as much as $216 billion."[23]

What about faith-based education in America? I readily admit my bias on this topic because I am the product of public school education, and proud of it. The first religious school I attended was at the university level. Nevertheless, there is compelling evidence that students fare better in faith-based schools. In one measurement, the combined average SAT score of students from faith-based schools was 134 points

HISTORICAL NOTE: Did you know Christians established the first universities? The system of education emerged first in Paris in the 1100s and into the 1200s, and not long after in Oxford and Cambridge. There had been gifted teachers and philosophers in the Greco-Roman world; however, they did not create permanent institutions, as the church did. What's more, Christianity also innovated the principle of education for both males and females, a revolutionary practice in a Roman world where few women were taught anything. Later, Christian reformers like Martin Luther and John Calvin pushed for mandatory education for all children, graded education, and tax-supported education. Organized education for the deaf and blind became a reality also because of committed Christians.

higher than the average score of public school students.[24] Another study found fewer instances of violent crime and bullying in religious schools.[25] More than six million students are enrolled in US religious schools (or homeschooled)—Catholic, Protestant, or Jewish—and if these students were to enroll in public education in the coming term it would cost the government an additional $630 million.[26]

In big and smaller cities today, Jesus' compassion for the sick and hurting lives is reflected in the names of hospitals, such as *Baptist, Lutheran, Methodist, St. Joseph's, St. Luke's,* and so on. Christianity's impact on medical care worldwide is profound. During my recent speaking tour in the United Kingdom, I stayed in the Bankside area of London. The Saint Thomas Hospital, which I was delighted to see houses the Florence Nightingale Museum, was located just a few blocks from my hotel. Nightingale, considered the founder of modern nursing, was only seventeen when she felt God call her to future service. For the rest of her life, she exemplified the Christian commitment to care for the sick and dying.

Today, health-care providers with an active religious affiliation (not just Christian in name) are a major part of our medical system.[27] For example, the US Catholic Health Association's 2017 report noted their mission is to "transform hurt into hope." They operate more than 1,600 care facilities, including nearly 649 hospitals, as well as 156 clinics for low-income individuals and families. By their estimates, one in six American patients every day is cared for in a Catholic hospital.[28] I hate to imagine what would happen if faith-based providers vanished from America's increasingly secularized health-care system.

So why do Christians care so much about the sick, poor, marginalized, and dying? As discussed earlier, in ancient times, the Greco-Roman gods were not seen as loving; they felt no compassion for people. In the world of Jesus and the early church, to hear that God—any god—loved you would have been a completely foreign concept. That changed when Jesus began preaching and teaching "For God so loved the world . . ."

I have written extensively in academic circles on Jesus' proclamation of the "kingdom of God."[31] At its essence, the kingdom of God

HISTORICAL NOTE: There was no such thing as humanitarian aid in the ancient world. Outside of caring for certain aristocrats, or soldiers, medical services were almost nonexistent. If you were sick, a Roman would go out of his or her way to avoid you and you would likely have died without care.[29] From its earliest days, though, "Christianity demanded that all of its adherents aid needy and sick people," says medical historian Guenter Risse. The early Christians read the New Testament in such a way that they interpreted and put into practice its command to welcome the outsider and alien and to build "special communal shelter(s) and nursing services."[30] These shelters became the hospitals we depend on today.

was seen in this light: God is loving; human life (that is, all life—old, young, sick, healthy, disabled, afflicted) is sacred to God; and Christians continued preaching and believing the kingdom of God was coming and yet was already in their midst, so they prepared by caring for the sick, marginalized, and hurting, *immediately*.

Still today the kingdom of God is itself the gospel, the good news for the world: "The time is fulfilled, and the kingdom of God is at hand; repent, and believe the gospel."[32] Jesus' message of a new kingdom reflects the good news proclaimed in the book of Isaiah. The good news (or good tidings) is the appearance of God,[33] the announcement of God's rule and reign,[34] and his saving, redemptive work.[35]

Study the Gospels and you will find the *kingdom of God* or *kingdom of heaven* mentioned fourteen times in Mark, thirty-two times in Luke, and fifty-four times in Matthew. It can hardly be overstated how relevant and convicting Jesus' message was not only for his immediate hearers but also for those generations of Jesus followers that came after. Consider the following verses:

> He called the twelve together and gave them power and authority over all demons and to cure diseases, and he sent them out to proclaim the kingdom of God and to heal. And they departed and went through the villages, preaching the gospel and healing everywhere.
>
> Luke 9:1–2, 6

> He [Jesus] had compassion on them, and healed their sick.
>
> Matthew 14:14

> And Jesus went about all the cities and villages, teaching in their synagogues and preaching the gospel of the kingdom, and healing every disease and every infirmity. When he saw the crowds, he had compassion

for them, because they were harassed and helpless, like sheep without a shepherd.

Matthew 9:35–36

Over and over again, Jesus showed compassion for the sick, the hurting, the diseased, and the outcasts. His actions and message resonated in the first century because the Roman world was a culture of death. In the Roman mindset, life was cheap and expendable. One-fourth of the Roman Empire was sick, dying, or in need of immediate medical attention on any given day. It was against this contextual backdrop that the message of an altogether new life in Christ revolutionized the ancient world and continues to bless "all the families of the earth,"[36] whether they express faith or not.

There is no qualifier with Jesus' striking message, "For God so loved the world . . ." (John 3:16). Importantly, Roman leaders did not appreciate the way in which the early Christian movement cared for all people. In fact, they brutally attempted to suppress early Christianity, which they viewed as a disgusting superstition.

So what caused the Christian movement to be successful? Why did anyone convert to Christianity in the first place? What is it about this new hope that attracted so much hate and persecution? To these answers we now turn.

CHAPTER 13
New Hope: Jesus and His Proclamation

I n AD 30 or AD 33 (experts disagree on the exact year), Jesus of Nazareth, who had been proclaiming the arrival of the kingdom of God, was condemned to death on a Roman cross. A few days later, his followers claimed that he had been raised from the dead and that he really was God's Son and Israel's Messiah.

Initially, most of those who heard this scoffed. Jews rejected it because the awaited Messiah was not supposed to die. His death at the hands of the Romans surely meant that he had been defeated. To Greeks, the idea of resurrection was preposterous and simply unbelievable. *A dead body raised?* It was absurd. Romans, too, understandably scoffed, for death on a cross signified disgrace as well as defeat.

Despite this, the followers of Jesus formed the Christian church, and within three centuries it had swept the Roman Empire.[1] The church did this without resorting to violence. Early Christians not only multiplied in the face of opposition that resulted in social, political, and economic disadvantages, they also risked imprisonment, torture, and martyrdom. Yet the church grew by leaps and bounds. Why?

In a recent study, noted New Testament scholar Larry Hurtado asks, "Why on earth would anyone become a Christian in the first three hundred years of the church?"[2] It is a great question that leads to insights for living a life of faith today.

What Was It about Christianity That Romans Didn't Like?

In the time of Jesus and his first followers, people had hundreds of gods to choose from. Naturally some gods were more popular than others. At the top of the hierarchy were gods who nearly everybody worshiped. This would include Zeus, as the Greeks called him, or Jupiter, as the Romans called him. Another favorite was Apollo, son of Zeus. Artemis and Venus were favorites among the female gods. Dionysus, the god of wine, was another favorite.

Most Greeks and Romans worshiped these gods, along with a few regional and municipal deities. Jews and Christians, however, did not worship these gods. In fact, they did not even acknowledge their existence. Because of a long-standing relationship with Rome, the Jewish people could ignore the Greco-Roman gods, as long as they were not too noisy about it. But as we saw in chapter 4, "A World of Inequality," Roman tolerance did not extend to atheists and other "destroyers of the gods," such as Christians, members of a new and detestable "superstition."

Christians were accused of strange, shameful rites. Before Christian apologist Justin Martyr was executed in AD 160, he alluded to pagan claims that Christians indulged in "promiscuous intercourse and eating human flesh."[3] Justin added that some pagans thought a Christian was one "who counts it good to feast on human flesh."[4] Indeed, he said mockingly, "We slay a man and . . . drink our fill of blood."[5] Christians "are assailed in every kind of way."[6]

Accusing Christians of cannibalism was not hard to do. After all, the eating of raw flesh, even human flesh, was supposedly the practice of some pagan mystery cults. Among these, the cult of Dionysus was especially well-known.[7] Moreover, precedent had already been established, for pagans sometimes accused Jews of cannibalism (and the horrifying story of the starving Jewish woman who ate her infant during the Roman siege of Jerusalem in AD 70 would only have confirmed the slander).[8]

Christian observation of Eucharist, or the Lord's Supper, made the accusation of cannibalism especially easy. "This is my body which is given for you," said Jesus to his disciples. "This cup is the new covenant in my blood."[9] Even worse is what Jesus said on the occasion of multiplying the loaves and fishes: "He who eats my flesh and drinks my blood has eternal life."[10] That Jesus was speaking metaphorically was beside the point.[11]

Critics of Christianity had a lot of fun with the words of institution. Commenting on Jesus' strange saying, arch-critic Porphyry remarks: "Truly this saying is not merely beast-like and absurd, but it is more absurd than any absurdity, and more beast-like than any fashion of a beast, that a man should taste human flesh and drink the blood of members of the same tribe and race, and that by doing this he should have eternal life."[12]

The allegations of these critics were taken very seriously and sometimes led to harsh interrogation, even torture and execution. An example of this is found in Pliny the Younger's correspondence with Emperor Trajan (who reigned AD 98–117). Dispatched to Bithynia and Pontus in Asia Minor (modern Turkey), Pliny set to work to restore law and order. The principal problem is that the temples were largely deserted, sacrifices were not being offered, and the gods were not being honored. The culprits, it seemed, were members of a strange new superstition. They were called "Christians," so named after their founder. Pliny had them brought before him. If they refused to recant, they were executed. If they were Roman citizens, they were sent to Rome for trial. Exasperated by their obstinacy (it seems the governor discovered that true Christians simply will not recant), Pliny interrogated/tortured them and discovered, among other things, that the Christians assembled together "to take food of an ordinary, harmless kind."[13]

Governor Pliny's description of "ordinary, harmless" food was in reference to the widespread rumor that Christians were cannibals. Although in his time as governor Pliny found no truth in the ugly allegation, the accusation of cannibalism persisted. Almost half a century later, Justin Martyr would still be fending off the charge.

The charge apparently was based not only on the words of institution of the Lord's Supper, but on the Christian practice of rescuing infants and young children who were cast out. Justin spoke to this as well: "We have been taught that to expose the newborn is wicked." It was wicked not only because many of those exposed died, but those rescued by pagans almost always were reared for prostitution. Although this was the fate of most females who were cast out, males too were recovered by pagans for the purpose of prostitution.[14] The practice was hateful to Christians.[15]

A generation later, Tertullian (c. AD 160–225), a North African Latin-speaking Christian apologist, complained that pagan critics continued to slander Christians with regard to infanticide and cannibalism: "Monsters of wickedness, we are accused of observing a holy rite in which we kill a little child [*infanticidii*] and then eat it; in which, after the feast, we practice incest. . . . This is what is constantly laid to our charge, and yet you take no pains to elicit the truth of what we have been so long accused."[16] Tertullian then rails against the pagan practices of infanticide, including killing "by drowning, or by exposure to cold and hunger and dogs."[17]

Apart from the outrageous slander of cannibalism, the accusations brought against Christians tended to be vague generalities. According to Justin Martyr, Christians were regularly accused of "impious" and "infamous deeds," but no actual evidence was proffered.[18] So what exactly were these impious deeds? Justin adds that Christians were often punished simply for being Christians, not for any specified crimes. He notes further that if a person is accused of being a Christian and then denies that he is, he is released. The implication is that simply being a Christian was the crime.[19] In essence, the Romans were engaging in identity politics.

If the accused confessed that he was a Christian, he would be punished either through imprisonment, confiscation of property, or execution. Justin Martyr tells his readers: "We know that the penalty appointed for a confessor [i.e., one who confesses that he is a Christian] is death"; "we alone are hated on account of the name of Christ, and, although we do nothing wrong, we are killed as sinners"; we "die gladly in the confession of Christ"; "death had been decreed against those who taught or simply confessed the name of Christ."[20]

A most disturbing and grotesque passage in ancient literature describes the action that the hated emperor Nero took against Christians in the aftermath of a fire, which broke out in the early hours of July 19, AD 64, and destroyed more than half of the city of Rome. The passage, which appears in Tacitus, *Annals* 15.44, and its broader context require careful analysis, for they reveal much about the world in which the early Christian movement arose. The passage is usually discussed because of its reference to Jesus, crucified under Pontius Pilate, but its real value in my estimation lies in what it tells us about the dangers Christians faced in the Roman Empire.

First, it is important to understand the context of the passage, which begins with the devastating fire in Rome. Tacitus describes it in his

Annals, book 15, chapters 38–43. The length of his description is remarkable. Major wars in his *Histories* and *Annals* sometimes receive briefer coverage. That Tacitus devoted six chapters to this event indicates the magnitude of the fire and the impact it had on the Roman population.

Tacitus begins by referring to the event as a disaster, whose origin was either "due to chance or to the malice of the sovereign," that is, Emperor Nero.[21] Tacitus himself takes no side, but many of his contemporaries believed that Nero was indeed responsible for the fire.[22] There is little doubt that many in Rome believed the hated emperor set the fire. We are told that Nero was cursed, though not explicitly by name.[23]

It is hard to exaggerate the devastation. The fire burned for seven days. About two-thirds of the city was destroyed—historic buildings, monuments, museums, shrines, and trophies. One naturalist lamented the loss of a priceless grove of trees. Countless numbers of people perished in the flames. Others were trampled to death in the panic. In some cases, soldiers who were supposed to assist in putting out the fire added to the fire so that they might loot the ruins. The emperor also may have profited from stolen property. Some claimed that Nero ascended to the top of his palace, or stage, and sang.[24]

Nero did at least make an effort to show concern. He provided temporary shelter for many of the displaced. He lowered the price of public grain. He promised to have the debris and the dead removed at his own expense. He also led a series of religious services that were intended to satisfy the gods and secure their blessing.[25] Much of this was likely for show. These efforts notwithstanding, most Romans remained convinced that the fire had been intentionally set and that it had been set under the orders of the emperor. Tacitus remarks that nothing "could stifle scandal or dispel the belief that the fire had taken place by order."[26]

Fearing overthrow or assassination, Nero decided to fasten blame on the Christians. No one tells it better than the early second-century

Roman historian Tacitus. The passage is lengthy, but it is necessary to quote and to offer a few comments along the way.[27]

> Therefore, to squelch the rumor [that he had started the fire], Nero substituted as culprits, and punished with the utmost refinements of cruelty, a class of people, loathed for their vices, whom the crowd called Christians.

Our earlier review of the charges brought against Christians, such as cannibalism, gross immorality, and refusal to worship the Greco-Roman gods, clarifies what Tacitus means when he says the Christians are "loathed for their vices." It has been suggested that Tacitus uses such strong language here because of the second Jewish rebellion underway in North Africa at the time of writing. Most Romans assumed that Christianity was a Jewish sect and therefore bore some responsibility for the rebellion, whether or not Christians took an active part.[28] The "utmost refinements of cruelty" will be made clear in what follows.

Tacitus then explains to his readers where the name or title *Christian* comes from:

> Christus, the founder of the name, had undergone the death penalty in the reign of Tiberius, by sentence of the procurator Pontius Pilate, and the pernicious superstition was checked for the moment, only to break out once more, not only in Judea, the home of the disease, but in the capital itself, where all things horrible or shameful in the world collect and are celebrated.

Tacitus is surprisingly well informed at most points. He correctly states that Christus was the "founder of the name" *Christian*. About twenty years before the fire of Rome, the followers of Jesus, or "the Way" as the movement was known at first, came to be called Christians in Antioch.[29] Tacitus's chronology is also correct; he knows that Jesus was crucified under Pontius Pilate in Judea (governor from AD 25 to 37), which was during the reign of Emperor Tiberius (AD 14 to 37).[30] He gives Pilate the rank of *procurator*, when it should have been *praefectus*, but that is only a minor error.[31] Tacitus describes the Christian movement in the worst possible light, calling it a "pernicious superstition"[32] and "disease," saying that it and all things "horrible and shameful in the world" find their way to the capital of the empire, that is, Rome.

> First, then, the confessed members of the sect were arrested; next, on their disclosures, vast numbers were convicted, not so much on the count of arson as for hatred of the human race.

By *confessed*, Tacitus means those who confess Christus (i.e., Jesus Christ), as opposed to Caesar and the Roman gods. A number of examples were cited above, in which Christians were charged for confessing Christ.[33] That in itself was a crime; no other charge was needed. Tacitus also speaks of "vast numbers."[34] This is very important, for his language speaks to the rapid growth of the Christian movement, even in the city of Rome itself. Recent estimates are unrealistic that suggest, for example, that there were no more than a few hundred Christians in all of Egypt at the end of the first century and probably no more than that in Italy or in Asia Minor.[35] After all, the Christians in Bithynia and Pontus were of such numbers that they brought the pagan sacrificial system to a standstill. In his letter to Emperor Trajan, the legate Pliny the Younger also speaks of "multitudes" who have become Christians and for this reason are being brought to trial.[36]

Tacitus also claims that the Christians "were convicted, not so much on the count of arson as for hatred of the human race."[37] This harsh language sharply contrasts with the more sympathetic tone expressed in Pliny's letter to Trajan. What we probably have here in Tacitus is his unrestrained anti-Semitism. One recent writer has suggested that the passage in Tacitus "is really more anti-Semitic than anti-Christian, since Tacitus knew so little about the Christian sect."[38] I agree. One suspects this is the case when Suetonius, writing only three or four years earlier, says Claudius expelled the Jews from Rome (c. AD 49) because they "constantly made disturbance at the instigation of Chrestus."[39] "Chrestus" probably refers to Jesus (i.e., Christus, which in Greek and Latin was sometimes spelled Chrestus). There is nothing in Suetonius that suggests a distinction between Jews and Christians. He seems to think that controversy centered on Jesus Christ is ethnically speaking a Jewish matter.[40]

Elsewhere, Tacitus speaks of the Jewish people, who he admits are compassionate toward one another, "but toward every other people they feel only hate and enmity."[41] Jews "despise the gods," "disown their country" (that is, the country in which they live, not Israel), and "regard as impious those who make . . . representations of gods."[42] In the mind of Tacitus, those who make images of gods are not impious; on the contrary, they are very pious. The Jewish people, to whom the Christians belong, are hateful. Accordingly, they are loathed by Romans. Nero's choice of them as scapegoats, even if dubious, makes sense.

And derision accompanied their end; they were covered with wild beasts' skins and torn to death by dogs; or they were fastened on crosses, and, when daylight failed, were burned to serve as lamps by night. Nero had offered his Gardens for the spectacle, and gave an exhibition in his Circus, mixing with the crowd in the habit of a charioteer, or mounted on his car. Hence, in spite of a guilt which had earned the most exemplary punishment, there arose a sentiment of pity, due to the impression that they were being sacrificed not for the welfare of the state but to the ferocity of a single man.

Here, Tacitus describes Nero's "refinements of cruelty" and the "exemplary punishment" directed against the Christians: torn to death by dogs and burned to death as "lamps." Tertullian (c. AD 200) urges his critics: "Consult your histories; you will there find that Nero was the first who assailed with the imperial sword [*Caesariano gladio*] the (Christian) sect, making progress then especially at Rome."[43] But for all his antipathy toward Jews and Christians, Tacitus has to admit that "there arose a sentiment of pity" for those cruelly punished. Evidently, many Romans rightly recognized that the Christians were being used as scapegoats, that their punishment had nothing to do with the security of Rome; rather, it had everything to do with Nero.[44]

Yes, there was much about the Christians that the Romans did not like: their close association with the Jewish people, the novelty of their "superstition," their refusal to worship the Greco-Roman gods and to confess the supremacy and divinity of Caesar, and the widespread suspicion that Christians indulged in unnatural practices. But the Christians' numbers continued to grow rapidly. The early faith proved to be irresistible.

Many Christians today face different forms of opposition than early followers. Perhaps you've been in parts of the world where Christians are persecuted and seen their dedication. You yourself might have had to stand alone for your faith. We should resolve to have a never-say-die faith. We should continue in the spirit of the early Christians and stand firm in the faith: "Let us hold fast the confession of our hope without wavering, for he who promised is faithful" (Hebrews 10:23).

CHAPTER 14
New Life: What Made Christianity Irresistible?

The disadvantages for Christians in the Roman Empire were numerous. Quite apart from persecution and martyrdom,[1] Christians faced social, economic, and political antipathy. It was especially dangerous for slaves who were Christians. As slaves, Christians could not legally resist their masters' sexual advances or refuse to participate in pagan religious practices. Even Roman citizens were not immune from prosecution and punishment.

So it is natural to wonder: *With so many disadvantages, why did Romans find the Christian faith appealing?* Four reasons come to mind:

- The belief that God loves humanity, individually and as a whole
- The teaching and practice that in the light of God's love it was incumbent upon the Christian to love all people, including those who were hateful and dangerous

- The teachings and deeds of Jesus that proclaimed him to be unrivaled as humanity's true benefactor
- The conviction that in the death and resurrection of Jesus Christ the believer is forgiven and will live forever in the presence of God

A Loving God

Previously, we reviewed pagan conceptions of the gods, noting especially how the gods were feared. They were viewed not only as potentially dangerous, jealous, and vindictive, but largely indifferent to humanity. The Greco-Roman gods felt no obligation toward humans. Of course, the gods could be placated, even cajoled, but almost always when they showed concern for humans or provided benefits; love for humanity had little or nothing to do with it.

The God of Israel stood out in sharp contrast to the gods of the Greeks and Romans. Throughout Israel's sacred Scriptures, we read of God's love for his people. Moses tells the people: "The LORD set his heart in love upon your fathers."[2] Countless times Israel's Scriptures speak of God's "steadfast love" or "loving-kindness," words that translate *hesed*. The God of Israel is a God of grace, mercy, faithfulness, and forgiveness.

Christian Scriptures share this view of God. "God is love," declares one letter writer.[3] We hear of the love of God in what is probably the most quoted verse of the Bible: "For God so loved the world that he gave his only Son, that whoever believes in him should not perish but have eternal life."[4] In his letter to the Christians of Rome, the apostle Paul declares: "God shows his love for us in that while we were yet sinners Christ died for us."[5] In another letter, the apostle says the love of God in Christ "surpasses knowledge."[6] In short, the quality of the love of God is incomprehensible. Importantly, God's love forms the very basis for God's redemptive work. God loves humanity, says the Christian church, and seeks to save humanity. Humanity is invited to turn to God and to be enveloped by his love.

There is nothing comparable to these beliefs in pagan religions. The Christian proclamation of the love of God, which in Christ is now freely available to all people, attracted people of all walks of life, even hard-nosed Roman pagans.

A Loving People

Christian teaching about love did not stop with how much God loves us. Early Christians believed it was necessary to love all people. They also believed that this love for people was ultimately sourced in God himself, as Paul put it in his letter to the Christians in Rome: "God's love has been poured into our hearts through the Holy Spirit which has been given to us."[7]

The requirement to love all is rooted in the teaching of Jesus. He not only endorsed the well-known command to love one's neighbor as one's self,[8] Jesus famously commanded his disciples, "Love your enemies and pray for those who persecute you."[9] Loving enemies and praying for persecutors were the kinds of things the Greco-Roman world did not practice and, for that matter, did not understand.

A Powerful Benefactor

In late antiquity, kings and emperors loved to speak of themselves as *benefactors*. This word comes from the Latin, meaning "doer of good." (The Greeks had an equivalent word.) To be called benefactor of a city or of a people was a great honor. For rulers, it had great political significance too. Typically, we find the language of benefaction in dedicatory inscriptions, in which the benefactions of the honorees are recounted, followed by a decree of some sort.[10]

Perhaps the most important inscription ever found is on the Rosetta Stone. The bilingual (Egyptian-Greek) text enabled scholars for the first time to decipher Egyptian hieroglyphics.[11] The Rosetta Stone is today housed in the British Museum. It was discovered in 1799, during Napoleon's invasion and exploration of Egypt. Along with a number of looted antiquities, it fell into British hands two years later and became the center of scholarly and popular attention. The inscription, which dates to 196 BC, recounts the many accomplishments and benefactions of King Ptolemy V, who reigned from 204 to 181 BC.[12] Part of the inscription reads: "King Ptolemy, the ever-living . . . has been a benefactor both to the temples and to those who dwell in them, as well as all those who are his subjects, being (himself) a god sprung from a god and a goddess."[13] Such language strikes us today as outrageous, perhaps even comical. But in antiquity, it was taken very seriously—for kings, pharaohs, and emperors were viewed as high priests and mediators between heaven and humanity. The divinity of the emperor in some sense guaranteed the blessings of the gods for his subjects, or at least it was hoped.

The Romans were influenced by the older Greek and Egyptian cultures. Not surprisingly, Roman emperors adopted some of the titles, including *benefactor*, in public inscriptions celebrating their achievements and their great piety toward the gods. Rome's first emperor was Octavian (63 BC–AD 14), who after gaining complete control over the empire became Caesar Augustus (reigned absolutely 28 BC–AD 14).

In celebration of Caesar's birthday, several inscriptions were set up in key locations in the empire. The Greek inscription begins:

Providence, which orders all our lives, has in her display of concern and generosity on our behalf adorned our lives with the highest good, (by giving us) Augustus, whom she has filled with virtue for the benefaction of humanity and has granted us and those who will come after us a Savior who has made war to cease and who shall put everything in peaceful order.[14]

At the end of his life, Augustus wrote and had put on display a lengthy list of his achievements and benefactions as emperor. The inscription is in Latin and Greek, and begins with the words (in the Greek version): "Translated and inscribed below are the achievements and gifts of the god Augustus."[15] In the birthday inscription, it is asserted that the achievements and benefits of Augustus are so numerous they cannot be counted and so great his successors have no hope of ever equaling them.

Another interesting example involved Nero, who participated in the Corinthian games in Greece in AD 67. Nero must have been the greatest athlete of all time, for he won first prize in every event in which he competed. We are told that he took home 1,800 trophies! Not to miss the opportunity for grand speechmaking, the emperor addressed the crowd: "It is goodwill, not pity, that prompts me to be your benefactor. . . . Your gods . . . have granted me the opportunity to practice benefactions on an unparalleled scale." A Greek high priest responds: "Nero—Lord of all the Cosmos, Supreme Emperor . . . Father of his country, a New Sun that brightens Greece, chosen to be benefactor of Greece."[16] The priest goes on to speak of Nero as "Zeus Savior" and "Zeus Liberator." In Ptolemais, Egypt, a papyrus was found that describes Nero as "Emperor, Savior, and Benefactor of the inhabited world."[17] It is remarkable to think that less than one year after this love-in, the Roman Senate would condemn Nero the great Benefactor as an enemy of the state.

It is in reference to these ideas and expressions of *benefactor* and *benefaction* that Jesus exhorts his disciples: "The kings of the Gentiles exercise lordship over them; and those in authority over them are called benefactors. But not so with you; rather let the greatest among you become as the youngest, and the leader as one who serves. For which is the greater, one who sits at table, or one who serves? Is it not the one who sits at table? But I am among you as one who serves."[18]

Romans no doubt laughed at this teaching. For many, it reflected weakness. To serve someone was shameful and degrading. Service was no path to greatness. I am confident that Plato, the famous Greek philosopher of the fourth century BC, spoke for many when he asked, "How can one be happy when he has to serve someone?"[19] The implication is clearly "One cannot be happy serving someone." Jesus taught otherwise.

Jesus tells his disciples that he has not come to lord over others. Referring to himself as the Son of Man, Jesus explains, "For the Son of Man also came not to be served but to serve, and to give his life as a ransom for many."[20] This statement is remarkable on many levels. For one, Jesus is alluding to a passage in the book of Daniel that describes the mysterious being as "one like a son of man" who approaches the throne of God and receives power and authority so that all nations and peoples might serve him.[21] There is little doubt that Jesus saw himself as this figure. But what is surprising is that Jesus asserts that before he is honored and served, he must first serve others. And not only serve others, he must give his life as a ransom, or payment, for the sin of others.

This leads to a second important observation about his statement. In speaking of ransom, Jesus has alluded to the famous prophecy of the Suffering Servant in the book of Isaiah.[22] He has combined the two great prophecies. All nations will serve the Son of Man, but only after he has first served humanity and, as the Suffering Servant, has suffered on humanity's behalf.

The benefaction that Jesus offered his world was nothing like what the emperors claimed to have provided. One of the things Jesus offered humanity was life—eternal life. No imperial benefaction came close to this.

A Living Hope

In a previous chapter, I discussed health and longevity in the ancient world, or perhaps I should say the *lack* of health and longevity. I also discussed people's fear of death and the faint hope for an afterlife. All this made Jesus as Healer and Jesus the Resurrected One a revolutionary reality.

In Professor Hurtado's book that asks why anyone would become a Christian in the first three hundred years of the church's existence, he explores healing and resurrection.[23] I believe these played an important part in convincing the Roman world that Jesus truly is God's Son and the world's Savior. In him there is hope.

Early Christians proclaimed the healing power of Jesus and the reality of his resurrection. Both of these elements—healing and life—were evidence of God's love for humanity and the true benefaction that God offers humanity through the person and work of his Son. Let's consider both of these elements, beginning with healing.

Some might say that the healing that took place "in the name of Jesus" was not especially significant or decisive. After all, as Hurtado says, "Miracle-working was by no means confined to Christianity. . . . Miracles were on offer from various sources."[24] Perhaps, but the healing that took place in the name of Jesus was nothing like the healing that supposedly took place through the powers and agency of other healers. In fact, non-Christian exorcists and healers invoked the name of Jesus. Some scholars have suggested that Apollonius of Tyana (c. 40–110) may have been comparable. But a critical sifting of the evidence shows that we know almost nothing of this man, and the biography of his life written by Philostratus of Athens (c. 180–244) more than a century after the death of Apollonius is "highly untrustworthy."[25] In any event, even if the miracles attributed to him are taken at face value (and no historian does this),[26] they are little more than tricks and stunts designed to impress an audience. Some are bizarre and grotesque.[27]

The miracles of Jesus attracted a large following during his public ministry. None of Jesus' contemporaries denied that Jesus performed miracles and healed people. His contemporary critics attributed his power to Satan,[28] while later critics accused Jesus of black magic, perhaps learned in Egypt.[29] But no one doubted that he did these things. There were simply too many witnesses and too many people healed to cast it all aside.

The miracles performed in his name, after the resurrection of Jesus, drew many converts. (A number of examples are in the book of Acts.) But it was the resurrection and what it meant for humanity that the Roman world found especially compelling.

As stated earlier, most Romans had no confidence in an afterlife. None that we know of believed in resurrection. Even in mythology, stories of a return to life were rare and did not reflect beliefs with respect to mortals. A common motto found on epitaphs in Roman late antiquity reads: "I was not, I was; I am not, I care not."[30] I suspect, however, that such passivity is more affectation than genuine personal indifference. If nothing else, it is an expression of hopelessness.

But the resurrection of Jesus changed everything. With his resurrection the promise of an authentic, verified afterlife for the followers of Jesus gained a whole new degree of gravitas. What Jesus offered was not pie in the sky but a promise grounded in a real event—an event witnessed firsthand by several witnesses, not all friendly.[31]

Not surprisingly, pagan critics reacted with mockery. And no one made mockery a greater art form than Celsus, whose polemical *True Word* was published sometime in the 170s. All that survives of this energetic and entertaining attack against Christianity are quotations, mostly found in Origen's equally energetic and entertaining response called *Against Celsus*. Celsus asks the question if "anyone who was really dead ever rose with a real body?"[32] He doubts that has happened and does not believe Jesus is an exception. Boiled down, Celsus offers three arguments against the resurrection.

The first objection concerns an apparent lack of logic: If a living, miracle-performing Jesus cannot save himself from the cross, how can a dead Jesus raise himself up? The second objection is concerned with the quality of the witnesses to the resurrection of Jesus. Who were they? A frantic woman, and perhaps another equally addled woman.[33] Such a dubious roster of witnesses inspires no confidence. Why should anyone believe such a story? The third objection follows up on the second objection: Had Jesus really been raised from the dead, one would have expected him to show himself to those who had ordered his death. Surely, appearing to the officials who had him crucified would have been very impressive and very convincing. Writing a generation later, Porphyry wonders the same thing: Why didn't Jesus confront Pilate?[34] Celsus concludes that the story of the resurrection is either based on delusion or on deceit.

The objections of Celsus are reasonable and, on his terms, are probably unassailable. But if the activities, teachings, and events relating to Jesus are properly understood in historical and social context, the objections carry no weight. Let me explain.

The first objection misses the point that it was God who raised Jesus, not Jesus himself. Jesus had faith in God and taught his disciples to have faith in God. The ultimate test of Jesus' faith was expressed as he died on the cross: "Father, into thy hands I commit my spirit!"[35] The second and third objections—that the first witnesses to the empty tomb and to the risen Jesus were frightened women and not men of status—actually cut against Celsus. He argues that the story of the resurrection is either delusion or deceit. If so, then why not tell a better story? Why give such prominence to women? Given the prejudice against women in late antiquity, as plainly evident in Celsus himself, one would expect a fabricated story to feature credible men, including Jewish and Roman officials who were not among the following of Jesus. The restrained Passion accounts we find in the Gospels point toward truth, not deceit, delusion, or embellishment.

The fact that the Christian church grew rapidly implies that the objections of Celsus did not enjoy much success. In his derisive criticisms, carried to even greater extremes in Porphyry, I sense a rearguard action; one might even say arguments in retreat. Mockery is usually a sign that the argument is not being won.

Worshiping a crucified Savior, confessed as God's unique Son, struck many in the Roman world as ludicrous. Lucian of Samosata (c. 115–185), writing about the same time as Celsus, tells his readers that Christians "worship that crucified sophist."[36] Other critics assert that Christians worship the "head of an ass."[37] One of the best known graffiti recovered from the ruins of Rome was found on the Palatine Hill. Dating to the end of the second century, it depicts a Christian slave saluting a crucified figure with the head of a donkey. Beneath the crude etching is the inscription that reads: "Alexamenos worships his god."[38] I have no doubt that his fellow slaves thought it very funny and that Alexamenos was a fool. This is why the apostle Paul, writing in the middle of the first century, said of himself and all Christians, "We are fools for Christ's sake."[39] This is why, in writing to the Christians of Rome, he declares, "I am not ashamed of the gospel."[40] He says this because contemporary culture regarded the death of Jesus as shameful and, therefore, belief in him as foolish.

But the mockery, misrepresentations, caricatures, persecutions, and occasional martyrdoms could not stop the Christian movement. Its message of a loving God, the example of a loving community, in which every man, woman, and child was wanted and valued, and the hope of life in this world and beyond, thanks to the resurrection of Jesus, were irresistible. Many mocked but far more believed. They believed (if I may appeal to Paul once again) because they discovered that the gospel "is the power of God for salvation."[41]

As we can see, the reactions to Jesus were varied and mixed. Some liked him, some did not; but it seems all agreed that there was no one like him. It was this "no one like him" that in the end overwhelmed the Roman Empire. Its emperors were phony sons of god and make-believe benefactors who promised good news but never delivered. The teachings and deeds of Jesus, in contrast, were on a completely different level. The message of Jesus was relevant, even if unexpected, unusual, and contrary to the conventions of the time.

For all their bravado, Romans faced an uncertain world and looked for answers wherever they could find them. Among the papyri recovered from the trash heaps of Egypt, we find a category of writings dubbed "Questions to Oracles." Here are a few examples: In the Fayum district a man addresses "Sokanobhoneus the great, great god. Answer me, shall I remain in Bacchias? Shall I meet him? Answer me this."[42] Another in Fayum petitions: "O lords Dioscuri, is it fate for him to depart to the city? Bring this to pass, and let him come to an agreement with your brother."[43] Others ask "Lord Serapis" or "Zeus Helios" for business advice.[44]

The people of the Roman Empire were seeking answers. Their gods and emperors were not providing them. Then they heard about this crucified Jew from Israel. What his followers said about him was like nothing they had heard before. It got them thinking. Added to this, they saw the compassion and concern that early Christians had for human life, at times requiring great sacrifice. It had a profound effect on the world, including Romans following Jesus of Nazareth.

CHAPTER 15
Christianity Ends Racism and Slavery

My wife and I first met Sujo John less than two months after he survived the 9/11 terrorist attacks. Sujo was at work that morning, on the eighty-first floor of Tower 1 of the World Trade Center in New York City, when the first plane struck just two floors above him. Sujo and others raced down the stairs, but just before he could vacate the building, the tower collapsed and he was buried in debris until finally escaping. Sujo had flown to our city to share his survival story with the church where we served on the pastoral staff. To say his story is powerful would be a significant understatement. Over dinner the night before our Sunday services, Audrey and I found it difficult to eat, even breathe at times, as we listened to Sujo recount his firsthand experience with the grim events of 9/11. The *New York Times* flew a reporter to our church, and later ran the story: "A NATION CHALLENGED: THE SURVIVOR; In Pulpits, a Grateful Christian Testifies to Deliverance."[1]

Sujo's story of survival and abiding faith in God while facing certain death continues to capture the hearts and minds of men and women all over the world, but he is not defined exclusively as a 9/11 survivor. Sujo is now using his gifts and global opportunities to combat a far greater evil than extremist terrorism: human trafficking and slavery.

Sujo and his wife, Mary, parents of three beautiful children, founded an international human rights organization called You Can Free Us, which is fighting human trafficking around the world through advocacy, rescue, rehabilitation, and prevention. Over 45 million people are enslaved in the world today—more than any other time in history. What's more, 80 percent of those enslaved are used in sexual exploitation. Women and children make up 95 percent of modern-day slaves.

Of course, slavery is hardly only a modern-day problem. It was ubiquitous in Roman times and even further back in Greek history. Plato's will revealed that he had five slaves, and Aristotle had fourteen slaves when he died.[2] However, Plato did not consider an individual wealthy unless he owned fifty slaves.[3] Yet it might shock you to learn that slaves are much more affordable (even accessible) today than in the Roman Empire. In Roman times, slaves cost up to 175,000 denarii.[4] Hundreds of years later, during the transatlantic slavery period, slaves were still quite expensive, selling for what amounts to an estimated $40,000 in today's economy.[5] Sadly today, slaves can be purchased for ninety dollars, or the equivalent cost of a pair of Nike shoes. My own home city of Houston is one of the busiest hubs for human trafficking in the United States. During my interview with Sujo, he pointed out that in 2009, human-trafficking was a 32 billion dollar industry worldwide but had recently surged to over $150 billion. The problem is real. It is the evil of our time.

Sujo showed me a video filmed inside a modern-day brothel, where child prostitutes were caged in cells. The feeling I experienced while watching that video clip matched what I felt just one other time in my life, when I visited a concentration camp. I was reminded of how Jesus showed his love for children when he told his disciples, "Let the children come to me, and do not hinder them; for to such belongs the kingdom of heaven."[6]

You Can Free Us is not an exclusively Christian organization. To be successful, it has to work with numerous organizations to save lives and rehabilitate women and children for reentry into the civilized world. Yet Sujo's life and worldview is shaped by God's love, that all people—every man, woman, and child—are inherently valuable. One life lost to trafficking is unacceptable. Humans are not to be exploited.

From only one religion or belief system historically emerged the conclusion that slavery was absolutely evil: Christianity. In contrast, Islam does not consider slavery to be a sin. Muhammad personally owned and sold slaves.[7] The Qu'ran, Hadith, and Sira (Islamic trilogy) contain the most elaborate and comprehensive slave code in the world.[8] Islam has enslaved more people than any other culture and still practices it in areas of Saudi Arabia, Mauritania, and the Sudan.[9]

Christianity has successfully abolished slavery not once, but twice before—in late antiquity and again in the 1800s, with the elimination of the transatlantic slave trade after the American Civil War. Much more could be said (and has been written) about the efforts of Christian leaders like William Wilberforce and John Wesley, who tirelessly worked in the eighteenth and nineteenth centuries to abolish slavery. More recently, a third wave of Christians are at the forefront of ending slavery in the marginalized world.

It should be noted that Wilberforce and Wesley lived during the so-called Age of Enlightenment. Were secular philosophers of the time "enlightened" to the evils of slavery? The simple answer is no. A "Who's Who" of major enlightenment figures supported slavery:

Thomas Hobbes, John Locke, Voltaire, David Hume, and Edmund Burke, among others.[10]

Many evils are overlooked when it is deemed certain men and women have no right to exist (see Part Two of this book). May we never forget that ordinary Christians courageously and vigorously opposed slavery. I am inspired by Rodney Stark's assertion that the "potent capacity of monotheism, and especially Christianity, to activate extraordinary episodes of faith have shaped Western civilization."[11]

What Stopped Racism Then? What Can Stop It Now?

As you may recall, as far back as our available sources take us, philosophers, politicians, and playwrights expressed racist opinions and dogmas. But starting in the fourth century, widespread racism ended for hundreds of years. Why was this?

That's when the Christian movement emerged as a dominant cultural force in the Roman Empire, and the bold socio-theological statement "There is neither Jew nor Greek"[12] took hold. Unfortunately, racist ideology, and with it justification for slavery in the West, reemerged in the eighteenth and nineteenth centuries. The influential voices that spouted this new racist ideology—all of them European—were atheists who explicitly rejected the notion that humanity had been created in the image of God. Humanity is not special. Human beings are not equal. Humanity is not one, but is made up of various races or subspecies, some of which are inferior to White Europeans. It was in this post-Christian thinking that the ugly racism of antiquity made its comeback, laying a foundation on which the horrors and tragedies of the twentieth century could take place.

This point has weighed heavily on me during the writing of this book, so much so that I made the trip to Baylor for the academic round table on this very issue. I was encouraged when the eminent sociologist and historian Rodney Stark called this point "pure gold."

Our society is fractured by modern-day racism. Christians today must lead the way in the same spirit of our Christian ancestors and work tirelessly to see the stain of racism removed. It must begin in our homes and churches. Will you make a fresh commitment to end racism in your community? As followers of Jesus, we must come to the aid of anyone who is marginalized or victimized through racism. And make no mistake, silence is support. We cannot and must not look the other way.

Skeptics like to point out Christians who supported slavery, as if that undercuts the spirit and theological emphasis of the New Testament. Alvin Schmidt's important work *How Christianity Changed the World* rightly says that erring Christians who either ignored the teachings of Christ or were ignorant of Paul's words should not be projected on the church as a whole.[13] There is no scriptural basis for slavery and racism, but there are several passages against slavery, including Philemon 16: "No longer as a slave, but better than a slave, as a dear brother" (NIV).

Seek Out Ways to End Slavery, Racism, and Oppression

We live in difficult times that remind us daily of the hurt and despair experienced around the globe. Many cry for help—a twelve-year-old Georgia girl took her life on Facebook Live; a collection of misfits who broadcast the torture and kidnapping of a mentally disabled man. As Christians, we have to, like Sujo John, run toward the darkness and be willing to sacrifice ourselves to eliminate evil. The Lord did not transform our lives so that we could remain in a comfort zone. I think of two important examples.

At the height of its power, the Roman Empire ruled over 2.5 million square miles. The low view of human life, along with the toxic mixture of racism and slavery, gave birth to the Roman gladiatorial contests that came to define the power of the empire for well over five hundred years from 264 BC to AD 378. I have stood in the Roman Colosseum, which was dedicated by Emperor Titus in AD 80. How did the Romans pay for and build the Colosseum? With Jewish gold and on the backs of Jewish slaves taken in the aftermath of the Jewish rebellion of AD 66–70. With a seating capacity reaching 70,000 and a structural height of 170 feet, nothing like it had ever been constructed in the ancient world. Thousands upon thousands of gladiators died not only in the Colosseum but in similar venues around the empire. The legal status of all gladiators? They were slaves.

Gladiators always fought to the death in one-on-one brawls. The armor used by gladiators surely was impressive. Precious few armor pieces have survived, yet one original helmet recovered from Pompeii carries a weight of nine pounds. Even though the gladiatorial contests were ingrained in the Roman cultural DNA, this did not stop the early Christian movement's tireless efforts to see the end of the games. Early church fathers like Athenagoras and Tertullian spoke out against the games and forbade Christians from enjoying this grotesque "entertainment." And the Christian movement eventually succeeded when the games were officially ended under Theodosius I.[14]

An example from our own time is Tim Tebow's "Night to Shine," which inspires individuals and churches around the world to create a prom-like atmosphere for individuals with special needs. The Tim Tebow Foundation website discusses the one-night event, where hundreds of churches participate, motivated by the love of God for all people to give the "royal" treatment to those struggling with special needs. On a late-night TV talk show, Tebow enjoyed an impromptu prom dance with Judy, who has special needs. The clip has been viewed nearly half a million times on YouTube.[15] Watching, I couldn't help but remember that in ancient times, infanticide, child abandonment, and abortion was common, especially for children with special needs. Christians rescued these "unwanted" children then, and we see Christians leading the way today, showing that every person is uniquely special and valuable.

In every corner of society, even those that are darkest, Christians are working to end suffering and bring justice. I personally believe this is the strongest evidence of Christianity—the fact that faith is a force for God, transforming lives and societies.

When Paul wrote to the Thessalonian church, he reminded them that their love compelled them to share "not only the gospel of God but our lives as well."[16] Let us never forget that our message is not only in word but also in deed and action. We should pray daily that God would make us the embodiment of the gospel. I hope before you turn the page, you will stop and reflect on where God would have you go to end oppression and show mercy to forgotten individuals. The words of Micah 6:8 should cause us to reflect and repurpose our efforts: "And what does the LORD require of you but to do justice, and to love kindness, and to walk humbly with your God?"

CHAPTER 16
Without Jesus, Women Would Not Be Free

W omen eat outside!" the Dunkin' Donuts manager screamed. My friend Misty was with her husband, Brandon, trying to enjoy a powdered-sugar donut and escape the suffocating heat of Riyadh, Saudi Arabia, when it really hit Misty that they were in a whole different world. The American couple was working in Riyadh, pastoring the only aboveground Christian church in the Kingdom of Saudi Arabia. The country is home to 27 million people, including an estimated 1.5 million Christians. Misty was wearing her thick abiyah (a heavy cloak worn by women in the Muslim world) and nehab (a veil with slits for the eyes), so the otherwise petite, blonde woman was unrecognizable.

Misty was sharing this story with me in our studios at Houston Baptist University, and began to cry. "It is a man's society. Only men can sit at a table," she explained. "Women cannot drive. Only men work in the department stores. There are no fitting rooms for women."

Back to the scene at Dunkin' Donuts: The pavement is simmering from the heat, creating a hazy effect, and the male manager suddenly chases Misty outside. *Where does she sit to enjoy her quickly melting donut?* She and Brandon find a parking lot curb, but she can hardly endure the heat. A minute later, the donut has disintegrated all over her black abiyah.

"I have never felt so much shame," Misty told me. "And why? Because I am a woman."

Misty's experience is emblematic of the harsh treatment of women in countries around the world where Christianity is not the recognized religion or prevailing influence. It should be noted in the Islamic holy text there are four explicit passages endorsing sex-slavery:

O Prophet! Surely we have made lawful to you your wives whom you have given their dowries, and those whom your right hand possesses out of those whom Allah has given to you as prisoners of war.

Qur'an 33.50

And if you fear that you cannot act equitably towards orphans, then marry such women as seem good to you, two and three and four; but if you fear that you will not do justice [between them], then [marry] only one or what your right hands possess; this is more proper, that you may not deviate from the right course.

Qur'an 4.3

And all married women except those whom your right hands possess [this is] Allah's ordinance to you, and lawful for you are (all women) besides those, provided that you seek [them] with your property, taking [them] in marriage not committing fornication. Then as to those whom you profit by, give them their dowries as appointed; and there is no blame on you about what you mutually agree after what is appointed; surely Allah is Knowing, Wise.

Qur'an 4.24

Successful indeed are the believers, Who are humble in their prayers, And who keep aloof from what is vain, And who are givers of poor-rate, And who guard their private parts, except before their mates or those whom their right hands possess, for they surely are not blamable.

Qur'an 23.1–6

However, it is not only in Islam that women are treated as less than human. As I described in chapter 4, women did not enjoy the same freedoms as men in late antiquity either; and in our own day, there are many places in the non-Christian world where women are treated with injustice, and certainly not equal.

As a historian and Bible scholar, I can assert that where women enjoy many of the same freedoms today as men, it is only because of Jesus Christ and his influence on the world. When Jesus came, he elevated women.

Jesus was not a political revolutionary, as some of his followers wanted. They thought he would drive the Romans out of Israel and overthrow the corrupt, abusive high priesthood. They wanted Jesus to vanquish the Jewish enemies and restore Jerusalem to its glory. Likely, Judas betrayed Jesus because Judas desired a conqueror.

But many did not understand Jesus' kingdom message and ministry. Jesus said his kingdom was not of this world.[1] The power of Jesus was in his message, not his might. He would not overcome the powers of evil by brute force but through love and equality, by changing the core spiritual DNA of society. It was his message that captured hearts and minds, crushed social prejudices, and revolutionized ancient customs, not the least of which was the horrific treatment of women. Without the influence of Jesus, women likely would have remained without freedom.

A Central Role

It is a remarkable omission today that so many self-described feminists utterly disregard the revolutionary influence of Jesus on female equality. Equally disturbing to me are the voices in conservative circles calling for the subordination of women. There are political and social reasons for both of these cultural realities, yet what cannot be ignored is the central role women played in Jesus' ministry and the greatest event in human history, his physical resurrection from the dead.

Taking a step further back, we see the significance of women in Jesus' life and ministry:

Jesus' incarnation (Mary and Elizabeth[2])

His upbringing (Anna the prophetess[3])

Accommodating his ministry (Peter's mother-in-law[4])

His miracles (healing the son of the widow of Nain[5])

Redeeming the "sinful woman"[6]

His financial needs were met by women[7]

He allowed a woman to "touch him" to heal her hemorrhaging[8]

He taught women (Mary and Martha[9])

He healed a woman who had been crippled[10]

His parables highlighted women[11]

It was the women who courageously waited with Jesus in his death,[12] and the same women who financially supported Jesus' ministry were the first eyewitnesses of the empty tomb[13]

We must not let these passages slide by too quickly, without appreciating how out of place these scenes must have been in the first century. And notice I have only highlighted the gospel of Luke; women also play a major role in the other Gospels and Luke's sequel, the book of Acts, where an additional thirteen women or groups of women are featured. The centrality of women in Jesus' life and ministry is nothing short of astonishing for that time.

Among the better known early objectors of the risen Lord were Celsus (writing c. AD 178) and Porphyry (c. AD 232–303), philosophers who ridiculed the Christian proclamation of the resurrection of Jesus, saying it rested on little more than the confused and contradictory testimony of frightened women: "But who really saw [the resurrection]? A hysterical woman."[14] In the first-century world, a woman would have been an embarrassing first witness of such a monumental event. Women were not viewed as reliable sources.

Women and the Early Church

Women outnumbered men in the early church, and they also held positions of honor and authority. The Christian population was likely 64 percent female by AD 80.[15] This is remarkable in light of Christianity's early competitor, the Roman Cult of Mithras, which was men-only; females were excluded.

The apostle Paul regularly included women in his praise of those who sacrificially served and led the early church movement. Women, as well as men, were freely encouraged to be baptized and partake in Communion (the Lord's Supper). Women prayed and worshiped in the worship context.[16] In Romans 16:1–7, 12, women are specifically mentioned for their leadership, wisdom, and service in ministry. Notice in Romans 16:1, Phoebe in Cenchrea is called by a historically male title, a deacon (lit. *diakonos* in Greek, not deaconess, to be clear), which is the oldest term used in the New Testament for "leader," most often translated in English as a "minister." Phoebe likely couriered the book of Romans from Corinth to Rome some four hundred miles, which is remarkable considering the social alienation of women in his day. Romans 16:3 remembers Priscilla and Aquila, and I note that Priscilla is mentioned before Aquila both here and in Acts 18:26, by Luke.

More examples of women in the early church include Mary, who is commended in Romans 16:6 as having "worked hard among you." Andronicus and Junia are also recognized as "outstanding among the apostles" (16:7 NIV). Two sisters (possibly twins), Tryphaena and Tryphosa, are greeted, as well as Persis (16:12 NIV). Of note, the book of Romans was not written to the church of Rome, so Pauline scholars like Robert Sloan and Tom Wright believe those greeted in Romans 16 were all leaders of household churches.

In several other places, Paul recognizes female leadership in the church, such as Philippians 4:2–3, where Euodia and Syntyche were ministers in the church of Philippi. According to Paul, Timothy's mother and grandmother passed on their great legacy of faith to young Timothy: "I am reminded of your sincere faith, a faith that dwelt first in your grandmother Lois and your mother Eunice and now, I am sure, dwells in you."[17] Paul thanks Lois and Eunice by name for inspiring Timothy to walk a life of faith. Another fascinating point, often neglected, is after Paul asks women to "submit yourselves to your own husbands as you do to the Lord," he takes nine verses describing how men should love their wives. Indeed, husbands should "love your wives, just as Christ loved the church and gave himself up for her."[18] This teaching was utterly unique in the Roman world of Jesus' day. Not only are women equal, but they should be honored, adored, cherished, cared for, and if necessary, husbands should even die for their wives. No wonder Christianity expanded so rapidly.

Another reason the early church grew so quickly was because of the child-rescue programs enacted by courageous followers of Jesus. As discussed earlier, being female in the Roman world more often than not was a death sentence ("If it is a boy, keep it. If it is a girl, throw it out!"). When the new converts of Christianity stopped practicing infanticide, especially female infanticide, the number of Christians grew exponentially. In fact, there was a shortage of Christian men available for marriage. It is quite interesting that 1 Peter 3:1–6 and 1 Corinthians 7:6–24 give detailed exhortations encouraging women to stay married to "unbelieving" husbands. The faithfulness of the women could melt the cold heart and bring their husbands to faith. We know from church history that due to the shortage of males, many women married pagans and even pagan priests. Oftentimes, those men were converted—and the church grew.

It has been said that Christianity gave back the concept of humanity to its converts. As we have seen, the Roman world was inhumane, and women continue to be marginalized and oppressed in non-Christian countries today. One lasting legacy of the early Christian movement was its resolve to restore virtue, dignity, and equality to women. For example, I used to be a professor at Acadia University, founded in 1838 by Baptists. Acadia was the first university in the British Empire to admit women into the BA program. The charge was led by Christians.

I personally am indebted to my mother and wife, for the faithful love and commitment to Jesus Christ they exemplify on a daily basis. In the fall of 2000, as a freshman at Liberty University, I was contemplating walking away from my Christian faith. For a variety of reasons, I became increasingly disillusioned with Christians and Christianity. On December 7, 2000, my mother flew into the Roanoke, Virginia, airport and we began a two-day journey home from college. Somewhere in that 1,042-mile journey, I rededicated my life to Jesus Christ, largely because I sensed God speaking to me, healing me, forgiving me, through my mother and her profound faith. What can be said for sure is that I would not be a follower of Jesus today had my mother not inconvenienced herself and focused on me at such an important juncture of my life.

Finally, my wife Audrey's unwavering commitment to Christ continues to embolden me. While I was completing my doctoral residency in Oxford, there were several moments where the stress level was so high I contemplated quitting the program. It was a challenge. Audrey kept my eyes on the end game. Accomplishing the goal of PhD was the only option. Audrey's prayers and faith carried me through those formative days. I am thankful for the women of God in my life and the profound influence of women in the historic Christian faith.

CHAPTER 17
Healing the Unimaginable in Your Life

The first descriptor that should permeate our minds when we think of Christianity should forever be *transformation*. What is utterly unique about the Christian movement—and in my opinion the greatest evidence for the Christian faith—is the holistic transformation the Jesus factor unleashes in life. Nothing else compares. Jesus of Nazareth constantly and audaciously transcended cultural barriers to bring his message of freedom. Not a temporary freedom, but a restorative grace, forgiveness, and altogether new life. His mission of forgiveness, which began in the first century and continues in our day, resonates.

The ultimate purpose of *Unimaginable* is to shed new light on old questions: Does God love me? How do I know? Does God still work in the world? Is there a divine purpose to my life? And . . . if Jesus had not come, would life really be that much different? As we have seen, the world in which we live would be a much darker place were it not for Christianity.

To be sure, we face significant challenges. People groups remain marginalized. Evil regimes continue to inflict suffering, even on their own people. There are countries where women are still not considered equal, let alone free. Yet, we have hope because the spirit of Jesus is vibrant throughout the world, especially when one considers the Christian faith is expanding at a rate of seventy thousand new converts per day.[1]

Our journey through the preceding pages has allowed us to measure what our world would be like without Christianity, which should leave us with a profoundly new level of gratitude and appreciation for the faith we share.

More than a century ago, Ferdinand Schenck, a professor at Rutgers College, was ahead of his time when he wrote *Christian Evidences and Ethics* in a question-and-answer style. Schenck's chapter 7, "Practical Evidence of Christianity," has become a classic in Christian literature. Of his seven compelling evidences for Christianity, I am particularly interested in point five: "Sociological, showing the effects of Christianity on society."

What man feels, thinks and wills concerning God and himself has a great effect upon his social life: morality is based upon religion, wrong views of God lead to wrong views of the nature and worth of man. Wrong views of both God and man lead to wrong conduct.[2]

Only in viewing God rightly can we view ourselves correctly and learn to love rather than hate those around us, who are also beloved by a heavenly Father.

One of the most captivating stories is found in Schenck's recollection of a quote about the impact of Christianity by then US Minister to England James Russell Lowell, who served in the 1880s. Lowell, a celebrated poet, politician, Harvard professor, and abolitionist, said,

I challenge you to find on the face of the earth a single place ten miles square where a decent man may live in safety and happiness where the Bible has not gone before to make that security and morality possible.[3]

Indeed, we should close this book highly motivated to continue the legacy of Christianity by doing good in our own communities. We can leave these pages speaking more articulately and intelligently about the tremendous blessing Christianity casts on the world. American historian and Yale Divinity School professor Kenneth Scott Latourette (1884–1968) summarized the life-giving power of Christianity:

> More than any other religion or, indeed, than any other element in human experience, Christianity has made for the intellectual advance of man in reducing languages to writing, creating literatures, promoting education from primary grades through institutions of university level, and stimulating the human mind and spirit to fresh explorations into the unknown. It has been the largest single factor in combating, on a world-wide scale, such ancient foes of man as war, disease, famine, and the exploitation of one race by another. More than any other religion, it has made for the dignity of human personality. This it has done by a power inherent within it of lifting lives from selfishness, spiritual mediocrity, and moral defeat and disintegration, to unselfish achievement and contagious moral and spiritual power [and] by the high value which it set upon every human soul through the possibilities which it held out of endless growth in fellowship with the eternal God.[4]

Perhaps you have experienced something *unimaginable* in your life, something that seems impossible to overcome. Perhaps you have done something unimaginable. My farewell message to you is to invite Jesus into that unimaginable experience, hopefully encouraged by this final story.

I could not have been more excited to speak at Twin Lakes Church in Santa Cruz, California, for two reasons. First, the church has a long, rich legacy of transformational ministry dating back to 1890, when it was known as the Little Brown Church by the Sea. The church has grown tremendously over the years and is known on the West Coast for phenomenal outreach and teaching. Second, Santa Cruz is heralded as the surfing capital of the world. Need I say more?

One of the best parts of traveling and speaking globally is the opportunity to meet so many fascinating followers of Jesus. You learn very quickly how vast the kingdom of God truly is throughout the world. In the book-signing line following my message at Twin Lakes Church, I met Lynn, and her story is one I will never forget because it shows the difference Jesus brings in the most tragic, unimaginable circumstances.

She told me that less than two weeks after 9/11, Lynn and her husband, Dan, along with their teenage daughters, Carrie and Mandie, were returning home from attending Luis Palau's evangelistic outreach Beachfest Santa Cruz. It had been a great family weekend with twenty-thousand other attendees. They piled into their minivan, buckled their seatbelts, but didn't make it home as a whole family.

The Wagner family was driving north on Cayuga Street around ten at night. As they pulled into an intersection, a Chevy Suburban from the east ran a stop sign and barreled into them. The vehicle never braked. No skid marks were found at the scene. It was later revealed that the driver, a woman named Lisa, was high on coke, meth, and alcohol. According to newspaper reports, the Wagners' van "spun around and crashed into a light pole, toppled a street sign and struck a parked Volvo, ultimately coming to rest in the front yard of a house at the corner."[5] The noise of the crash in the quiet area caused neighbors to run to the scene, some even barefoot. They found Carrie and Mandie dead and Lynn and Dan seriously hurt.

News of the tragic accident spread quickly. The next night, Luis Palau announced at the close of the two-day outreach event that "something terrible happened here last night," as photos of the girls were shown on video screens. Then Luis said, "Mandie and Carrie went straight to the Lord at that very moment."

Dan and Lynn had been rushed from the scene to Dominican Hospital, both with head injuries, and Lynn suffering a broken tailbone, three fractured ribs, and a broken pelvis. Dan also had a neck injury, a sprained coccyx, and embedded safety glass. Both had no memory of the accident.

When Lynn woke up in ICU that Sunday morning and was told about the accident, the first words she was able to muster to a friend were, "Are they in Jesus' arms?"

Sharon replied, "Yes, they are."

"God is a good God," Lynn responded.

Dan did not wake up until Monday morning. His pastor tried to gently let him know about the girls, but it wasn't sinking in. In a reflection he shared with me from something he wrote later, Dan said, "The first time I remember grasping it was when someone visiting me in my hospital room had said they were sorry for my loss. I had asked, 'What loss?' They told me I had lost my girls."

As a parent of five, when I put myself in Dan's situation, I think I would have preferred death to trying to carry on without my children. Dan told me he was battered by what-ifs. "Why didn't God let me drop my keys walking to my car that night or have me see a friend to delay my departure by thirty seconds?" Would this tragedy rip Dan and Lynn's marriage apart? So often, when a married couple loses a child, the marriage is ultimately lost too.

The driver of the Suburban eventually pleaded guilty and went to state prison. Dan admitted, "My anger and resentment toward God began slowly as I read Scripture after Scripture of God's promises—promises that apparently didn't apply to us." Lynn recounted how difficult the first Christmas without the girls was. *How can we celebrate? How will we survive? Will we lose our faith?* Anger turned from the driver to God, who could have stopped the accident, Lynn reasoned. *Why did he take our girls?* Meanwhile, counselors visited Dan and Lynn for the first year. Their church held them close, supporting them, loving them "like a mother loves her child," Dan said, "and God began to do his work in us."

He shared a glimpse of how he processed the grief:

> My own thoughts and feelings want me to believe that perhaps:
>   God did not have the power to stop the accident,
>   or God did not know it was going to happen,
>   or God was tied up with other business and could not attend to us
> at that time, or God did not have the authority to stop the accident,
>   or he simply didn't care.
>
> Or I can choose to believe what God said about himself in the Bible:
>   He is all-powerful—he could have stopped it;
>   He is all-knowing—he certainly knew it was going to happen;
>   He is everywhere at all times—he was there then;
>   He is sovereign—he had the authority to stop it;
>   He is love—therefore his action or nonaction was an expression of
> his love.[6]

It was not overnight, but Dan and Lynn chose to trust God in the face of their greatest adversity. Not only that, they chose to forgive Lisa. Here's where their story transcends ordinary human logic. In August of 2008, the Wagners learned that Lisa would be released from prison after serving 85 percent of her sentence. According to the parole office, the Wagners had a most unusual request. God protected the Wagners so they never had to appear in the courtroom to relive the tragedy and therefore they had never met Lisa. The Wagners wanted to meet her.

Only days before the seven-year anniversary of the tragedy, Dan and Lynn met Lisa under the supervision of her parole officer. When they hugged Lisa, a flood of emotions filled Dan's heart and he began to weep. They learned Lisa had come to faith in Christ while in prison. Dan and Lynn forgave Lisa for killing their two daughters and forgave her for all the pain. As Dan and Lynn turned to leave their meeting with Lisa, the parole officer exclaimed, "I've never seen anything like this, and it happened only because of our faith. We serve a God of reconciliation" (note the officer included himself in "our" faith). What a testimony. Lynn wrote in her story *Not Wasted*, "*That* woman is now like a daughter to me, and I know she will be here for Dan and me no matter what." Lynn and Dan forgave Lisa because God not only commanded it, but they themselves have received the eternal forgiveness offered through the death, burial, and resurrection of Jesus Christ.

Forgiveness was freeing for the Wagners. Their marriage has never been stronger. They volunteer in ministries and touch the lives of multitudes of people. What's more, Dan and Lynn, with Lisa, have shared their story of tragedy and forgiveness in churches. The Wagners are quick to say, "This is not Plan B. This was Plan A, all along." Lynn says, "If our aim is to bring others to Jesus, then how we respond to suffering is so important to those around us who don't yet know him."[7] Dan and Lynn reflected on the hope of the resurrection of Jesus. They will see their girls again. Our eventual resurrection is linked with Jesus' resurrection. Dan and Lynn understand that life is not about the eighty years on this earth. Life is about eternity. Life is about bringing honor and glory to God today despite the most difficult, unimaginable circumstances.

As I left Santa Cruz and drove toward the San Jose airport, I wept thinking about the Wagners. No story is more illustrative of the difference the Jesus factor makes in the world. We can invite Jesus into a situation that appears to be wrecked, and he will make sense of it. In this book we have seen both at macro and micro levels, how Christianity brings hope and healing to the world.

Now, what about you? Have you made your decision to trust in Jesus Christ and begin a relationship with him? If you are a follower of Jesus, will you stop and at this moment and recommit your heart and life to live for him? We do not worship Christianity, we worship and follow Jesus Christ. He is the one who makes the difference. There is no perfect church, because the church is made of imperfect people; however, we see the Spirit of Jesus at work in the world through flawed, ordinary people every single day. Ask Jesus to enter your unimaginable circumstance. He will bring you forgiveness, hope, healing, and transformation.

ACKNOWLEDGMENTS

I have had the good fortune to spend time researching in some very well-resourced locations. These include Oxford University and its fabled Bodleian Library; Yale University and its Beinecke Rare Book and Manuscript Library; Vaughan Memorial Library of Acadia University; and the Lanier Theological Library here in Houston, where I have the opportunity to serve on the faculty of Houston Baptist University as Associate Professor of Early Christianity.

I thank Dr. Rodney Stark, distinguished professor of sociology at Baylor University, who invited me to Waco, Texas, to share aspects of my research with him and his colleagues. It was stimulating and very affirming.

I thank Jeff Braun, my editor and friend. His insights and perceptive editorial work have been so effective and important. His encouragement throughout the project was infectious.

I also want to thank Jonathan Sandys and Wallace Henley for meeting with me to discuss Sir Winston Churchill, Britain's famous wartime prime minister and Jonathan's great-grandfather. I am not sure the West appreciates how indebted it is to the courage and leadership of that great man.

I also thank my mentor and dear friend Craig Evans. Meeting Craig changed my life forever, and it is an honor to co-labor with him in both academic and popular circles. Craig is a true scholastic, in every sense of the word.

I thank Robert B. Sloan, president of Houston Baptist University, whose vision and dedication inspire us all. Working as the special assistant to the president at HBU is a role I continue to cherish. Dr. Sloan continually offered stimulating and encouraging answers as we discussed the formation of this book.

I thank Christian Thinkers Society for the platform and opportunity to spread the message of *Unimaginable* throughout the world.

I am profoundly grateful for the Museum of the Bible, based in Washington, DC, and their mission to encourage all people to engage with the Bible—its narrative, history, and impact.

I wish to express my gratitude to my parents, Jerry and Christie Jo, for encouraging me to always persevere.

Finally, I thank God for my wife, Audrey, and our five children, Lily Faith, Justin, and the Texas triplets: Abel, Ryder, and Jaxson. They are and will always be my first focus and ministry.

Jeremiah J. Johnston
Christian Thinkers Society

NOTES

Introduction

1. Sarah Pulliam Bailey, "Mark Zuckerberg Shares the Prayer He Says to His Daughter Every Night," *The Washington Post*, May 25, 2017, https://www.washingtonpost.com/news/acts-of-faith/wp/2017/05/25/mark-zuckerberg-shares-the-prayer-he-says-to-his-daughter-every-night/.

2. Ruth Gledhill, "Scandal and Schism Leave Christians Praying for a 'New Reformation,'" *The Times*, April 6, 2010, https://www.thetimes.co.uk/article/scandal-and-schism-leave-christians-praying-for-a-new-reformation-lflgv79r7js.

3. Victor Davis Hanson, "No Glory That Was Greece," and Josiah Ober, "Conquest Denied," in Robert Cowley, ed., *What If? The World's Foremost Military Historians Imagine What Might Have Been* (New York: Berkley Books, 1999), 15–36 and 37–56, respectively.

4. Cecelia Holland, "The Death that Saved Europe," in Cowley, ed., *What If?* 93–106. Holland likens the thirteenth-century Mongols to the twentieth-century Khmer Rouge, which ravaged and depopulated Cambodia.

5. I cite from *Mein Kampf*, with Introduction by D. Cameron Watt; Ralph Manheim, trans. (London: Pimlico, 1992).

6. Ibid., 129. Hitler here refers to a missed opportunity in 1904, asserting, "The bloodshed in the year 1904 would have saved ten times as much in the years 1914 to 1918."

7. Ibid., 171. With all due modesty and reservation, Hitler tells his readers: "More than once I was tormented by the thought that if Providence had put me in the place of the incapable or criminal incompetents or scoundrels in our propaganda service, our battle with Destiny would have taken a different turn."

8. Matthew 5:45.

9. "World Watch List 2017," Open Doors, https://www.opendoorsusa.org/christian-persecution/world-watch-list/.

10. Christopher Hitchens, *God Is Not Great: How Religion Poisons Everything* (New York: Twelve, 2007). The subtitle of Hitchens' book recalls the dark opinion of Friedrich Nietzsche (1844–1900), who asserted that Christianity is a poison that has infected the whole world. See F. Nietzsche, *The Birth of Tragedy and the Genealogy of Morals*, Francis Golffing, trans. (New York: Doubleday, 1956, German orig. 1872 and 1887), 185. Nietzsche gives expression to similar ideas in *The Anti-Christ*, R. J. Hollingdale, trans. (New York:

Penguin, 1968, German orig. 1895). Here the clergy are described as poisoners of humanity. We shall take a hard look at this angry, sick little man in a later chapter.

11. The first is seen in Hindu polytheism; the second is seen in Islamic violence.

12. John 10:10.

Part I: The World Before Christianity
Chapter 1: Our Sense of the Divine

1. Sometimes a wife would address her husband as *brother*. See another example on papyri, P. Lond. 42 (168 BC). Older family friends might be addressed as *mother* or *father*.

2. Addressing Berous as *my lady* was a mark of courtesy. See another P. Leip. 110, as well as 2 John 1:5.

3. For photo, see Adolf Deissmann, *Light from the Ancient East* (London: Hodder & Stoughton, 1927), fig. 26 (between 168 and 169). The penmanship is workmanlike, but there are a few slips (e.g., the accusative *you* in line 8, where it should be the dative *to you*). The same grammatical slip is found in P. Oxy. 119, lines 4 and 5. The letter was originally published in B. P. Grenfell and A. S. Hunt, eds., *The Oxyrhynchus Papyri. Part IV*, OP 4 (London: Egypt Exploration Fund, 1904), 243–244 (= no. 744). It is reprinted, with brief notes, in A. S. Hunt and C. C. Edgar, *Select Papyri I*, LCL 266 (Cambridge, MA: Harvard University Press, 1932), 294–295 (= no. 105). I follow these translations (which do not always agree), but in a few places I go my own way. For further discussion of the text, see Stanislaus Witkowski, *Epistulae Privatae Graecae* (Berlin: Teubner, 1906), 97–98; George Milligan, *Selections from the Greek Papyri* (Cambridge: Cambridge University Press, 1910), 32–33 (= no. 12); Adolf Deissmann, *Light from the Ancient East*, 167–170.

4. The meaning here is uncertain. Milligan (*Selections*, 33) suggests "Good luck to you!" Hunt and Edgar (*Select Papyri*, 295) render "If by chance." Witkowski (*Epistulae Privatae Graecae*, 98) thinks the Greek words are the equivalent of the Latin *quod bene vertat*.

5. *De Ira* 1.15.2 (LCL, 214; 144–145).

6. *The Twelve Tables* (LCL, 329; 440–441).

7. The word *hierarchy* means "sacred" or "priestly rule."

8. For discussion and photos of the neolithic temple at Göbekli Tepe, see Charles C. Mann, "The Birth of Religion," *National Geographic* 214, no. 6 (June 2011): 34–59.

9. See Wilhelm Schmidt, *The Origin and Growth of Religion* (London: Methuen, 1931).

10. C. J. Gadd, "Hammurabi and the End of His Dynasty," in I. E. S. Edwards, ed., *The Cambridge Ancient History*, Vol. 1 (Cambridge: Cambridge University Press, 1973), 176–227; Jack M. Sasson, "King Hammurabi of Babylon," in Jack M. Sasson, ed., *Civilizations of the Ancient Near East*, Vol. 2 (New York: Charles Scribner's Sons, 1995), 901–915.

11. L. W. King, trans., *The Code of Hammurabi* (1915; reprint edition by J. S. Pereira, 2011), 32.

12. Exodus 20:2.

13. Richard Taylor, *Ethics, Faith, and Reason* (Englewood Cliffs, NJ: Prentice-Hall, 1985), 83–84.

Chapter 2: A World of Suffering

1. In this part of my chapter, I depend on Craig A. Evans, "The Talking Dead," a chapter found in his book *Jesus and the Remains of His Day* (Peabody, MA: Hendrickson, 2015), 203–236.

2. *Epigrammata Graeca* 646.

3. *Studia Pontica* 145a.

4. *Epigrammata Graeca* 56.

5. *Carmina Latina Epigraphica* 801.

6. *Corpus Inscriptionum Latinarum* I, 2 1222.

7. There is more to the story of Asclepius, but for our purposes what I summarize here is sufficient. For a concise abstract of the Asclepius myth, see Robert Graves, ed., *New Larousse Encyclopedia of Mythology* (New York: Prometheus, 1968), 163; Robert Graves, *The Greek Myths*, 2 vols. (London: Folio Society, 1996), 1:168–171.

8. For a helpful overview of the subject, see John J. Pilch, *Healing in the New Testament: Insights from Medical and Mediterranean Anthropology* (Minneapolis: Fortress, 2000). For an overview of disease in ancient history and in various geographical settings, see Roland K. Harrison and Edwin M. Yamauchi, "Diseases and Plagues," in Edwin M. Yamauchi and Marvin R. Wilson, *Dictionary of Daily Life in Biblical and Post-Biblical Antiquity*, Volume II:De–H (Peabody, MA: Hendrickson, 2015), 63–84.

9. See Mark 4:1.

10. See Mark 5:24–34.

11. See Mark 2:1–12.

12. E. P. Sanders, *Jesus and Judaism* (London: SCM, 1985), 164.

13. For discussion of the role Christian miracles played in converting Romans prior to Constantine, see Ramsay MacMullen, *Paganism in the Roman Empire* (New Haven, CT: Yale University Press, 1981), 94–112; *Christianizing the Roman Empire (AD 100–400)* (New Haven, CT: Yale University Press, 1984), 3, 22, 25–30, 40, 60–61, 132–134.

14. Mark 9:38–40. After hearing Paul preach, the seven sons of a Jewish high priest named Sceva attempted to invoke the name of Jesus, but with negative results. See Acts 19:13–17.

15. See the discussion of this evidence in Craig A. Evans, "Jesus, Healer and Exorcist: The Non-Christian Archaeological Evidence," in Daniel A. Warner and Donald D. Binder, eds., *A City Set on a Hill: Essays in Honor of James F. Strange* (Fayetteville, AR: BorderStone, 2014), 55–77. See also my Bible study *The Dark Side*, Bible Studies for Life (Nashville: LifeWay, 2017).

16. The first-century apocryphal work known as the *Testament of Solomon* catalogues evil spirits, maladies they cause, and steps that must be taken to thwart them.

17. Hippocrates, *Jus jurandum* 1–5, 18–22.

18. Hippocrates, *De morbis* 1.2; *De natura hominis* 4.

19. Hector Avalos, *Illness and Health Care in the Ancient Near East: The Role of the Temple in Greece, Mesopotamia, and Israel*, Harvard Semitic Monographs, 54 (Atlanta: Scholars Press, 1995).

20. Mark 5:25–26.

21. *Naturalis historia* 29.7.14.

22. See Mark 1:40–45; Luke 17:11–19. For an Old Testament example, see 2 Kings 5:1–14.

23. For discussion of the discovery of this tomb, called the "Shroud Tomb," see Shimon Gibson, *The Final Days of Jesus: The Archaeological Evidence* (New York: HarperOne, 2009), 139–147.

24. Suetonius, *Titus* 8.

25. Harrison and Yamauchi, "Diseases and Plagues," 78.

26. Matthew 8:14; Mark 1:30; Luke 4:38; John 4:52; cf. Acts 28:8.

27. The scholarly literature is vast. I suggest Marvin W. Meyer and Paul Mirecki, eds., *Ancient Magic and Ritual Power*, Religions in the Graeco-Roman World 129 (Leiden: Brill, 2001); Andrew T. Wilburn, *Materia Magica: The Archaeology of Magic in Roman Egypt, Cyprus, and Spain*, New Texts from Ancient Cultures (Ann Arbor: University of Michigan Press, 2012).

28. For more on first-century life expectancy, see my book, *Unanswered: Lasting Truth for Trending Questions* (New Kensington, PA: Whitaker House, 2015), 73–74.

29. For more on afterlife traditions and post-mortem beliefs, see my book, *The Resurrection of Jesus in the Gospel of Peter: A Tradition-Historical Study on the Akhmîm Gospel Fragment*, Jewish and Christian Texts in Contexts andd Related Studies, vol. 21 (London: Bloomsbury, 2016), 65–110.

30. Aeschylus, *Eumenides*, 647–648. The text is cited and discussed by F. F. Bruce, *Paul: Apostle of the Heart Set Free* (Grand Rapids, MI: Eerdmans, 1977), 246–247; Stanley E. Porter, "Resurrection, the Greeks and the New Testament" in Stanley E. Porter, Michael A. Hayes, and David Tombs, eds., *Resurrection*, JSNTSup 186; RILP 5 (Sheffield, UK: Sheffield Academic Press, 1999), 52–81, here, 52; and Evans, "The Talking Dead," 204–211.

31. *Eumenides* 649–651. Translation is based on Richmond Lattimore, *Aeschylus I* (New York: Washington Square Press, 1967), 172.

32. Mark 5:21–43.

33. Luke 7:11–17.

34. John 11:1–44.

35. Acts 4:20 NIV.

Chapter 3: A World of Fear

1. Jean-Pierre Vernant, *Mortals and Immortals: Collected Essays*, ed. Froma I. Zeitlin (Princeton, NJ: Princeton University Press, 1991), 273: "A [Greek] god is a power that represents a type of action, a kind of force."

2. For an overview of the Greco-Roman gods, see Robert Graves, ed., *New Larousse Encyclopedia of Mythology* (New York: Prometheus, 1972) 85–221. For a current treatment of Roman religions, see Mary Beard, John A. North, and Simon Price, *Religions of Rome* (Cambridge: Cambridge University Press, 1998).

3. 1 Peter 1:19.

4. Thelma Sargent, trans., *The Homeric Hymns* (New York: Norton, 1975), 190–192.

5. Acts 17:22.

6. The gods did not impose morality on humans. "Piety" with regard to the gods had nothing to do with human behavior. See Ramsay MacMullen, *Paganism in the Roman Empire* (New York: Yale University Press, 1981), 58.

7. One of the most graphic examples is the god Pan raping a goat (on display in the Naples Museum).

8. At Pompeii, we find examples of erect phalli framed in miniature stone reliefs that resemble temples. See Michael Grant and Antonia Mulas, *Eros in Pompeii: The Erotic Art Collection of the Museum of Naples* (New York: Stewart, Tabori, and Chang, 1997); Antonio Varone, *Eroticism in Pompeii: Getty Trust Publications* (Los Angeles: J. Paul Getty Museum, 2001). For an entertaining but very informed depiction of life in Pompeii shortly before the eruption of Vesuvius, see Keith Hopkins, *A World Full of Gods: The Strange Triumph of Christianity* (New York: Plume, 1999) 7–45, 333–337, notes.

9. Peter G. Bolt, "Jesus, the Daimons and the Dead," in A. N. S. Lane, ed., *The Unseen World: Christian Reflections on Angels, Demons, and the Heavenly Realm* (Grand Rapids, MI: Baker, 1996), 75–102.

10. They are reviewed in Bolt, "Jesus, the Daimons and the Dead."

11. Suetonius, *Caligula* 58–59. The passage is discussed in Evans, *Jesus and the Remains of His Day: Studies in Jesus and the Evidence of Material Culture*, 229–230.

12. Pliny the Younger, *Epistles* 5.5.5–6.

13. As in the ghost of the murdered rapist who haunted the people of Temesa. See Pausanius, *Description of Greece* 6.6.7–9. The spirit of Achilles, whose body had not been properly buried, haunted the Greeks until a maiden was sacrificed. See Ovid, *Metamorphoses* 13.441–480.

14. Mark 5:1–20; 9:14–29.

15. For further discussion of these practices, see Evans, *Jesus and the Remains of His Day*, 234–235.

16. Fear of the "evil eye" permeated Jewish as well as pagan culture. On the latter, see Matthew W. Dickie, "Heliodorus and Plutarch on the Evil Eye," *Classical Philology* 86 (1991): 17–29. For a comprehensive study, whose volumes are still appearing, see John H. Elliott, *Beware the Evil Eye: The Evil Eye in the Bible and the Ancient World*, 5 vols. (Eugene, OR: Cascade Books, 2015).

17. Matthew 6:23 (KJV).

18. John H. Elliott, "The Evil Eye and the Sermon on the Mount," *Biblical Interpretation* 2 (1994): 51–84. It is important to note that many Bible versions do not translate *evil*, even though it is the proper translation of *poneros*.

19. On this strange subject, one should consult John G. Gager, *Curse Tablets and Binding Spells from the Ancient World* (Oxford: Oxford University Press, 1992). On the general topic of magic, one should see Christopher A. Faraone and Dirk Obbink, eds., *Magika Hiera: Ancient Greek Magic and Religion* (Oxford: Oxford University Press, 1991).

20. *PGM* XII.376–96. For examples, see Craig A. Evans, "Jesus, Healer and Exorcist: The Non-Christian Archaeological Evidence," in Daniel A. Warner and Donald D. Binder, eds., *A City Set on a Hill: Essays in Honor of James F. Strange* (Mountain Home, AR: BorderStone, 2014), 55–77, here, 61–62.

21. In this wickedly funny satire, Seneca suggests that at death Claudius was not transformed into a god (called *apotheosis*) but rather into a pumpkin (*apocolocyntosis*).

22. In the paragraphs that follow, I rely on Matthew Dennis, *The Twelve Caesars: The Dramatic Lives of the Emperors of Rome* (New York: St. Martin's Griffin, 2012).

23. Suetonius, *Vespasian*, 23.4.

24. Ludwig Feuerbach, *Lectures on the Essence of Religion* (New York: Harper & Row, 1967), 187. The whole sentence reads: "God did not, as the Bible says, make man in His image; on the contrary man, as I have shown in *The Essence of Christianity*, made God in his image." Feuerbach refers to his *Das Wesen des Christenthums* (1841; 2nd ed., 1848), which appears in English as *The Essence of Christianity* (1854; 2nd ed., 1881) (New York: Prometheus, 1989). Feuerbach, of course, is contradicting Genesis 1:26, "Then God said, 'Let us make man in our image.'"

Chapter 4: A World of Inequality

1. See Acts 19 for Paul's gospel encounter with the sale of mini Diana (Artemis) shrines.

2. Frank Cowell, *Life in Ancient Rome* (New York: Berkley Publishing Group, 1961), 97.

3. Galatians 3:28.

4. Throughout this section I rely on John F. DeFelice Jr., "Slavery" in Edwin M. Yamauchi and Marvin R. Wilson, eds., *Dictionary of Daily Life in Biblical and Post-Biblical Antiquity*, Volume IV: O–Z (Peabody, MA: Hendrickson, 2016), 191–215.

5. For a number of graphic examples in Homer, see *Odyssey* 4.244–246; 14.324–343; 22.35–41, 462–473; 24.249–250; *Iliad* 1.12–13; 2.699; 6.654–655; 7.472–475.

6. *Politica* 1253b.

7. *Ethica nicomachea* 8.11.

8. *Odyssey* 1.147; 7.104–109, 340–342; 10.123; Hesiod, *Opera et dies* 405–409, 458–461, 469–471, 502–503, 571–573, 597–599.

9. Jo-Ann Shelton, *As the Romans Did* (Oxford: Oxford University Press, 1998), 163.

10. Walter Scheidel, "Human Mobility in Roman Italy, II: The Slave Population," *Journal of Roman Studies* 95 (2005): 64–79. Scheidel's conservative estimates are probably too low.

11. Roman law regulated such establishments. See *Digesta* 5.27.1. The *Digesta* is a sixth-century AD compilation of Roman law, but much of its contents date to the first through third centuries.

12. As articulated in *Digesta* 48.5.6.1; 48.5.35.

13. Dio Chrysostom, *Orationes* 7.133–152.

14. *Digesta* 11.4.1–3.

15. The very charge was leveled against Alexander Jannaeus, the Hasmonean, when he assumed the Jewish high priesthood. See Josephus, *Jewish Antiquities* 13.373.

16. As quoted by Rodney Stark, *For the Glory of God: How Monotheism Led to Reformations, Science, Witch-Hunts, and the End of Slavery* (Princeton, NJ: Princeton University Press, 2003), 297.

17. In the paragraphs that follow, I rely on Robin G. Branch and Emerson B. Powery, "Wealth and Poverty" in Yamauchi and Wilson, eds., *Dictionary of Daily Life in Biblical and Post-Biblical Antiquity*, Volume IV: O–Z, 367–392, especially 377–383.

18. Richmond Lattimore, *Greek Lyrics* (Chicago: University of Chicago Press, 1949), 44.

19. Ibid., 30.

20. Aristophanes, *Wealth*, 362–363.

21. 1 Timothy 6:10. See also Hebrews 13:5: "Keep your life free from love of money, and be content with what you have."

22. Cicero, *De officiis* 1.150.

23. Seneca, *De vita beata* 24.1.

24. Polybius, *Historiae* 31.25.

25. Luke 16:3.

26. Luke 16:19–30. One also thinks of metaphors exchanged between Jesus and the desperate Syrophoenician woman, who speak of bread thrown to the dogs outside and crumbs that fall from the table that indoor dogs lick up while the family eats dinner.

27. Juvenal, *Satirae* 5.11. For more examples, see Marvin R. Wilson, "Beggars and Alms," in Yamauchi and Wilson, eds., *Dictionary of Daily Life in Biblical and Post-Biblical Antiquity*, Volume I: A–Da, 157–166.

28. Sophocles, *Ajax* 292–293.

29. Democritus, Frag. 110–111.

30. Yeshua ben Sira, Sir 26:14.

31. Yeshua ben Sira, Sir 7:19; 25:8, 13, 16, 20, 23, 25; 26:1, 2, 3, 6, 7, 8, 15, 16; 40:19; 42:6.

32. *Sipre Deut.* 235 (on Deuteronomy 22:13).

33. *t. Berakoth* 6:18. The parallels and contrast with Paul's declaration in Galatians 3:28 have often been pointed out. Prior to his encounter with Christ on the road to Damascus, Saul of Tarsus may well have agreed with the views expressed by Rabbi Judah.

34. *y. Sota* 3.19a.

35. *BGU* 1104.

36. *Leges Duodecim Tabularum*, Table IV.1.

37. *Didache* 2:2b

38. *Barnabas* 19:5c.

39. *Didache* 5:2.

40. Wisdom of Solomon 12:5.

41. There may have been some human sacrifice practiced in Egypt in the Roman period. See also the reference in Wisdom of Solomon 14:23, where killing children "in their initiations" and "secret mysteries" probably refer to Greek mystery religions, especially the cult of Dionysus, whose followers at one time supposedly ripped their victims apart and ate them raw.

42. According to Cicero, *De natura deorum* 1.85.121.

43. Plato, *Phaedo* 117A–118A.

44. Philo, *Quod omnis probus liber sit* 127.

45. Plato, *Apologia* 26C.

46. The reference is to *Sisyphus* frag. 19, but the authorship of this work is disputed.

47. For example, Philo speaks critically of "the opinion which denies any god" (*De migratione Abrahami* 69). Indeed, "[A]theism is the beginning of all iniquity" (*De decalogo* 91). In another context, Philo describes atheism, often associated with men who study philosophy, as "the greatest of all vices" (*De specialibus legibus* 1.32). Philo's comments clearly presuppose the existence of atheists in Egypt at this time.

48. On atheism in late antiquity, see Jan N. Bremmer, "Atheism in Antiquity," in Michael Martin, ed., *The Cambridge Companion to Atheism* (Cambridge: Cambridge University Press, 2007), 11–26.

49. Larry Hurtado, *Destroyer of the Gods: Early Christian Distinctiveness in the Roman World* (Waco, TX: Baylor University Press, 2016), 56–57.

50. *Martyrdom of Polycarp* 3:2. The story is retold in Eusebius, *Historia Ecclesiastica* 4.15.6; cf. 4.15.18.

51. *Martyrdom of Polycarp* 9:2; 10:1.

52. Ibid., 12:2.

53. As seen in his correspondence with Emperor Trajan. Pliny, *Epistulae* 106–197.

54. Justin Martyr, *1 Apologia* 6.1.

55. Ibid., 13.1.

56. Ibid., 46.2

57. Justin Martyr, *2 Apologia* 3. The story is retold in Eusebius, *Historia Ecclesiastica* 4.16.3.

58. Tatian, *Oratio ad Graecos* 27.1.

59. Athenagoras, *Legatio pro Christianis* 4–30.

60. Acts 19:25–27.

61. *Martyrdom of Polycarp* 9:3. When asked to revile Christ, Polycarp replied: "For eighty-six years I have been his servant, and he has done me no wrong. How can I blaspheme my King, who saved me?"

Chapter 5: A World of Bondage: Racism

1. Galatians 3:28.

2. As seen in George M. Frederickson, *Racism: A Short History* (Princeton, NJ: Princeton University Press, 2002). On page 17, Frederickson states: "It is the dominant view among scholars who have studied conceptions of difference in the ancient world that no concept truly equivalent to that of 'race' can be detected in the thought of the Greeks, Romans, and early Christians."

3. A compelling case for protoracism in antiquity has been made in Benjamin Isaac, *The Invention of Racism in Classical Antiquity* (Princeton, NJ: Princeton University Press,

2004). I have benefited greatly from Isaac's well-documented study and have made use of it throughout the first section of the present chapter.

4. Matthew 6:22.

5. Often in Greek literature, *barbaros* was used in reference to the Persians, a powerful and threatening people to the east.

6. That is, to "stutter" or "babble." See the lengthy lexical treatment in Hans Windisch, "Barbaros," in Gerhard Kitte, ed., *Theological Dictionary of the New Testament*, 10 vols. (Grand Rapids, MI: Eerdmans, 1964–1976), 1:546–53. Plato openly speaks of Greek hatred of the barbarian (*Menexenus* 254c–d). Aristotle assures his readers that barbarians are far more suited to slavery (*Politica* 1285a). For a bibliography on this topic, see Isaac, *The Invention of Racism*, 3–4, n. 6.

7. Aristotle, *Physiognomonica* 806b.

8. Ptolemy, *Tetrabiblos* 2.3.65–66.

9. For texts, notes, and brief comments, see Isaac, *The Invention of Racism in Classical Antiquity*, 157–158, nn. 409–411.

10. Plato, *Respublica* 546d–547a.

11. *Politica* 1334b–1335b.

12. Aristotle, *Politica* 1327b; see also 1,252b; 1,255a; 1,285a. For scholarly discussion, see Peter Garnsey, *Ideas of Slavery from Aristotle to Augustine* (Cambridge: Cambridge University Press, 1996), 105–127; Malcolm Heath, "Aristotle on Natural Slavery," *Phronesis* 53 (2008): 243–270.

13. Exodus 34:24; Leviticus 18:24; Numbers 24:8; Deuteronomy 4:38; 7:1, 22; 8:20; 9:1; 19:1.

14. Genesis 26:4; 27:29; Leviticus 26:45; Deuteronomy 7:6; 14:2; 1 Kings 3:8.

15. The apostle Paul, a "Hebrew of Hebrews" (Philippians 3:5), appeals to Israel's Scriptures to make the case that God in his sovereignty may choose Gentiles, as well as Israel, for blessing and salvation. See Romans 9:14–29.

16. As in Exodus 33:16b: "Is it not in thy going with us, so that we are distinct, I and thy people, from all other people that are upon the face of the earth?"

17. Exodus 33:19b.

18. Isaiah 19:22.

19. Isaiah 19:25.

20. 1 Kings 8:41–43a.

21. Isaac, *The Invention of Racism in Classical Antiquity*, 8–14.

22. Georges-Louis Leclerc, "La dégénération des animaux" in Buffon, *Histoire naturelle* 14 (1766).

23. For discussion and bibliography, see Isaac, *The Invention of Racism in Classical Antiquity*, 9–11, includes footnotes 14–20.

24. Hume, "Essay XXI. Of National Characters," 240.

25. Voltaire, *Essai sur les moeurs et l'esprit des nations*, tome 1 (Paris: Stoupe, 1792, orig. 1756). "Voltaire" is the *nom de plume* of François-Marie Arouet.

26. Isaac, *The Invention of Racism in Classical Antiquity*, 11.

27. *The Cambridge Companion to Voltaire* (Cambridge: Cambridge University Press, 2009), 199.

28. As quoted by Paul Edwards, *God and the Philosophers* (Amherst, NY: Prometheus, 2009), 145.

29. *Dublin Review: A Quarterly and Critical Journal* (1840), 208.

30. Léon Poliakov, *The History of Anti-Semitism: From Voltaire to Wagner* (New York: Routledge & Kegan Paul, 1975), 88–89; Dennis Prager and Joseph Telushkin, *Why the Jews? The Reason for Antisemitism* (New York: Simon & Schuster, 1983), 128–189.

31. Immanuel Kant, *Beobachtungen über das Gefühl des Schönen und Erhabenen* (Königsberg: Johann Jacob Kanter, 1764). The quotation is from the English version by John T. Goldthwait, *Observations on the Feeling of the Beautiful and the Sublime* (Berkeley: University of California Press, 1960), 110. How exactly does Kant know that Blacks have no deep feelings? By "feelings" Kant means thought as much as emotion. His assertion is utterly gratuitous.

32. Karl Vogt, *Untersuchungen über Thierstaaten* (Frankfurt, Germany: Literarische Anstalt, 1851), 29–31. The English title: "Studies on Animal States."

33. As quoted in Annette Wittkau-Horgby, *Materialismus: Entstehung und Wirkung in den Wissenschaften des 19. Jahrhunderts* (Göttingen: Vandenhoeck & Ruprecht, 1998), 90. The English title: *Materialism: Origin and Function in the Scholarship of the Nineteenth Century*. Vogt, of course, was borrowing the famous line from Anthelme Brillat-Savarin (1755–1826), French lawyer, gourmet, and author of *The Physiology of Taste* (1825). Vogt's meaning, however, was quite different. It is speculated that Vogt's expression was inspired by Feuerbach's famous—and oft misunderstood—aphorism "Man is what he eats" (*Der Mensch ist, was er isst*). However Feuerbach should be understood, it nevertheless reflects the idea that a human is no more than a biological machine, an idea that Vogt accepted and advanced enthusiastically.

34. Karl Vogt, *Vorlesungen über den Menschen, seine Stellung in der Schöpfung und in der Geschichte der Erde*, 2 vols. (Giessen: J. Richer, 1863), 1:295. The work appeared in English as *Lectures on Man: His Place in Creation and in the History of the Earth* (London: Anthropological Society of London, 1864). The proof Vogt offers for his assertion is highly dubious.

35. Ludwig Büchner, *Force and Matter, or Principles of the Natural Order of the Universe* (London: Trubner, 1864; New York: 1950). In German, the book appeared as *Kraft und Stoff: Empirisch-naturphilosophische Studien* (Frankfurt am Main: Meidinger Sohn, 1855), then later as *Kraft und Stoff oder Grundzüge der natürlichen Weltordnung*, 20th ed. (Leipzig: Theodor Thomas, 1902). Büchner's goal was to advance a more consistent materialist explanation of the universe, including human life.

36. As seen, for example, in Büchner, *Natur und Geist: Gespräche zweier Freunde über den Materialismus* [*Nature and Spirit: Conversations among Friends on Materialism*] (Frankfurt am Main: Meidinger Sohn, 1857); *Aus Natur und Wissenschaft: Studien, Kritiken, Abhandlungen und Entgegnungen* [*From Nature and Science: Studies, Critiques, Treatises, and Replies*] (Leipzig: Theodor Thomas, vol. I., 1862; vol. II., 1884); *Der Fortschritt in Natur und Geschichte im Lichte der Darwinschen Theorie* [*Progress in Nature and History in the Light of the Darwinian Theory*] (Stuttgart: E. Schweizerbart, 1884), among others.

Part II: The World Without Christianity
Chapter 6: A Slippery Slope

1. Quoted in Andrew Roberts, "The Death of Winston Churchill Was the Day the Empire Died," *The Telegraph*, January 18, 2015, www.telegraph.co.uk/history/11351639/The-death-of-Winston-Churchill-was-the-day-the-Empire-died.html.

2. Speech delivered October 29, 1941, at Harrow School. See https://www.national churchillmuseum.org/never-give-in-never-never-never.html.

3. Winston Churchill, "We Shall Fight on the Beaches" (speech to the House of Commons, London, June 4, 1940). The full text of this speech can be found online at www .winstonchurchill.org/resources/speeches/1940-the-finest-hour/we-shall-fight-on-the-beaches.

4. For an assessment of the life and thought of Ludwig Feuerbach, see Van A. Harvey, *Feuerbach and the Interpretation of Religion* (Cambridge: Cambridge University Press, 1995).

5. Ludwig Feuerbach, *The Essence of Christianity*, M. A. Evans, trans. (New York: Calvin Blanchard, 1855), 269. Evans varied the spelling of her first name.

6. Alluding to and contradicting Genesis 1:26. See Ludwig Feuerbach, *Lectures on the Essence of Religion* (New York: Harper & Row, 1967), 187. The English translation is based on Feuerbach, *Vorlesungen über das Wesen der Religion. Nebst Zusätzen und Anmerkungen* (Stuttgart: Frommann, 1908).

7. Charles Lyell, *Principles of Geology*, 3 vols. (London: John Murray, 1830–1833). The first volume appeared shortly before Darwin's voyage. The second and third volumes appeared during the voyage.

8. Throughout his life, Darwin had great respect for Charles Lyell.

9. Charles Darwin, *On the Origin of Species* (London: John Murray, 1859). Charles Lyell assisted Darwin in getting his book published.

10. Darwin, *On the Origin of Species*, 488.

11. Charles Darwin, *The Descent of Man* (London: John Murray; New York: Appleton, 1871), 204–205. It is an interesting statement: "The Simiadae then branched off into two great stems, the New World and Old World monkeys; and from the latter, at a remote period, Man, the wonder and glory of the University, proceeded."

12. Darwin Correspondence Project: Letter to John Fordyce (7 May 1879), letter 1,2041.

13. Ibid.

14. For a helpful overview, see Alfred Kelly, *The Descent of Darwin: The Popularization of Darwinism in Germany, 1860–1914* (Chapel Hill: University of North Carolina Press, 1981).

15. For further discussion, see Isaac, *The Invention of Racism in Classical Antiquity*, 29–30, including footnotes 74–77.

16. It is important to remark that "human races do not occur in reality . . . race is not a biological reality." I have quoted Isaac, *The Invention of Racism in Classical Antiquity*, 34.

17. On the nonsense regarding humans and apes, see Kelly, *The Descent of Darwin*, 32.

18. For a lengthy and learned study of Charles Darwin, see Adrian Desmond and James Moore, *Darwin: The Life of a Tormented Evolutionist* (London: Norton, 1991).

19. Francis S. Collins, *The Language of God: A Scientist Presents Evidence for Belief* (New York: Free Press, 2006).

20. Guillermo Gonzalez and Jay W. Richards, *The Privileged Planet: How Our Place in the Cosmos Is Designed for Discovery* (Washington, DC: Regnery, 2004); Roy A. Varghese, *The Wonder of the World: A Journey from Modern Science to the Mind of God* (Fountain Hills, AZ: Tyr, 2004); Denyse O'Leary, *By Design or By Chance? The Growing Controversy on the Origins of Life in the Universe* (Minneapolis: Augsburg, 2004).

21. Only if the Bible is interpreted in an uncritical, hyperliteral manner.

22. Marx composed notes called "Theses on Feuerbach," which served as an outline for a series of manuscripts by Marx and Engels called *Die Deutsche Ideologie* ("The German Ideology"), composed in 1846. The material, which was chiefly concerned with a materialist understanding of history, was not published until 1932. For more on Feuerbach's influence on Marx, see Van A. Harvey, "Ludwig Feuerbach and Karl Marx" in Ninian Smart et al., eds., *Religious Thought in the West*, vol. 1 (Cambridge: Cambridge University Press, 1986), 291–328.

23. Georg Wilhelm Friedrich Hegel (1770–1831) conceived of history largely as a struggle between opposing forces, as thesis versus antithesis finally producing synthesis. Hegel's ideas left a lasting impression on German thinking in many fields, including philosophy and theology. It is pure ideology, of course. There is nothing scientific about it and it finds

no support in any objective study of history. Nevertheless, the concept remained very influential for generations.

24. Bauer's work gave major impetus to what is today called Mythicism. See especially Bruno Bauer, *Kritik der evangelischen Geschichte der Synoptiker*, 2 vols. (Leipzig: Otto Wigand, 1841); *Christus und die Cäsaren: Der Ursprung des Christenthums aus dem römischen Griechenthum* (Berlin: Eugen Grosser; 1877; 2nd ed., 1879). The title of the first book in English is *Criticism of the History of the Synoptic Gospels*. The title of the second is *Christ and the Caesars: The Origin of Christianity from the Roman-Greek Culture*. Today these books are viewed as eccentric. The "last gasp" of what might be regarded as mainstream Mythicism was seen in Artur Drews, *Die Christusmythe* (Jena: Diederichs, 1909; 3rd ed., 1924); English: *The Christ Myth* (London: Unwin, 1910). Mythicism today has few scholarly adherents.

25. In one incident the drunken Bauer and Marx rode donkeys through the streets of Berlin. See David McLellan, *Karl Marx: Biography*, 4th ed. (Basingstoke: Palgrave Mac-Millan, 2006), 32–33.

26. *Das Kapital* appeared in three installments. The first in 1867, the second and third in 1885 and 1894, after Marx's death. They were edited by Engels. The English edition is *Capital: A Critique of Political Economy* (New York: Modern Library, 1906).

27. For a concise assessment of Marx's scholarship and tendency to misquote and misrepresent his sources, see Paul Johnson, *Intellectuals: From Marx and Tolstoy to Sartre and Chomsky* (New York: HarperCollins, 1988), 52–81.

28. Ibid., 54.

29. As quoted by Johnson, ibid.

30. Ibid., 55.

31. German: *Sie ist das Opium des Volkes*. Marx is not the originator of the well-known saying; he borrowed it from Heinrich Heine. See Johnson, *Intellectuals*, 56. Many of Marx's famous quips came from others, almost never with acknowledgment.

32. Karl Marx, *Critique of Hegel's Philosophy of Right*, Annette Jolin, trans.; Joseph O'Malley, ed. (Cambridge: Cambridge University Press, 2009), 131. English translation of "Zur Kritik der Hegelschen Rechtsphilosophie," *Deutsch-Französische Jahrbücher* (February 1844): 378–391, here, 378–379. The words in italics are italicized in the original German.

33. It is ironic in this connection to note that Marx was not personally acquainted with any factory workers or coal miners, whose economic lives so greatly concerned him. The only working-class person he knew was his maid, whom he never paid a penny.

34. Jim Yardley, "Praising Pope, Cuban President Says He Might Return to Church," *New York Times* (11 May 2015): A4.

Chapter 7: Dehumanizing Humanity

1. Sigmund Freud, *Civilization and Its Discontents*, James Strachey, ed. and trans. (New York: (Norton, 2010, German orig. 1930), 67.

2. Freud, *Civilization and Its Discontents*, 57, 66–67. See also Freud's comments on 36, 56–58.

3. Jörg Salaquarda, "Nietzsche and the Judaeo-Christian Tradition" in Bernd Magnus and Kathleen Higgins, eds., *The Cambridge Companion to Nietzsche* (Cambridge: Cambridge University Press, 1996), 90–118, here, 99. For extensive evaluation of Nietzsche's views of the New Testament, see Hans Hübner, *Nietzsche und das Neue Testament* (Tübingen: Mohr Siebeck, 2000). I am not aware of an English translation.

4. Friedrich Albert Lange, *Geschichte des Materialismus und Kritik seiner Bedeutung in der Gegenwart* (Iserlohn: J. Baedeker, 1866). In English the title is "History of Materialism and Criticism of its Importance in the Present." Although a materialist, Lange rejected Marx's understanding of materialism. Lange's book was republished in an expanded two-volume edition in 1873–1875. A three-volume English translation appeared in 1877–1881. The 1950 English reprint includes an Introduction by atheist Bertrand Russell.

5. In a letter he wrote to Hermann Mushacke in 1868, Nietzsche described Lange's book as "the most significant philosophical work to have appeared in recent decades." See Giorgio Colli and Mazzino Montinari, eds., *Nietzsche Briefwechsel: Kritische Gesamtausgabe* (Berlin and New York: de Gruyter, 1975), 1:2. In English, the title means "The Nietzsche Correspondence: A Critical General Edition."

6. For original publications, see Friedrich Nietzsche, *Jenseits von Gut und Böse: Vorspiel einer Philosophie der Zukunft* (Leipzig: C. G. Naumann, 1886); *Zur Genealogie der Moral: Eine Streitschrift* (Leipzig: C. G. Naumann, 1887); *Götzen-Dämmerung: Wie man mit dem Hammer philosophirt* (Leipzig: C. G. Naumann, 1888); *Der Antichrist: Versuch einer Kritik des Christentums* (Leipzig: Alfred Kröner, 1895). The last title in German is ambiguous. It can mean either "Anti-Christ" or "Anti-Christian." Even Nietzsche enthusiasts admit that in some places in this book the author sounds insane. Although written in 1888, it was not published until 1895. The subtitle for *Götzen-Dämmerung* (*The Twilight of the Idols*) means "How to Do Philosophy with a Hammer."

7. All of Nietzsche's books initially appeared in German. A few of them were translated and published in English. Perhaps the most famous of his works is *Also Sprach Zarathustra* (Chemnitz: Ernst Schmeitzner, 1883). For an English translation, see Walter Kaufmann, *Thus Spoke Zarathustra: A Book for All and None* (New York: Random House, 1966), reprinted numerous times. There are several English translations. *Ecce Homo* was published posthumously in 1908. Not surprisingly, atheists and moral relativists are enamored with Nietzsche's thought.

8. Supposedly brought on by seeing a horse being whipped.

9. Dimitri Hemelsoet, Koenraad Hemelsoet, and Daniël Devreese, "The Neurological Illness of Friedrich Nietzsche," *Acta Neurologica Belgica* 108 (2008): 9–16.

10. Some have argued that Nietzsche's insanity was the result of his philosophy. For example, see René Girard, *To Double Business Bound: Essays on Literature, Mimesis, and Anthropology* (Baltimore, MD: Johns Hopkins University Press, 1978), in chap. 4: "Strategies of Madness—Nietzsche, Wagner, and Dostoevski" (61–83). This chapter appeared earlier as "Superman in the Underground: Strategies of Madness—Nietzsche, Wagner, and Dostoevski," *Modern Language Notes* 91 (1976): 1,161–1,185.

11. Although I have read widely on Nietzsche, in this chapter I am deeply indebted to Richard Weikart's incisive chapter "Superman's Contempt for Humanity," in Weikart, *The Death of Humanity and the Case for Life* (Washington, DC: Regnery, 2016), 185–213. For an analysis of the psychology of Nietzsche, see Paul C. Vitz, *Faith of the Fatherless: The Psychology of Atheism*, 2nd ed. (San Francisco: Ignatius Press, 2013), 34–40.

12. Weikart, "Superman's Contempt for Humanity," 189, with quotation from Nietzsche, *Thus Spake Zarathrustra*, Walter Kaufmann, trans. (New York: Penguin, 1976), 125.

13. Nietzsche, *Beyond Good and Evil*, Walter Kaufmann, trans. (New York: Vintage, 1966), 201; Weikart, "Superman's Contempt for Humanity," 189.

14. Nietzsche, *Will to Power*, 872, as quoted in Weikart, "Superman's Contempt for Humanity," 191.

15. Nietzsche, *The Genealogy of Morals*, Francis Golffing, trans. (Garden City, NY: Doubleday, 1956), 210, as quoted by Weikart, "Superman's Contempt for Humanity," 191.

16. Weikart, "Superman's Contempt for Humanity," 190.

17. Nietzsche, *Antichrist*, Karl Schlechta, ed. (Munich: Carl Hanser, 1966), 2:1, as translated by Weikart, "Superman's Contempt for Humanity," 191.

18. Nietzsche, *Twilight of the Idols*, Walter Kaufmann, trans. (New York: Penguin, 1976), 536–537, as quoted and discussed in Weikart, "Superman's Contempt for Humanity," 192.

19. Weikart draws our attention to Michael Lackey's absurd claim that Nietzsche's "philosophy mandates an extremely respectful relationship between people, which calculated to ennoble." To this misrepresentation, Weikart responds: "Except, Lackey forgot, if those people happen to be sick, weak, disabled, female, or part of the masses." Weikart also appeals to critic Simon May, who rebuts Nietzsche's apologists: "With Nietzsche there is not even an attempt to produce a safety net against cruelty . . . the supreme value he places on individual life-enhancement and self-legislation leaves room for, and in some cases explicitly justifies, unfettered brutality." Simon May, *Nietzsche's Ethics and His War on 'Morality'* (Oxford: Oxford University Press, 1999), 132.

20. May, *Nietzsche's Ethics and His War on 'Morality'*, 132.

21. To this end, see Richard Wolin, *The Seduction of Unreason: The Intellectual Romance with Fascism from Nietzsche to Postmodernism* (Princeton, NJ: Princeton University Press, 2004). See especially the chapter "Zarathustra Goes to Hollywood: On the Postmodern Reception of Nietzsche," 27–62.

22. Freud's middle name *Schlomo* reflects the Hebrew form of the name Solomon.

23. The literature on this troubling topic is enormous. I suggest Marie E. Tomeo, Donald I. Templer, Susan Anderson, and Debra Kotler, "Comparative Data of Childhood and Adolescence Molestation in Heterosexual and Homosexual Persons," *Archives of Sexual Behavior* 30 (2001): 535–541; William C. Holmes and Gail B. Slap, "Sexual Abuse of Boys: Definition, Prevalence, Correlates, Sequelae, and Management," *Journal of the American Medical Association* 280 (1998): 1,855–1,862.

24. Freud's fullest statement on the psychology of religion is found in his *Die Zukunft einer Illusion* (Leipzig: Internationaler Psycholoanalytischer Verlag, 1927). The work has been translated into English as *The Future of an Illusion*, W. D. Robson-Scott, trans. (London: Hogarth, 1928), James Strachey, rev. and ed. (Garden City, NY: Anchor Books, 1964).

25. Freud, *The Future of an Illusion*, 71.

26. Freud, *Civilization and Its Discontents*, James Strachey, trans., 22, 36; *The Future of an Illusion*, 86.

27. Freud, *The Future of an Illusion*, 76–82. For comment, see Steven D. Kepnes, "Bridging the Gap between Understanding and Explanation: Approaches to the Study of Religion," *Journal for the Scientific Study of Religion* 25 (1986): 504–512, especially 510.

28. On this point, see Peter Gay, *A Godless Jew: Freud, Atheism, and the Making of Psychoanalysis* (New Haven, CT: Yale University Press, 1987), 4–5. Belief in God, says Freud, will often "overwhelm Reason and Science." See Freud, *Moses and Monotheism*, Katherine Jones, trans. (New York: Vintage Books, 1967), 157. In this book, Freud offers a critique of Judaism as well as Christianity. For a critical evaluation of *Moses and Monotheism*, Freud's last book on religion, see R. Z. Friedman, "Freud's Religion: Oedipus and Moses," *Religious Studies* 34 (1998): 135–149. He finds Freud's critique intellectually flawed and politically misdirected.

29. Gay, *A Godless Jew*, 37.

30. Vitz, *Faith of the Fatherless*, 11–17, 165–169. Vitz remarks: "As a statement about the origins of religion, Freud's interpretation is thoroughly rejected by anthropologists," 14.

31. Freud, *Civilization and Its Discontents*, 109. For critical discussion, see Ernest Wallwork, "Thou Shalt Love Thy Neighbor as Thyself: The Freudian Critique," *Journal of Religious*

Ethics 10 (1982): 264–319; Timothy Patrick Jackson, *Love Disconsoled: Meditations on Christian Charity*, Cambridge Studies in Religion and Critical Thought 7 (Cambridge: Cambridge University Press, 1999), 56–70. Both foreign words are Greek, with the first, *agape*, and its cognate verb, occurring more than two hundred times in Christian Scripture and the second, *eros*, never occurring. For Freud, *eros* is the "life instinct" that for most people overcomes the "death instinct." See Freud, *Beyond the Pleasure Principle*, James Strachey, trans. and ed. (New York: Norton, 1961), 73. Freud's simplistic reductionist understanding of humanity is strange.

32. Freud and Bonaparte (2009), 238–239.

33. Peter J. Swales, "Freud, Minna Bernays, and the Conquest of Rome: New Light on the Origins of Psychoanalysis," *The New American Review* (Spring/Summer 1982): 1–23. There is some evidence that the affair resulted in Minna Bernays' having an abortion.

34. Ernest Jones, *Sigmund Freud: Life and Work*, vol. 1 (London: Hogarth, 1953), 94–96.

35. Jones, *Sigmund Freud*, 86–108; Robert Byck, *Cocaine Papers by Sigmund Freud* (New York: Stonehill, 1974); Elizabeth Thornton, *Freud and Cocaine: The Freudian Fallacy* (London: Blond & Briggs, 1983), 45–46.

36. Although he continued to use the drug from time to time. See Jeffrey M. Masson, ed., *The Complete Letters of Sigmund Freud to Wilhelm Fliess, 1887–1904* (Cambridge, MA: Harvard University Press, 1985), 49, 106, 126–127, 132, 201.

37. Wilhelm Fliess, *Neue Beiträge zur Klinik und Therapie der nasalen Reflexneurose* (Leipzig: Franz Deuticke, 1893). The English title is "New Contributions to the Clinic and Therapy of Nasal Reflex Neuroses."

38. Gay, *A Godless Jew*, 84–87.

39. Ibid., 650–651.

40. Minna apparently confessed the affair to Carl Jung in 1907. It should be noted that the Freud–Minna Bernays correspondence (1893–1910), which would provide the clearest evidence of the affair, has been stolen and perhaps destroyed. Even without this evidence, other correspondence and journal entries strongly support the conclusion that Freud and Minna were involved.

41. The whole sordid affair is described, with detailed and convincing documentation, in E. Michael Jones, *Degenerate Moderns: Modernity as Rationalized Sexual Misbehavior* (South Bend, IN: Fidelity, 2012), 139–212. Carl Jung (1875–1961) confessed to Freud his sexual affair with his patient Sabina Spielrein, only to learn that Freud, whom Jung viewed as a father figure, was himself entangled in an affair. Jung lost respect for Freud, while he himself went on to have affairs with other women, some of them his patients.

Chapter 8: Atheism and the Broken Soul

1. Paul Johnson, *Intellectuals* (New York: Harper, 2007), 342.

2. E. Michael Jones, *Degenerate Moderns* (San Francisco: Ignatius Press, 1993).

3. One will find variations of this statement, depending on which version of Freud's works one consults. I am quoting verbatim from Freud, *Leonardo da Vinci: A Psychosexual Study of an Infantile Reminiscence*, A. A. Brill, trans. (New York: Moffat, Yard, 1916), 103. A version of the statement is quoted and discussed in Paul C. Vitz, "Freud and the Psychology of Atheism," in Mark Andrew Holowchak, ed., *Radical Claims in Freudian Psychoanalysis: Point-Counterpoint* (Lanham, MD: Jason Aronson, 2011), 129–144, here, 138.

4. John Cottingham, "Reply to Dr. Vitz," *Radical Claims in Freudian Psychoanalysis*, 151.

5. C. S. Lewis, *Surprised by Joy: The Shape of My Early Life* (New York: Harcourt Brace, 1956).

6. Richard Dawkins, *River out of Eden: A Darwinian View of Life* (New York: Basic Books, 1995), 133.

7. Johnson, *Intellectuals*; Jones, *Degenerate Moderns*; James Spiegel, *The Making of an Atheist*, 70–80.

8. See the convenient thumbnail sketches provided in Spiegel, *The Making of an Atheist* (Chicago: Moody, 2010), 71–72.

9. Aldous Huxley, *Ends and Means: An Inquiry into the Nature of Ideals and into the Methods Employed for Their Realization* (New York: Harper & Bros., 1937), 316 (with italics added); cited by Spiegel, *The Making of an Atheist*, 73.

10. Huxley, *Ends and Means*, 312 (with italics added); again cited by Spiegel, *The Making of an Atheist*, 73.

11. Margaret Mead, *Coming of Age in Samoa: A Psychological Study of Primitive Youth for Western Civilization* (New York: Blue Ribbon Books, 1928), 222.

12. Jones, *Degenerate Moderns*, 19–40; Spiegel, *The Making of an Atheist*, 74–76.

13. Jones, *Degenerate Moderns*, 37: "Mead's anthropological conclusions were drawn primarily from her own personal unresolved sexual conflicts." See also the comments in Spiegel, *The Making of an Atheist*, 75–76. The incompetent, if not fraudulent nature of Mead's study in Samoa was exposed in Derek Freeman, *Margaret Mead and Samoa: The Making and Unmaking of an Anthropological Myth* (New York: Penguin Books, 1983). Although not itself without faults, the major conclusions of Freeman's book are now widely accepted. That the academy did not discover Mead's deceit for half a century is a disgrace.

14. The *Kinsey Reports* are found in Alfred Kinsey, Wardell Pomeroy et al., *Sexual Behavior in the Human Male* (Bloomington: Indiana University Press, 1948) and *Sexual Behavior in the Human Female* (Bloomington: Indiana University Press, 1953).

15. As Kinsey openly states. See Cornelia Christenson, *Kinsey: A Biography* (Bloomington: Indiana University Press, 1971), 6–7. For a devastating critique, see Jones, *Degenerate Moderns*, 83–108.

16. In one especially troubling case, Kinsey draws up a report based on a journal kept by a pedophile (and misleadingly presents it as a compilation of confessions from several persons). If the information comes from the recollections of pedophiles, it is scientifically worthless. If it comes from experiments conducted by Kinsey and/or his colleagues, it is criminal. See Jones, *Degenerate Moderns*, 99–105. For an especially negative evaluation of Kinsey's work, see Judith A. Reisman and Edward W. Eichel, *Kinsey, Sex and Fraud: The Indoctrination of a People* (Lafayette, LA: Huntington House, 1990). In view of Reisman's findings, Patrick Buchanan wonders if "Kinsey will wind up on the same ethical and scientific shelf now reserved for the German doctors who conducted live experiments on Jewish children." See Patrick Buchanan, "Kinsey: Medical Pioneer or Criminal Fraud?" *Human Events* (July 2, 1983): 14.

17. However, there were some serious academic critiques of the *Kinsey Reports*. See Abraham H. Maslow and James M. Sakoda, "Volunteer Error in the Kinsey Study," *Journal of Abnormal Psychology* 47 (1952): 259–262; Peter Gay, *The Bourgeois Experience: Victoria to Freud*, vol. 2: *The Tender Passion* (New York: Oxford University Press, 1986), 447: Kinsey's findings are "far from persuasive." Also see Jones, *Degenerate Moderns*, 96.

18. I thank Dr. Peter J. Williams, principal of Tyndale House, Cambridge, for this insightful point.

19. I have consulted a number of sources, but I rely heavily on Johnson, *Intellectuals*, 197–224, with notes on 355–358.

20. Ibid., 217–218.

21. Bertrand Russell, *Why I Am Not a Christian, and Other Essays on Religion and Related Subjects*, Paul Edwards, ed. (New York: Simon & Schuster, 1957). The principal essay, "Why I Am Not a Christian," was delivered as a public lecture in 1927.

22. Sartre recalled that as young child he said remarkable things that people wrote down and memorized. Others, however, do not have the same recollection. For a critical review of Sartre's life and thought, see Johnson, *Intellectuals*, 225–251, with notes on 358–360.

23. Vitz, *Faith of the Fatherless*, 146–150.

24. Khwaja Maṣud, "Remembering Che Guevara," *The News International* (October 9, 2006).

25. Weikart, *Death of Humanity*, 198–204.

26. Johnson, *Intellectuals*, 246.

27. Ibid., 246–247, 340–341. Sartre called on students to engage in violence: "Violence is the only thing remaining to the students who have not yet entered into their fathers' system." Johnson is quoting from Annie Cohen-Solal, *Sartre: A Life* (London: Heinemann, 1987), 459.

28. As quoted by Weikart, *Death of Humanity*, 204. For source, see Jean-Paul Sartre, *Talking with Sartre: Conversations and Debates*, John Gerassi, trans. and ed. (New Haven, CT: Yale University Press, 2009), 14–15.

29. Johnson, *Intellectuals*, 250.

30. Richard Dawkins, *The God Delusion* (Boston: Houghton Mifflin Harcourt, 2006).

31. Johanthan Leake, "Dawkins Evolves Into Single Man After 'Amicable' Split with Time Lady," *The Times*, July 17, 2016, https://www.thetimes.co.uk/article/dawkins-evolves-into-single-man-after-amicable-split-with-time-lady-sp911k2nt.

32. Vitz, *Faith of the Fatherless*, 78–80, with quotation from 80.

33. Daniel C. Dennett, *Breaking the Spell: Religion as a Natural Phenomenon* (New York: Viking, 2006).

34. Christopher Hitchens, *God Is Not Great: How Religion Poisons Everything* (New York: Twelve, 2007).

35. Vitz, *Faith of the Fatherless*, 157.

36. MDMA = Methylenedioxymethamphetamine, on the street known as "ecstasy."

37. In chronological order: Sam Harris, *The End of Faith: Religion, Terror, and the Future of Reason* (New York: Norton, 2004); *Letter to a Christian Nation* (New York: Knopf, 2006); *Waking Up: A Guide to Spirituality without Religion* (New York: Simon & Schuster, 2014); *Islam and the Future of Tolerance* (Cambridge, MA: Harvard University Press, 2015).

38. Sam Harris, *The Moral Landscape: How Science Can Determine Human Values* (New York: Free Press, 2010). Friedrich Nietzsche, Sigmund Freud, and a host of other atheists in the nineteenth and twentieth centuries were convinced that "science can determine human values." The result was gross immorality, intellectual deceit and fraud, racism, eugenics, slavery, war, and mass murder—not a benevolent, enlightened society. Finding a humane morality based on an atheistic worldview will continue to prove elusive, despite the best efforts of well-meaning philosophers and scientists like Sam Harris.

39. For examples, see Peter Foster, "Sam Harris's Brave New World," *National Post* (October 29, 2010); K. A. Appiah, "Science Knows Best," *The New York Times* (October 1, 2010); Simon Blackburn, "Morality without God," *Prospect* (March 23, 2011); H. Allen Orr, "The Science of Right and Wrong," *New York Review of Books* (May 2011); Scott Atran, "Sam Harris's Guide to Nearly Everything," *The National Interest* (March/April 2012).

40. Even in the case of a theist of the intellectual stature of Albert Schweitzer, a morality based on reason, without recourse to God, really doesn't work. Schweitzer, a great thinker and humanitarian, with three earned doctorates (in philosophy, theology, and medicine),

attempted to ground humanitarian ethics on rational thought, summed up by his well-known descriptor "reverence for life." Schweitzer made a valiant effort, to be sure, but in the end it failed to convince. The reason such an approach falls short is that a human ethic that is truly human and humane must be grounded in God, who alone provides a fixed moral point of reference. See Benjamin L. Hall, *Reverence for Life: An Examination of Albert Schweitzer's Attempt to Ground Ethics in Rational Thought* (unpublished doctoral dissertation; Durham, NC: Duke University, 1985).

41. Spiegel, *The Making of an Atheist*, 64–87.

Chapter 9: "Superman" Arrives

1. J. Rufus Fears, *The Wisdom of History*, lecture 3 (Chantilly, VA: The Great Courses, 2007).

2. Some think that Maria, a housekeeper in a Jewish home, may have become pregnant by the family's son Leopold Frankenberger. See Ron Rosenbaum, *Explaining Hitler: The Search for the Origins of His Evil* (London: Harper Perennial, 1999), 21. The evidence for this is much disputed, however. Even the existence of Leopold Frankenberger is in doubt.

3. *Hitler*, also spelled Hittler or Hüttler, is a real name, though understandably not many today go by this notorious nomen. There are also few families in Germany and Austria today that have the name *Hiedler*.

4. Richard J. Evans, "How the First World War Shaped Hitler," *The Globe and Mail* (June 22, 2011). Evans is a distinguished British professor of history. Hitler claimed that Germany, though unbeaten on the battlefront, was "stabbed in the back" at home by Jews and Marxists. See Ian Kershaw, *Hitler: A Biography* (New York: Norton, 2008), 61–63; Michael Kellogg, *The Russian Roots of Nazism: White Émigrés and the Making of National Socialism, 1917–1945* (Cambridge: Cambridge University Press, 2005), 203.

5. Indeed, Hitler was profoundly grateful for the war, as he states in *Mein Kampf*: "I fell down on my knees and thanked Heaven from an overflowing heart for granting me the good fortune of being permitted to live at this time." The quotation is found on page 148 of my English edition of *Mein Kampf*. Full bibliographical details of both German and English editions will be provided below. The nature of the times did indeed favor Hitler. Richard J. Evans rightly remarks that the angry, uneducated Austrian "would have remained a disregarded figure on the lunatic fringe of German politics but for the Depression of 1929–1933 and the attendant crisis of the Weimar Republic." See Richard J. Evans, *In Defence of History* (London: Granta, 2000, orig. 1997), 188.

6. Alan Bullock, *Hitler: A Study in Tyranny* (London: Penguin, 1962), 121.

7. It is still maintained by some historians. See Richard Steigmann-Gall, *The Holy Reich: Nazi Conceptions of Christianity, 1919–1945* (Cambridge: Cambridge University Press, 2004). For a critique of Steigmann-Gall, see Richard Weikart's review in *German Studies Review* 27 (2004): 174–176; and Mark Edward Ruff, "The Nazis' *Religionspolitik*: An Assessment of Recent Literature," *Catholic Historical Review* 92 (2006): 252–266.

8. The best treatment available on this subject is Richard Weikart, *Hitler's Religion: The Twisted Beliefs that Drove the Third Reich* (Washington, DC: Regnery History, 2016). I have greatly benefited from this learned study.

9. As quoted by Weikart, *Hitler's Religion*, 72. See also "Programme of the NSDAP, 1920," in Peter Matheson, ed., *The Third Reich and the Christian Churches* (Grand Rapids, MI: Eerdmans, 1981), 1.

10. See, for example, Norman H. Baynes, ed., *The Speeches of Adolf Hitler, April 1922–August 1939*, 2 vols. (Oxford: Oxford University Press, 1942): 1:19–20, 402.

11. William L. Shirer, *The Rise and Fall of the Third Reich* (London: Secker & Warburg, 1960), 238–239. In reference to faith in Jesus Christ, Kerrl remarked: "That makes me laugh."

12. Shirer, *The Rise and Fall of the Third Reich*, 238–239. Rosenberg was the author of *Der Mythus des 20. Jahrhunderts: Eine Wertung der seelisch-geistigen Gestaltenkämpfe unserer Zeit* (Munich: Hoheneichen, 1930), a religious-sounding anti-Semitic rant that even Hitler described as incomprehensible. See Albert Speer, *Inside the Third Reich: Memoirs by Albert Speer*, Richard and Clara Winston, trans. (New York: Macmillan, 1970), 115. The English title of Rosenberg's book is "The Myth of the Twentieth Century: An Evaluation of the Mental and Spiritual Forms of Struggle in Our Time."

13. Shirer, *The Rise and Fall of the Third Reich*, 234.

14. Heinz Hürten, "'Endlösung' für den Katholizismus? Das nationalsozialistische Regime und seine Zukunftspläne gegenüber der Kirche," *Stimmen der Zeit* 203 (1985): 534–546. The English title of this article is "'Final Solution' for Catholicism? The National Socialist Regime and its Future Plans against the Church."

15. Robert Cecil, *The Myth of the Master Race: Alfred Rosenberg and Nazi Ideology* (London: Batsford, 1972), 119.

16. Ian Kershaw, *Hitler 1936–1945* (London: Norton, 2000), 40.

17. These include Carl Spiecker, *Hitler gegen Christus: Eine katholische Klarstelllung und Abwehr* (Paris: Société d'éditions européennes, 1936); and Waldemar Gurian, *Hitler and the Christians* (London: Sheed & Ward, 1936). The English title of Spiecker's book is "Hitler against Christ: A Catholic Clarification and Defence." I should note that Spiecker wrote under the Latin pseudonym Miles Ecclesiae ("Soldier of the Church").

18. Fred Taylor, *The Goebbels Diaries 1939–1941* (London: Hamish Hamilton, 1982), 340. Here Goebbels also describes Hitler as an opponent of Christianity.

19. As noted in Richard Overy, *The Dictators: Hitler's Germany and Stalin's Russia* (London: Allen Lane, 2004), 281: "Hitler was politically prudent enough not to trumpet his scientific views publicly, not least because he wanted to maintain the distinction between his own movement and the godlessness of Soviet Communism." The same point is affirmed by Laurence Rees, *The Dark Charisma of Adolf Hitler* (London: Ebury Press, 2012), 135: "Hitler, as a politician, simply recognised the practical reality of the world he inhabited. . . . Thus his relationship in public to Christianity—indeed his relationship to religion in general—was opportunistic. There is no evidence that Hitler himself, in his personal life, ever expressed any individual belief in the basic tenets of the Christian church."

20. It is debated whether or to what extent Hitler may have read any of Nietzsche's works. Whether he did or did not, I have no doubt that Hitler was influenced by Nietzsche. In *Mein Kampf* the future führer states: "The weakness and half-heartedness of the position taken in old Germany towards so terrible a phenomenon [i.e., racial impurity] may be evaluated as a visible sign of a people's decay. *If the power to fight for one's own health is no longer present, the right to live in this world of struggle ends.* This world belongs only to the forceful 'whole' man and not to the weak 'half' man." Nietzsche himself could not have stated this better. The translation comes from the 1992 Pimlico edition (234; italics in the original German). More will be said about this edition below. Further evidence of Hitler's fascination with and admiration of Nietzsche is seen in a photograph in which Hitler looks upon the bust of Nietzsche with evident respect. That this is the point seems certain because the photo appears in the propaganda picture book, *Hitler wie ihn keiner kennt* (1938), edited by Heinrich Hoffmann. Beneath the photograph, the "caption claims that Nietzsche was a forerunner of Nazism." See Weikart, *Death of Humanity*, 188. More will be said on Hoffmann's book below.

21. Again, as noted in Overy, *The Dictators*, 281: Hitler's "few private remarks on Christianity betray a profound contempt and indifference." Overy adds: "Hitler believed that all religions were now 'decadent.'"

22. Ian Kershaw, *Hitler: A Biography* (London: Norton, 2008), 295.

23. Ibid., 295.

24. See Alan Bullock, *Hitler: A Study in Tyranny* (New York: Harper Perennial, 1991), 219: "In Hitler's eyes, Christianity was a religion fit only for slaves. . . . Once the war was over, he promised himself, he would root out and destroy the influence of the Christian churches." The first edition of Bullock's book appeared in 1952. It was revised in 1962 and has been reprinted numerous times.

25. Hitler sometimes spoke of doing "the Lord's will" and of "Providence." The former was said in mockery, the latter was Hitler's way of speaking of his destiny, which was part of his pagan animism. See Allan Bullock, *Hitler and Stalin: Parallel Lives* (London: Fontana Press, 1993), 412.

26. Ibid., 412.

27. Overy, *The Dictators*, 281: Hitler believed that Christianity was collapsing in Europe in his time because of science.

28. Heinrich Hoffmann, *Hitler wie ihn keiner kennt: 100 Bilddokumente aus dem Leben des Führers* (Berlin: Zeitgeschichte-Verlage, 1935). In English the title means "Hitler as No One Knows Him: 100 Images from the Life of the Führer."

29. Ibid., 57. In the German caption, *Marienkirche* is actually misspelled as *Marinekirche*.

30. Weikart, *Hitler's Religion*, 68: "Hoffmann's claim that this was a 'chance event' is rather suspicious."

31. Hoffmann, *Hitler wie ihn keiner kennt*, 2nd ed. (1938), 73. Once again, in the German caption, *Marienkirche* is misspelled.

32. Translation by Weikart, *Hitler's Religion*, xviii. For German text, see Werner Reichelt, *Das braune Evangelium: Hitler und die NS-Liturgie* (Wuppertal: Peter Hammer Verlag, 1990), 134–133. Note how apt the title of Reichelt's book is: *The Brown Gospel: Hitler and the NS-Liturgy*. *Brown*, of course, refers to the Brownshirts (aka the SA or *Sturmabteilung*, lit. "Storm Detachment"), paramilitary wing of the Nazi Party. The Brownshirts, many of whom were little more than street thugs, were superseded by the more professional, better trained SS.

33. So impressed after reading Hitler's *Mein Kampf* in the fall of 1925, Joseph Goebbels writes in his diary: "Who is this man? Half plebian, half God! Actually the Christ, or only John (the Baptist)?" Weikart, *Hitler's Religion*, xviii. The source is Elke Fröhlich, *Die Tagebücher von Joseph Goebbels*, part 1: *Aufzeichnungen 1923–1941*, vol. 1: *June 1924–Dec. 1930* (Munich: K. G. Saur, 1987), 365.

34. A patriotic Nazi song, penned by Horst Wessel in 1929. After Wessel's murder, it became known as the "Horst-Wessel-Lied" (in English: "The Horst Wessel Song").

35. As translated and quoted by Weikart, *Hitler's Religion*, 55, 212. The comment comes from Hitler's monologues. See Werner Jochmann, ed., *Monologe im Führerhauptquartier 1941–1944: Die Aufzeichnungen Heinrich Heims* (Hamburg: Albrecht Knaus, 1980), 40.

36. As believed by Alfred Rosenberg and Hans Frank. See Weikart, *Hitler's Religion*, 57, 312–313, notes 71–72.

37. Weikart, *Hitler's Religion*, 58. The reference is to Max Domarus, *The Complete Hitler*, 4 vols. (Wauconda: Bolchazy-Carducci, 2007), 1:29.

38. Weikart, *Hitler's Religion*, 219.

Chapter 10: Hitler's Hell on Earth

1. The standard English translation of *Mein Kampf* was done by Ralph Manheim, and first published by Houghton Mifflin in 1943. My Manheim edition was published by Pimlico in 1992, in one volume, and includes an excellent Introduction by D. Cameron Watt. The Pimlico edition contains 628 pages. All of my quotations and references are to this edition.

2. *Mein Kampf*, 295. Hitler is referring to African occupational troops that France brought in from Senegal. They were stationed in the Rhineland in the 1920s.

3. Ibid., 391; see also, 260: "Lowering of the level of the higher race."

4. For further evaluation of Hitler's warped use of science, see Richard Weikart, *From Darwin to Hitler: Evolutionary Ethics, Eugenics, and Racism in Germany* (New York: Palgrave Macmillan, 2004); Richard Weikart, *Hitler's Ethic: The Nazi Pursuit of Evolutionary Progress* (New York: Palgrave Macmillan, 2009).

5. *Mein Kampf*, 140. These "Jewish colonies," of course, facilitate the Jewish plan to gain control of Europe's finances. See *Mein Kampf*, 175–176, 187: "There is no making pacts with Jews; there can only be the hard either/or."

6. Ibid., 142. This curious language again reflects Hitler's pseudo anthropology, in which he imagines humanity made up of various subspecies. This language, of course, is consistent with Hitler's talk of "infection" (*Mein Kampf*, 569), referenced above. On occasion, Hitler also linked interracial marriage with prostitution, speaking—sometimes metaphorically and sometimes literally—of the spread of venereal disease. For example, Hitler asserts that the "profanation of the blood and the race" (of Aryans) can be thought of as the "syphilization of our people" (*Mein Kampf*, 226; see also, 227–231). Hitler speaks of the "black-haired Jewish youth" lurking "in wait for the unsuspecting [Aryan] girl whom he defiles with his blood." See *Mein Kampf*, 295.

7. Ibid., 105. The allusion is to Matthew 6:24; Luke 16:13.

8. In the Gospels, Jesus is warning his disciples that one cannot simultaneously serve God and wealth, for invariably these dual loyalties will come into conflict. In *Mein Kampf*, Hitler is speaking of the impossibility of being loyal to both Church and State. He is speaking in reference to the Christian Democratic Party of the 1920s.

9. The passage is found in *Mein Kampf*, 278.

10. Mark 11:15–18 and parallels.

11. Hitler, in fact, often appealed to Jesus and his whip. It was about the only thing about Jesus that Hitler liked, for it allowed Hitler to portray Jesus "as an Aryan fighter against materialism and a staunch opponent of the Jews." For discussion and primary literature, see Weikart, *Hitler's Religion*, 80–83, with quotation from 81. See especially the photograph on 82, in which Hitler poses with a whip.

12. Miklós Nyiszli, *Auschwitz: A Doctor's Eyewitness Account*, Tibère Kremer and Richard Seaver, trans. (New York: Arcade, 1960, 2011), 171. Nyiszli wrote his account in 1946.

13. Ibid., 181.

14. On the sordid story of Mengele and his Third Reich medical associates, see Robert Jay Lifton, *The Nazi Doctors: Medical Killing and the Psychology of Genocide* (New York: Basic Books, 1986); Gerald L. Posner and John Ware, *Mengele: The Complete Story* (New York: McGraw-Hill, 1986); Helena Kubica, "The Crimes of Josef Mengele," in Yisrael Gutman and Michael Berenbaum, eds., *Anatomy of the Auschwitz Death Camp* (Bloomington: Indiana University Press, 1994), 317–337.

15. Eugen Kogon, *Der SS-Staat: Das System der deutschen Konzentrationslager* (Munich: Karl Alber, 1946); English translation: *The Theory and Practice of Hell: The German Concentration Camps and the System Behind Them*, Heinz Norden, trans. (London: Secker

& Warburg; New York: Farrar, Strauss and Giroux, 1950). One might wish to see Kogon's related essay in Michael Kogon and Gottfried Erb, eds., *Eugen Kogon: Gesammelte Schriften*, 8 vols. (Berlin: Quadriga, 1995–1997), Vol. 1: *Ideologie und Praxis der Unmenschlichkeit: Erfahrungen mit dem Nationalsozialismus.* The English title of vol. 1 is "Ideology and Practice of Inhumanity: Experiences with National Socialism." One should also consult Nikolaus Wachsmann, *Hitler's Prisons: Legal Terror in Nazi Germany* (New Haven, CT: Yale University Press, 2004).

16. For Kogon's thoughts and reminiscences regarding his faith, among other things, see Michael Kogon and Gottfried Erb, eds., *Eugen Kogon: Gesammelte Schriften*, 8 vols. (Berlin: Quadriga, 1995–1997), 6:39–70.

17. Kogon, *TheTheory and Practice of Hell*, 49–50, 228. Kogon's account (225–235) of the brutality that took place at Buchenwald's so-called "Bunker" is beyond comprehension.

18. John 8:32. It reads in Luther's German translation: *und die Wahrheit wird euch frei machen.*

19. John 18:37–38.

20. Jonathan Sandys and Wallace Henley, *God and Churchill: How the Great Leader's Sense of Divine Destiny Changed His Troubled World and Offers Hope for Ours* (Carol Stream, IL: Tyndale, 2015). Until now, the topic has been left unexplored.

21. For a list of references to "Christian civilization" in Churchill's most important speeches, see ibid., 91–93. All of Churchill's speeches are available online at www.winston-churchill.org.

22. Sandys and Henley, *God and Churchill*, 91–92, 248, n. 3. The speech was given on October 5, 1938.

23. Winston Churchill, Speech to the House of Commons, May 13, 1940.

24. Winston Churchill, Speech to the House of Commons, June 4, 1940.

25. Winston Churchill, Speech to the House of Commons, June 18, 1940.

26. Sandys and Henley, *God and Churchill*, 92, 248, n. 4. The source is Richard M. Langworth, ed., *Churchill by Himself: The Definitive Collection of Quotations* (New York: Public Affairs, 2008), 170.

27. See, for example, Psalms 7:1; 16:1; 18:2; 36:7; 46:1; Proverbs 30:5.

28. Rodney Stark, Distinguished Professor of Sociology at Baylor University, has published a number of well-researched studies that document the many benefits the West has derived from Christianity. See, for example, Rodney Stark, *The Rise of Christianity: How the Obscure, Marginal Jesus Movement Became the Dominant Religious Force in the Western World in a Few Centuries* (New York: HarperCollins, 1996); *America's Blessings: How Religion Benefits Everyone, Including Atheists* (West Conshohocken, PA: Templeton, 2012); *How the West Won: The Neglected Story of the Triumph of Modernity* (Wilmington, DE: Intercollegiate Studies Institute, 2014).

29. Winston Churchill, Speech to the House of Commons, June 18, 1940.

30. See Larry P. Arnn, *Churchill's Trial: Winston Churchill and the Salvation of Free Government* (Nashville: Thomas Nelson, 2015).

31. Winston S. Churchill, *My Early Life: A Roving Commission* (London: Thornton Butterworth, 1930; London: Macmillan, 1941), 289–290.

Chapter 11: When Truth Is What You Want It to Be

1. Weikart, *Death of Humanity*, 187. For source, see Wolin, *Seduction of Unreason*, 27.

2. D. M. Smith, *Mussolini: A Biography* (New York: Knopf, 1982), 12–15.

3. See Ruth Ben-Ghiat, "A Lesser Evil? Italian Fascism in/and the Totalitarian Equation" in Helmut Dubiel and Gabriel Motzkin, eds., *The Lesser Evil: Moral Approaches to Genocide Practices* (London: Routledge, 2004), 137–153.

4. Jan Nelis, "Constructing Fascist Identity: Benito Mussolini and the Myth of Romanità," *Classical World: A Quarterly Journal on Antiquity* 100 (2007): 391–415; Nelis, *From Ancient to Modern: The Myth of Romanità during the Ventennio Fascista. The Written Imprint of Mussolini's Cult of the "Third Rome"*, Etudes d'Institue Historique Belge de Rome 1 (Turnhout: Brepols, 2011).

5. Jan Nelis, "Modernist Neo–Classicism and Antiquity in the Political Religion of Nazism: Adolf Hitler as *Poietes* of the Third Reich," *Totalitarian Movements and Political Religions* 9 (2008): 475–490.

6. Nelis, "Constructing Fascist Identity," 395, 405. See also Jan Nelis, "The Clerical Response to a Totalitarian Political Religion: *La Civiltà Cattolica* and Italian Fascism," *Journal of Contemporary History* 46 (2011): 245–270, here, 260–261: Rome's celebration of the life of Augustus made "an explicit identification between Augustan and fascist Rome."

7. Nelis, "The Clerical Response to a Totalitarian Political Religion," 267. For contemporary testimony, Nelis cites G. Messina, "L'apoteosi dell'uomo vivente e il Cristianesimo," *La Civiltà Cattolica* 3 (1929): 295–310.

8. Nelis, "Constructing Fascist Identity," 391–93.

9. Ibid., 397.

10. Ibid., 398.

11. Nelis, "The Clerical Response to a Totalitarian Political Religion," 249.

12. Nelis, "Constructing Fascist Identity," 399.

13. Ibid., 409.

14. Ibid., 398, 401.

15. Robert Himmer, "On the Origin and Significance of the Name 'Stalin'," *Russian Review* 45 (1986): 269–286.

16. Stephen Kotkin, *Stalin: Paradoxes of Power, 1878–1928* (New York: Penguin, 2014), 31–36.

17. Robert Conquest, *The Great Terror: A Reassessment* (Oxford: Oxford University Press, 2007), xvi.

18. "Soviet Ends Silence on Stalin Wife's Suicide," Reuters, April 14, 1988, www.nytimes .com/1988/04/14/world/soviet-ends-silence-on-stalin-wife-s-suidide.html.

19. Jasper Becker, *Hungry Ghosts: Mao's Secret Famine* (New York: Henry Holt, 1998), 81.

20. Becker, *Hungry Ghosts*, 86–93.

21. See Li Zhisui, *The Private Life of Chairman Mao*, Tai Hung-Chao, trans. (New York: Random House, 1995), 102. For a favorable review of this book, see Richard Bernstein, "The Tyrant Mao, as Told by His Doctor," *New York Times* (October 2, 1994).

22. Patrick Johnstone, *Operation World* (London: Paternoster, 2001), 168.

23. See my article, "Modern Day Martyrs: A Non-Christian's Chronicle of China's Dark Side," *Christian Research Journal*, 35 (2012), 60.

24. William J. Duiker, *Ho Chi Minh: A Life* (New York: Hachette, 2000).

25. See Johnson, *Intellectuals*, 340–341. The annoying irony here is not lost on Noam Chomsky, a radical leftist who is highly critical of the US and the West, and who cannot find fault with any Communist government or dictator. See Noam Chomsky, *Towards a New Cold War* (New York: New Press, 1982), 183, 213, 382, n. 73. For references, I depend on Johnson, *Intellectuals*, 365, nn. 76–79. Chomsky often indulges in outlandish special pleading and on occasion outright misrepresentation of the facts.

26. "Half-Kilometre Long Kim Jong-un Propaganda Message Visible from Space," *National Post* (November 23, 2012).

27. Stéphane Courtois, et al., *Le livre noir du Communisme: Crimes, terreur, répression* (Paris: Robert Laffont, 1997); English translation: *The Black Book of Communism* (Cambridge, MA: Harvard University Press, 1999).

28. Marius Stan and Vladimir Tismaneanu, "Coming to Terms with the Communist Past" in Lavinia Stan and Diane Vancea, eds., *Post-Communist Roman at Twenty-Five: Linking Past, Present, and Future* (Lanham, MD: Lexington Books, 2015), 23–39, here, 34.

29. On this important point, see Steven Lukes, "On the Moral Blindness of Communism," in Helmut Dubiel and Gabriel Motzkin, eds., *The Lesser Evil: Moral Approaches to Genocide Practices* (London: Routledge, 2004), 154–166. Lukes addresses the moral poverty of Communism, but much of what he says also applies to the Nazi and fascist regimes of Germany and Italy.

30. R. Z. Friedman, "Does the 'Death of God' Really Matter?" *International Philosophical Quarterly* 23 (1983): 321–332, here, 322.

31. Richard Taylor, *Ethics, Faith, and Reason* (Englewood Cliffs, NJ: Prentice-Hall, 1985), 83–84.

32. Paul Kurtz and William Lane Craig, "Is Goodness without God Good Enough?" in Robert K. Garcia and Nathan L. King, eds., *Is Goodness without God Good Enough? A Debate on Faith, Secularism, and Ethics* (New York: Rowman & Littlefield, 2009), 25–46, here, 32.

33. Ibid., 33.

34. Richard Dawkins, *The Blind Watchmaker* (London: Norton, 1986), 133.

35. Kurtz and Craig, "Is Goodness without God Good Enough?" 29. I mean no disrespect to Dr. Kurtz, but there is nothing he says in defense of morality based on atheism that could not be affirmed by the intellectuals who supported Hitler and Stalin. All of them "reasoned together" and "sought common ground." All acted for the supposed good of humanity, the betterment of civilization.

36. Paul Froese, *The Plot to Kill God: Findings from the Soviet Experiment in Secularization* (Berkeley: University of California Press, 2008), 176–177.

37. Ibid., 177.

38. He did crack down on dissent through his State Security secret police.

39. Sandys and Henley, *God and Churchill*, 152. The source is Tim Townsend, *Mission of Nuremberg: An American Army Chaplain and the Trial of the Nazis* (New York: HarperCollins, 2014), 11.

40. For an account of Monsignor O'Flaherty's daring exploits, see J. P. Gallagher, *Scarlet Pimpernel of the Vatican* (London: Souvenir Publishing; Toronto: Ryerson, 1967); later edition: J. P. Gallagher, *The Scarlet and the Black: The True Story of Monsignor Hugh O' Flaherty, Hero of the Vatican Underground* (San Francisco: Ignatius Press, 2009). The movie version, which emphasizes the rivalry between Herbert Kappler and Hugh O'Flaherty, was released in 1983 as *The Scarlet and the Black*. It features Christopher Plummer as Kappler and Gregory Peck as O'Flaherty. The name of the movie reflects the scarlet color of the monsignor's cassock and the black color of Kappler's SS uniform.

41. Tom Phillips, "China on Course to Become 'World's Most Christian Nation' within 15 Years," *The Telegraph* (April 19, 2014); Matthew Carney, "Chinese Communist Party Readies Crackdown on Christianity," *ABC News Net* (October 2, 2016).

42. Andrey Shirin, "Russia: The Other Christian Nation," *Christianity Today* (July 13, 2016); Marc Bennetts, "Who's 'Godless' Now? Russia Says It's the U.S.," *Washington Times*

(January 28, 2014). Recent surveys suggests that more than one half of the Russian population claims to be Christian. These surveys were conducted by Pew (2011), Ipsos (2011), Levada Center (2012), and Public Opinion Foundation (2013). Russian Muslims are also converting to Christianity.

43. Donald DeMarco and Benjamin Wiker, *Architects of the Culture of Death* (San Francisco: Ignatius Press, 2004).

44. See Wesley J. Smith, *Culture of Death: The Assault on Medical Ethics in America* (San Francisco: Encounter Books, 2000). The book has been reissued as *Culture of Death: The Age of "Do Harm" Harms Medicine* (San Francisco: Encounter Books, 2016). See also Wesley J. Smith, *Forced Exit: Euthanasia, Assisted Suicide, and the New Duty to Die* (New York: Times Books, 1997).

Part III: The World With Christianity
Chapter 12: Jesus' Tour de Force: Good News for All People

1. "Religion: Promises," *Time* (December 24, 1956).

2. Genesis 12:3 NASB, emphasis added.

3. NASB, emphasis added.

4. Genesis 26:4 ESV.

5. Genesis 28:14–15.

6. Acts 3:25 ESV.

7. Acts 3:13–15 ESV.

8. Galatians 3:8.

9. Luke 2:10.

10. "'Nones' on the Rise," Pew Research Report, October 9, 2012, page 60: http://www.pewforum.org/2012/10/09/nones-on-the-rise-religion/.

11. "What Would America Look Like, If We Were a Nation Without Faith?" Republican Study Committee, 2016, http://rsc.walker.house.gov/Americawithoutfaith/.

12. Ibid.

13. Ibid.

14. Ibid.

15. Brian Grim and Melissa Grim, "The Socioeconomic Contribution of Religion to American Society," *Interdisciplinary Journal of Research on Religion* 12 (2016): 2, http://www.religjournal.com/pdf/ijrr12003.pdf.

16. Ibid., 14.

17. Ibid., 10.

18. "What Would America Look Like If We Were a Nation Without Faith?"

19. Rodney Stark, *America's Blessings* (West Conshohocken, PA: Templeton, 2012), 168.

20. Sarah Kliff, "Seven Facts About America's Mental Health-Care System," *Washington Post*, December 17, 2012, https://www.washingtonpost.com/news/wonk/wp/2012/12/17/seven-facts-about-americas-mental-health-care-system/.

21. "What Would America Look Like If We Were a Nation Without Faith?"

22. Stark, *America's Blessings*, 109.

23. Ibid., 165.

24. Council for American Private Education, CAPE Outlook, *Students Significantly Exceed SAT Benchmark*, 1 (January 2015).

25. Council for American Private Education, CAPE Outlook, *Federal Report Looks at Crime and Safety in Schools*, 1 (January 2015).

26. Stark, 164.

27. Grim and Grim, 7.

28. Reported by Catholic Health Association of the United States, "U.S. Catholic Health Care, 2017," https://www.chausa.org/docs/default-source/default-document-library/cha _2017_miniprofile.pdf.

29. Howard W. Haggard, *The Doctor in History* (New Haven, CT: Yale University Press, 1934), 108.

30. Guenter Risse, *Mending Bodies, Saving Souls* (Oxford: Oxford University Press, 1999), 74.

31. Jeremiah J. Johnston, "Kingdom of God/Heaven," with Craig Evans, in S. E. Balentine, ed., *Oxford Encyclopedia of Bible and Theology*, 2 vols. (Oxford: Oxford University Press, 2015), vol. 2, cols. 1–9; Jeremiah J. Johnston, "Kingdom of God" in P. J. J. Geest, Bert Jan Lietaert Peerbolte, and David Hunter, eds., *Brill Encyclopedia of Early Christianity* (Leiden: Brill), forthcoming; Jeremiah J. Johnston, "Gottesherrschaft" in Jens Schröter and Christine Jacobi, eds., *Jesus Handbuch*, Theologen-Handbücher (Tübingen: Mohr Siebeck), forthcoming.

32. Mark 1:15.

33. Isaiah 40:9.

34. Isaiah 52:7.

35. Isaiah 61:1–2.

36. Genesis 12:3.

Chapter 13: New Hope: Jesus and His Proclamation

1. Rodney Stark, *The Rise of Christianity: How the Obscure, Marginal Jesus Movement Became the Dominant Religious Force in the Western World in a Few Centuries* (New York: HarperCollins, 1996); Stark, *The Triumph of Christianity: How the Jesus Movement Became the World's Largest Religion* (New York: HarperOne, 2011).

2. Larry W. Hurtado, *Why on Earth Did Anyone Become a Christian in the First Three Centuries?* (The Père Marquette Lecture in Theology, 2016) (Milwaukee: Marquette University Press, 2016); and, more fully, Hurtado, *Destroyer of the Gods: Christian Distinctives in the Roman World* (Waco, TX: Baylor University Press, 2016).

3. Justin Martyr, *1 Apologia* 26.7.

4. Justin Martyr, *2 Apologia* 12.1.

5. *2 Apologia* 12.5. Justin argues that Christians are (falsely) accused of doing the very things that some pagans in fact do in their perverse worship of Jupiter and other gods. In *Apologeticus* 9.1, Tertullian levels the same charge. On this topic, see James B. Rives, "Human Sacrifice among Pagans and Christians," *Journal of Roman Studies* 85 (1995): 65–85, here, 75–76. The pagan practice is also criticized by Tatian, Justin's disciple. See Tatian, *Oratio ad Graecos* 29.1. It is described by the pagan Dionysus of Halicarnassus, *Antiquitates* 4.49.2–3. Educated Greeks and Romans viewed cannibalism with horror, as we see in Juvenal, *Satirae* 15.78–83; Porphyry, *De abstinentia* 3.17.3; 4.21.4 (in reference to barbaric Scythians); cf. Tertullian, *Apologeticus* 9.9.

6. *2 Apologia* 12.6.

7. Graphically portrayed in Euripides, *Bacchae*, especially lines 1122–1147, where Agaue, possessed by the spirit of Dionysus, rips apart and devours portions of her son Pentheus. Another popular myth concerns the feast served Thyestes, guilty of adultery against his brother Atreus. After he eats his dinner, his brother informs him that he has devoured the flesh of his own sons (Aeschylus, *Agamemnon* 1590–1599; Seneca, *Thyestes*). A similar

legend is told of one Harpagus, who unwittingly "feasted on the flesh of his dearest" (as related in Macarius Magnes, *Apocriticus* 3.15).

8. The story is recounted in Josephus, *Jewish Wars* 6.201–213. On pagan slander against the Jewish people, see Pieter W. van der Horst, "The Myth of Jewish Cannibalism: A Chapter in the History of Antisemitism" in van der Horst, *Studies in Ancient Judaism and Early Christianity* (Leiden: Brill, 2014), 173–187. The accusation of cannibalism was not uncommon in contexts of slander. See Andrew McGowan, "Eating People: Accusations of Cannibalism against Christians in the Second Century," *Journal of Early Christian Studies* 2 (1994): 413–442.

9. The Words of Institution are found in the three Synoptic Gospels and in Paul: Matt 26:26–29; Mark 14:22–25; Luke 22:14–23; 1 Cor. 11:23–25.

10. John 6:54. The whole passage (i.e., John 6:48–58), if taken literally, could be construed in terms of cannibalism. Pagan critics of the early Christian movement were more than willing to do so.

11. In context, Jesus is comparing himself to the bread God provided Israel in the wilderness. Eating that bread, called manna, sustained life on a day-to-day basis (Numbers 16:13–30), but to "eat" Jesus, the bread of life (John 6:35), is to live forever.

12. Macarius Magnes, *Apocriticus* 3.15. The passage is cited in full and discussed in John Granger Cook, *The Interpretation of the New Testament in Greco-Roman Paganism*, Studies and Texts in Antiquity and Christianity 3 (Tübingen: Mohr Siebeck, 2000), 202–205. Although the "Greek" critic in the *Apocriticus* is not explicitly identified, it is believed that he is Porphyry (AD 234–305).

13. Pliny the Younger, *Epistulae* 10.96. 1–10. The reference to the "harmless [*innoxium*]" food is found at 10.96.7.

14. Justin Martyr, *1 Apologia* 27.1; 29.1; cf. Tertullian, *Apologeticus* 9.17. For scholarly discussion, see William V. Harris, "Child-Exposure in the Roman Empire," *Journal of Roman Studies* 84 (1994): 1–22. The reasons for abortion and infanticide varied. See Cornelia B. Horn and John W. Martens, *"Let the Little Children Come to Me": Childhood and Children in Early Christianity* (Washington, DC: Catholic University Press of America, 2009), 18–21.

15. See the Christian *Letter to Diognetus* 5:6: Christians "marry like everyone else, and have children, but they do not expose their offspring." Although Jews, so far as we know, did not rescue pagan infants, they did not practice abortion or infanticide. On this important point, see Daniel R. Schwartz, "Did the Jews Practice Infant Exposure and Infanticide in Antiquity?" *Studia Philonica Annual* 16 (2004): 61–95. Schwartz rightly criticizes some who have claimed that Jewish practices were almost as bad as pagan practices. The comments of Roman historian Tacitus (c. AD 56–118), who was no friend of the Jewish people, lends important support to the position taken by Schwartz. According to Tacitus, *Historiae* 5.5: Jews "take thought to increase their numbers, for they regard it as a crime to kill any ineligible child." By "ineligible" (*agnatus*) is meant a child not eligible to inherit. Such a child in late antiquity was far more in danger of exposure. One should also consult Strabo, *Geographica* 17.2.5. According to Seneca (*De ira* 1.15.2), only defective children should be exposed.

16. Tertullian, *Apologeticus* 8.1.

17. Ibid., 9.6–9. Readers will recall the pagan Hilarion's instructions to his pregnant wife: "If it is a boy, keep it; if it is a girl, throw it out" (P. Oxy 744, lines 9–10).

18. Justin Martyr, *1 Apologia* 3.1; 10.6; 23.3; 26.7; 27.5; 68.10; *2 Apologia* 10.5; 12.1–13.1.

19. Justin Martyr, *1 Apologia* 4.1–8; 7.3–4; 11.1; 24.1; 39.3; 45.5; *2 Apologia* 2.7, 10–13, 16–18.

20. Justin Martyr, *1 Apologia* 11.1; 24.1; 39.3; 45.5.

21. Tacitus, *Annales* 15.38.

22. Suetonius, *Nero* 38; Cassius Dio, *Historia Romana* 62.16.2; 62.17.3; Pliny, *Historia Naturalis* 17.1.5. At *Annales* 15.38, even Tacitus, who stops short of accusing Nero, admits that some men, openly throwing firebrands, shouted that they had authority to do so. Nero may have instigated the fire, perhaps with the intent of clearing an area in the city in which he hoped to build. If so, I surmise that the fire, fanned by strong winds, burned well beyond the original plan. Of course, there are doubts that Nero in fact started the fire. See Christian Hülsen, "The Burning of Rome under Nero," *American Journal of Archaeology* 13 (1909): 45–48; Hugh Last, "The Study of the 'Persecutions'," *Journal of Roman Studies* 27 (1937): 80–92, here, 89–90.

23. Cassius Dio, *Historia Romana* 62.17.3: "There was no curse that the populace did not invoke upon Nero, though they did not mention his name, but simply cursed in general terms those who had set the fire."

24. Pliny, *Historia Naturalis* 17.1.5; Suetonius, *Nero* 38; Tacitus, *Annales* 15.38–40; Cassius Dio, *Historia Romana* 62.16–18. Which song was sung is disputed.

25. Tacitus, *Annales* 15.44: "Means were sought for appeasing the gods . . . public prayers were offered . . . Juno was propitiated. . . . Ritual banquets and all-night vigils were celebrated."

26. Tacitus, *Annales* 15.44.

27. The passage makes up most of *Annales* 15.44. My translation is based on, with a few modifications, John Jackson, *Tacitus V: Annals Books 13–16*, LCL 322 (Cambridge, MA: Harvard University Press, 1937), 283, 285.

28. As plausibly suggested in Percival Frost, *The Annals of Tacitus, with a Commentary* (London: Whittaker, 1872), 440–441. Besides the North African rebellion (AD 115–117), Romans no doubt still recalled the horrifying war of AD 66–70.

29. As stated in Acts 11:26.

30. It is possible that Tacitus was familiar with the account that Josephus provides (in *Antiquitates Judaicae* 18.63–64), or the source on which Josephus himself had relied.

31. Beginning in AD 44, Rome appointed procurators over Israel (which now included Judea Samaria, Galilee, Gaulanitis, and Perea, essentially the same territory that had been governed by Herod the Great). Pilate's rank as *praefectus* was confirmed by the discovery of a dedication stone in Caesarea Maritima, in 1961.

32. "Superstition" (*superstitio*) was pejorative, implying that it was foreign or barbaric, and in any case, not Roman. See Suetonius, *Nero* 16.2: "Punishment was inflicted on the Christians, a class of persons given to a new and mischievous superstition [*superstitionis novae ac maleficae*]." On superstition in late antiquity, see L. F. Janssen, "'Superstition' and the Persecution of Christians," *Vigiliae Christianae* 33 (1979): 131–159. For a broader discussion of the topic, see Dale B. Martin, *Inventing Superstition* (Cambridge, MA: Harvard University Press, 2004).

33. As in Justin Martyr, *1 Apologia* 11.1; etc.

34. Livy speaks this way in reference to 7,000 persons. See Livy 39.13: *multitudinem ingentem*. Tacitus's *multitudo ingens* cannot apply to a few dozen. The Christian population in Rome must have been substantial by the 60s of the first century.

35. Roger S. Bagnall, *Early Christian Books in Egypt* (Princeton, NJ: Princeton University Press, 2009), 20. Bagnall estimates that at the beginning of the second century there were just over 750 Christians in Egypt. I suspect this number is much too small.

36. Pliny the Younger, *Epistulae* 10.96.9.

37. Latin: *odio humani generis*.

38. Ronald Mellor, *Tacitus' Annals*, "Oxford Approaches to Classical Literature" (Oxford: Oxford University Press, 2011), 56–57. Mellor adds that "Tacitus might well have seen the incipient spread of Christianity as another example of a growing acceptance of Jewish ideas" (59). Tacitus was deeply troubled, for example, when Pomponia Graecina was accused of embracing a foreign superstition. Tacitus despised all things non-Roman. See Tacitus, *Annales* 13.32.

39. Suetonius, *Claudius* 25.4: *Iudaeos impulsore Chresto assidue tumultuantis*.

40. It is possible that Suetonius actually thought that not only his followers, but Jesus himself, had been in Rome.

41. Tacitus, *Historiae* 5.5: *hostile odium*.

42. Ibid.

43. Tertullian, *Apologeticus* 5.3.

44. Writing more than one century after Tertullian, the great church historian Eusebius refers to the actions of Nero: "We boast that such a man was the author of our chastisement; for he who knows him can understand that nothing would have been condemned by Nero had it not been great and good." See Eusebius, *Historia Ecclesiastica* 2.25.4.

Chapter 14: New Life: What Made Christianity Irresistible?

1. In recent publications, Professor Candida Moss, University of Notre Dame, has argued that Christians faced little persecution in the Roman Empire in the first three centuries of the church. She says the narrative of a persecuted church, including the martyrdom of many Christians, is a myth that has had harmful consequences down through the centuries. See Candida Moss, *Ancient Christian Martyrdom: Diverse Practices, Theologies, and Traditions*, AYBRL (New Haven: Yale University Press, 2012); Moss, *The Myth of Persecution: How Early Christians Invented a Story of Martyrdom* (New York: HarperOne, 2013). Both of these books are problematic, especially the latter, more popular presentation. While there was admittedly a tendency in some Christian circles to embellish accounts of martyrdom and sometimes even invent stories of martyrdom, the evidence from pagan sources, such as Pliny the Younger and Tacitus, makes it clear that being a Christian in Rome in the first three centuries of the Christian movement was difficult and sometimes dangerous.
From a Christian point of view, one must ask how exaggeration of persecution and martyrdom served to attract new converts or reassure suspicious Roman officials. I think the majority opinion of historians—that there really was serious persecution—is correct. Christians did not invent a narrative of persecution; they attempted to make a virtue of it. Moss's books have been severely criticized, not least for the special pleading in the treatment of the ancient evidence. For an especially critical and insightful evaluation, see N. Clayton Croy's review in *Review of Biblical Literature* (posted October 2013). Although somewhat dated and cavalierly dismissed by Moss, a better treatment is found in Glen W. Bowersock, *Martyrdom and Rome*, Wiles Lectures, Queen's University of Belfast (Cambridge: Cambridge University Press, 1995). Bowersock is a widely respected classicist. In another study, Brent Shaw has argued that Emperor Nero did not persecute Christians. See Brent Shaw, "The Myth of the Neronian Persecution," *Journal of Roman Studies* 105 (2015): 73–100. The thesis is not convincing. For rebuttal, see Christopher P. Jones, "The Historicity of the Neronian Persecution: A Response to Brent Shaw," *New Testament Studies* 63 (2017): 146–152.

2. Deuteronomy 10:15. See also Deuteronomy 7:7–8.

3. 1 John 4:8, 16.

4. John 3:16.

5. Romans 5:8.

6. Ephesians 3:19.

7. Romans 5:5.

8. Matthew 19:19 and parallels in Mark and Luke. The command comes from Leviticus 19:18.

9. Matthew 5:44. The parallel in Luke 6:27 reads, "Love your enemies, do good to those who hate you." In Luke 6:35 Jesus adds, "Love your enemies, and do good, and lend, expecting nothing in return."

10. The best collection on this subject will be found in Frederick W. Danker, *Benefactor: Epigraphic Study of a Greco-Roman and New Testament Semantic Field* (St. Louis: Clayton, 1982).

11. The inscribed stone was found in Rosetta, Egypt. The ancient Egyptian is presented in the top and middle parts of the inscription, in hieroglyphic script and demotic script, respectively, and, at the bottom, in Greek. The parallel Greek and demotic script made it possible to understand the hieroglyphics.

12. For the original scripts and translations, see E. A. Wallis Budge, *The Rosetta Stone in the British Museum* (London: Religious Tract Society, 1929). For a popular treatment, see Carol Andrews, *The Rosetta Stone* (London: British Museum Press, 1981).

13. Lines 9–10 (of the Greek). The translation is from Andrews, *The Rosetta Stone*, 25. See also Budge, *The Rosetta Stone in the British Museum*, 54; Danker, *Benefactor*, 208.

14. Danker, *Benefactor*, 217. The Greek text will be found in *OGIS* 458 = Wilhelm Dittenberger, ed., *Orientis Graeci Inscriptiones Selectae: Supplementum Sylloges Inscriptionum Graecarum*, 2 vols. (Leipzig: S. Hirzel, 1903–1905), II, 48–60, here, 54.

15. For Greek and Latin texts, with English translation and commentary, see Alison E. Cooley, *Res Gestae Divi Augusti: Text, Translation, and Commentary* (Cambridge: Cambridge University Press, 2009). The quoted part is from 59.

16. *SIG* 814 = Wilhelm Dittenberger, ed., *Sylloge Inscriptionum Graecarum*, 4 vols. (Leipzig: S. Hirzel, 3rd ed., 1915–1924), II, 505–508, here, 507. I adapt the translation in Danker, *Benefactor*, 284.

17. *OGIS* 668 = Dittenberger, ed., *Orientis Graeci Inscriptiones Selectae*, II, 387. See also *SIG* 804 = Dittenberger, ed., *Sylloge Inscriptionum Graecarum*, II, 498, where Nero is addressed as "Benefactor of the fatherland, high priest of the gods."

18. Luke 22:25–27.

19. Plato, *Gorgias* 491e.

20. Mark 10:45.

21. Daniel 7:9–14.

22. Isaiah 52:13–53:12. For study of this important passage, see Darrell L. Bock and Mitch Glase, eds., *The Gospel According to Isaiah 53: Encountering the Suffering Servant in Jewish and Christian Theology* (Grand Rapids, MI: Kregel, 2012).

23. Hurtado, *Why on Earth Did Anyone Become a Christian in the First Three Centuries?* 108–129.

24. Ibid., 110–111.

25. Helmut J. Rix and Antony J. S. Spawforth, "Apollonius of Tyana" in Simon Hornblower and Antony Spawforth, eds., *The Oxford Classical Dictionary*, 3rd ed. (Oxford: Oxford University Press, 1996), 128.

26. For studies that argue that the Apollonian tradition is highly unreliable, see B. F. Harris, "Apollonius of Tyana: Fact or Fiction?" *Journal of Religious History* 5 (1969): 189–199; E. L. Bowie, "Apollonius of Tyana: Tradition and Reality," *Aufstieg und Niedergang der römischen Welt* 2.16.2. (1978): 1,652–1,699.

27. For a critical comparison of the miracles of Jesus and Apollonius, see Craig A. Evans, *Jesus and His Contemporaries: Comparative Studies*, AGJU 25 (Leiden: Brill, 1995),

245–250. It is suspected that Philostratus exaggerated the stories of Apollonius to make his works seem more impressive than those of Jesus. On the uniqueness of Jesus as healer, see Jan-Olav Henriksen and Karl Olav Sandnes, *Jesus as Healer* (Grand Rapids, MI: Eerdmans, 2016), especially 21–24, 124–30.

28. Matthew 12:24 and parallels.

29. I have in mind here Celsus (c. 140–200), as recounted in Origen, *Contra Celsum* 2.48–49.

30. Latin: *non fui, fui, non sum, non curo.* The saying was common. For discussion, see J. M. C. Toynbee, *Death and Burial in the Roman World* (Ithaca, NY: Cornell University Press, 1971), 34.

31. Most witnesses were friendly, including and especially his own disciples. But the risen Jesus was also seen by unbelievers, such as his brother James (and probably his brother Jude), and even a violent opponent in the person of Saul of Tarsus. Saul the convert, now known as Paul, states that on one occasion "more than five hundred" saw the risen Jesus (1 Corinthians 15:6).

32. Quotations and references to Celsus come from Origen, *Contra Celsum* 2.55.

33. In Macarius Magnes, *Apocriticus* 2.14, the Greek critic (probably Porphyry) identified the frantic woman as Mary Magdalene, "a coarse woman who came from a wretched village," and the other woman as "another utterly obscure Mary, who was herself a peasant woman." For critical discussion of the passage, see John Granger Cook, *The Interpretation of the New Testament in Greco-Roman Paganism* (Heidelberg: Mohr Siebeck, 2000), 198–200.

34. References to Celsus come from Origen, *Contra Celsum* 2.63. Porphyry's objections will be found in Macarius Magnes, *Apocriticus* 2.14. Some popular Christian writers and apologists responded to this criticism by rewriting and embellishing the Passion narratives, in which now the Jewish High Priest, the Jewish Sanhedrin, Roman soldiers, and Pontius Pilate himself, as well as the men who followed Jesus, all see, firsthand, supernatural events that take place during the trial and crucifixion of Jesus as well as on the day of the resurrection. Such popular writings include the *Gospel of Peter* (mid- to late-second century) and *Acts of Pilate* (late-second or early-third century). In these writings there is no shortage of credible witnesses to the resurrection of Jesus.

35. Luke 23:46.

36. Lucian, *De morte Peregrini* 13; see also 11: Christians "worship the man who was crucified in Palestine because he introduced this new cult into the world."

37. *The Octavius of Minucius Felix* 9: "I hear that they (Christians) adore the head of an ass, that basest of creatures, consecrated by I know not what silly persuasion."

38. For discussion of this important graffito, see John Granger Cook, "Envisioning Crucifixion: Light from Several Inscriptions and the Palatine Graffito," *Novum Testamentum* 50 (2008): 262–285, especially 282–285. When not visiting other museums, the Palatine Graffito is on display in the Palatine Museum overlooking the Roman Forum.

39. 1 Corinthians 4:10.

40. Romans 1:16a.

41. Romans 1:16b.

42. P. Fayum 137. For Greek text, notes, and English translation, see Bernard P. Grenfell, Arthur S. Hunt, and David G. Hogarth, *Fayûm Towns and their Papyri* (London: Egypt Exploration Fund, 1900), 292–293.

43. P. Fayum 138. For Greek text, notes, and English translation, see Grenfell, Hunt, and Hogarth, *Fayûm Towns and their Papyri*, 293.

44. From Oxyrhynchus, dating from the first and second centuries AD. See P. Oxy 1,148 and 1,149. For Greek texts and English translations, see A. S. Hunt and C. C. Edgar, *Select

Papyri: I. Non-Literary Papyri, Private Affairs, LCL 266 (Cambridge, MA: Harvard University Press; London: Heinemann, 1932), 436–437, nn. 193, 194.

Chapter 15: Christianity Ends Racism and Slavery

1. Dan Barry, "A Nation Challenged: The Survivor," *New York Times*, November 6, 2001, www.nytimes.com/2001/11/06/nyregion/nation-challenged-survivor-pulpits-grateful-christian-testifies-deliverance.html.

2. Rodney Stark, *For the Glory of God* (Princeton, NJ: Princeton University Press, 2003), 326–327.

3. Plato, *Respublica* 9.578.d.

4. Frank Cowell, *Life in Ancient Rome* (New York: Berkley, 1961), 97.

5. Texas State Historical Association, "Slavery," https://www.tshaonline.org/handbook/online/articles/yps01.

6. Matthew 19:14.

7. Bill Warner, *The Doctrine of Slavery: An Islamic Institution* (Nashville: CSPI, 2010), 13. Dr. Warner's book should be read for a complete perspective on slavery within Islam and its effect.

8. Ibid., 30–31.

9. Bill Warner, *Sharia Law for Non-Muslims* (Nashville: CSPI, 2010), 33.

10. Stark, *For the Glory of God*, 359–360.

11. Ibid., 365.

12. Galatians 3:28.

13. Alvin J. Schmidt, *How Christianity Changed the World*.

14. For a more detailed review, I recommend Schmidt, *How Christianity Changed the World*, chap. 2.

15. "Tim Tebow Surprises Inspirational Fan Judy with Prom Dance," https://www.youtube.com/watch?v=h2gq2PngXBQ.

16. 1 Thessalonians 2:8 NIV.

Chapter 16: Without Jesus, Women Would Not Be Free

1. John 18:36.

2. Luke 1:5–7, 13, 24–25, 36, 40–45, 56–61; 1:26–53.

3. Luke 2:36–38.

4. Luke 4:38–39.

5. Luke 7:11–17.

6. Luke 7:36–50.

7. Luke 8:1–3.

8. Luke 8:43–48.

9. Luke 10:38–42.

10. Luke 13:10–17.

11. Luke 15:8–10; 18:1–8; 21:1–4.

12. Luke 23:49, 55–56.

13. Luke 24:22–24.

14. Joseph Hoffmann, *Celsus on the True Doctrine* (New York: Oxford University Press, 1987), 61–62. Sometime in AD 175–181, the pagan philosopher Celsus wrote a hard-hitting critique of Christian faith entitled *The True Doctrine*, a work that is extant only in Origen's third-century response entitled *Contra Celsum*.

15. Rodney Stark, *The Rise of Christianity* (New York: HarperOne, 1996), 101.

16. Acts 1:14.
17. 2 Timothy 1:5.
18. Ephesians 5:22, 25–33 NIV.

Chapter 17: Healing the Unimaginable in Your Life

1. Richard Bauckham, *Jesus: A Very Short Introduction* (Oxford: Oxford University Press, 2011), 1.

2. Ferdinand S. Schenck, *Christian Evidences and Ethics* (New York: Young Men's Christian Association Press, 1910), 92.

3. Ibid., 85. This is an oft quoted (and misquoted) passage. But in researching the original source, I discovered the actual quote, which I still find compelling.

4. Kenneth Scott Latourette, *Advance Through Storm: A History of the Expansion of Christianity*, vol. VII (London: Eyre & Spottiswoode, 1939–45), 480–481.

5. Dan White, "Two Teens Killed in Crash," *Santa Cruz Sentinel* (CA), September 24, 2001.

6. Dan shared his personal reflection with me from *According to His Purpose*, and this comes from p. 3.

7. I am very thankful to Dan and Lynn Wagner for sharing their story with me, providing very helpful materials and information, including their pamphlet *Not Wasted*, Sentinel articles, and our follow-up interviews and emails.

ABOUT THE AUTHOR

Jeremiah J. Johnston, PhD, MA, MDiv, BA, is known for his unique communication skills and his infectious love for people. Pastors have remarked on the timely effectiveness of his ministry in their churches, often drawing record attendance due to his compelling content and fresh presentation.

Johnston is president of Christian Thinkers Society, a resident institute at Houston Baptist University (in the top ten most ethnically diverse campuses in North America), where he also serves as Associate Professor of Early Christianity. Jeremiah's passion is working with local churches and pastors in equipping Christians to give intellectually informed accounts of what they believe.

Jeremiah hosts the nationally syndicated *Jeremiah Johnston Show*, and has distinguished himself by speaking in churches of all denominations. As a theologian who has the unique ability to connect with people of all ages, and a culture expert, he has been interviewed numerous times and contributed articles across a spectrum of national shows, including: Fox News, CNN, *CBS This Morning*, *Vanity Fair*, *Premier Christianity Magazine* and Premier radio, *Relevant Magazine*, *Decision Magazine*, *The Christian Post*, Moody Radio Network, Salem Radio

Network, numerous network affiliate television stations, and is repeatedly quoted in *USA Today* and their associated *Faith & Reason* blog.

As a New Testament scholar, Johnston has published with Oxford University Press, E. J. Brill, Bloomsbury, T & T Clark, Macmillan, and Mohr Siebeck. He completed his doctoral residency in Oxford and received his PhD from Middlesex University (UK). He also earned advanced degrees in theology from Acadia University and Midwestern Baptist Theological Seminary. Jeremiah is married to Audrey, and they are parents to five children—including triplet boys!

 facebook.com/ChristianThinkersSociety

 twitter.com/_jeremiahj

 instagram.com/_jeremiahj

 ChristianThinkers.com

DID YOU LOVE
UNIMAGINABLE?
SPREAD THE WORD!

If you enjoyed *Unimaginable*, help us tell the world about it by taking a few moments to tweet, like, post, pin, and otherwise share the love in all your social media channels.

- Post about the book using the hashtag #Unimaginable

- Recommend *Unimaginable* to your friends, small group, and church. *Unimaginable* is ideal for sermon series, Bible studies, youth ministry, camps, conferences, and more. Start a conversation with your church or ministry leader today about how this book changed your worldview.

- Here are a few tweets to consider:

  † "A world without Christianity would be #**Unimaginable**. Find out why in the new book from @_JeremiahJ."

  † "What would our world be like without Christianity? #**Unimaginable** by @_JeremiahJ"

  † "Is Christianity good for the world? In his new book, @_JeremiahJ reveals why a world without Christianity would be #**Unimaginable**."

  † "If you care about social justice, women's rights, and the inherent value of human life, #**Unimaginable** by @_JeremiahJ is a must-read."

- Write a book review online

JEREMIAH WOULD LOVE TO CONNECT WITH YOU!

 Christian Thinkers Society

 @_JeremiahJ

 @_JeremiahJ

 Christian Thinkers Society

Amazon Author Page: Jeremiah J. Johnston

Visit christianthinkers.com for more great information, including videos, inspirational thoughts, answers to difficult questions, and apologetics materials.

#ChristianThinkersSociety